Economic Performance in Malaysia

PROFESSORS WORLD PEACE ACADEMY

Economic Performance in Malaysia

The Insiders View

Edited by Manning Nash

A PWPA Book

**Published by
Professors World Peace Academy**

Distributed by Paragon House

New York

Published in the United States by
Professors World Peace Academy
G.P.O. Box 1311
New York, NY 10116

Distributed by
Paragon House Publishers
90 Fifth Avenue
New York, NY 10011

A Professors World Peace Academy Book

The Professors World Peace Academy (PWPA) is an international association of professors, scholars, and academics from diverse backgrounds,
devoted to issues concerning world peace. PWPA sustains a program of
conferences and publications on topics in peace studies, area and cultural
studies, national and international development, education, economics, and
international relations.

Library of Congress Cataloging-in-Publication Data

Economic performance in Malaysia: the insiders view
  edited by Manning Nash
  p. cm.
  "A PWPA book."
  Includes index
  ISBN 0-943852-52-8. ISBN 0-943852-58-7 (pbk.)
  1. Malaysia—Economic conditions.   I. Nash, Manning.
HC445.5.E27 1988
330.9595'1053—dc19

Printed in the United States of America

Table of Contents

Introduction

Manning Nash

The papers in this volume are the result of two conferences. In May 1985 a group of twelve scholars met in Bangkok, Thailand for three days of seminar participation. Papers were read, commented upon, exchanged, and the participants returned to their respective home bases with a promise to reconvene with a rewritten set of papers. In February 1986 the authors of the papers in this volume met in Phuket, Thailand and repeated the process of intellectual and scholarly exchange. After revision and second and third and (sometimes more) thoughts and versions, the contributions assumed their present form.

There are several novel, unusual, and intellectually significant aspects of this project and these papers. First the project was conceived to throw new light on the mooted and tangled problems of economic development and cultural change between and among national entities, the usual units for social science comparison and theory building on this topic. In addition, the economic differentials among different groups within a national state was also a problem. When and how did different ethnic or "communal" categories or groups exhibit different economic performance over time, and why did glaring disparities of income and wealth continue to exist among such groups within a single nation-state? The Malay peninsula seemed, and is, a near laboratory situation for the exploration of these questions. Its history, demography, cultural variety, class structure, and communal differentials permit the focused use of controlled comparison which seeks to control as many variables in as many directions as possible. Furthermore, there is an excellent ethnographic record of the communities and peoples of the peninsula, well kept and detailed historical archives, and a continuous record of observers' accounts since early colonial days.

The papers in this volume speak for themselves and make their own telling points at various levels of generality and from various academic viewpoints. Rice production and its special place in the rural economy of Malays is explored; the planned and actual effects of the national New Economic Policy on the different "races" of Malaysia is well analyzed; the role of local communities in political activity aimed at economic development is discussed; Chinese and Malay managers are compared on the value systems that guide their day to day activity; women's roles in the new factories of an industrially growing Malaysia are studied and compared to women's roles elsewhere; the growth and composition of Malay entrepreneurship is sociologically portrayed since 1957 independence; rubber small holders, the dominant peasant activity in Malaya, is placed in a firm historical context. These papers run a chain and compass across the frontier Malaysian and Southeast Asian studies. They add fresh knowledge, cogent insight, and empirical generalization important to both scholars and planners.

What are the larger implications and meanings of these contributions to the problems of cultural change and economic development and to the question of relative economic performance (within the same context) of different "communal" "ethnic" or "cultural and religious" groups? This sort of problem has been part of the social science inquiry almost from the inception of modern, empirically oriented systematic social research. And, the Malaysian case, when placed in historical, political, economic, and social context provides fresh and novel insights and responses to these ever recurring general conundrums of historical activity.

Malaysia was absorbed into the British empire in bits and pieces and almost, it seems, absent mindedly as the British kept India, the jewel in the crown, as the center of the imperial network. The history, military and diplomatic, of the British expansion in Malaya, Borneo and other parts of Southeast Asia is well and widely chronicled. First the settlements of Singapore, Malacca and Penang formed the Straits Settlements, then the territories of the West Coast of the peninsula became the Federated Malay States; with the Eastern portion being the Unfederated Malay States. These three colonial entities have shown different degrees of involvement in the modern, international, and commercial economy, roughly corresponding to the time of their incorporation into the nexus of international trade via imperial connections. There was next a Malay federation, finally independence after World War II, and the emergency operation against communist guerrillas, then the formation of Malaysia with the inclusion of Sabah and Sarawk into East Malaysia. Singapore was for a brief period part of Malaysia before it became the Republic of Singapore.

When the British began imperial expansion into Malaya the chief occupants of the peninsula were Malays. There were Chinese, Indians, Orang Asli (as the Senoi, Temiar and other hunters and gatherers or shifting cultivators are called), Thai, and "other," all of whom are still in the census categories used to enumerate the population of Malaysia. The British considered the "Malays" the indigenous people of the peninsula and the rightful owners and rulers of the territory, a perception that has influenced the economic role of Malays in colonial and early independence times, and is of course the salient political heritage of those times. These categories of persons had only a loose identification within them, and hardly any action structures that included all of the category. They have over time, during political and economic process, moved from category to communal group, often with action programs that include large segments of the community. Of course there are other bases for social action — class, occupation, rural or urban residence, religion, and education and cross-cultural experience — but in the Malaysian context ethnicity or communal group enters into and helps define all other bases of social interaction in the political and economic arenas, and often in the domestic and personal spheres as well.

From about 1820 to 1920 there was relatively free immigration into parts of British Malaya. The discovery of tin in abundance in the 1850s and the growth of world demand spurred by the American Civil War needs for food packaged in "tin" cans required a large labor force for the mines. Chinese labor was the chief human element in tin mining, for the agricultural Malay was uninterested in labor at such low wages (here we find the familiar combination of cultural, social and economic factors that are always embedded in the economist's concept of opportunity costs.) The Chinese poured into the West Coast of Malaya under British aegis, and they were largely self-governed by "Captains China," local overlords and labor recruiters. In the 1870s rubber seedlings were transported to Malaya where they prospered, and the demand for rubber in the international market spurted in the wake of the automobile and its use of rubber tires. To work on the rubber estates, Indian labor was imported. The Indians were brought to Malaya with the assistance of the colonial administration and with the aid of private capitalists. Most of the workers on the plantation frontier were Tamils, and unlike the Chinese in the mines, there were many women rubber workers and in the early stages of the plantation, there was much more of a family life than there was in the mines. The plantation isolation of the Indian labor force and the urban clustering of Chinese miners still play a part in contemporary Malaysia. Of course other Indians worked in the railroads, as clerks, and as police, and as businessmen, professionals, while there were (and are) Chinese farmers, businessmen, professionals, as well as proletarians.

It is clear that the present population of peninsular Malaysia grew up in the wake of the expansion of capitalist enterprise under the protection of the colonial government of the British empire. While there was division of labor along ethnic lines, there did not evolve the "classic" plural society that J.S. Furnivall had described for Burma and Indonesia. The division of labor did not follow strict (classic plural society or export economy models) ethnic lines, although Chinese were predominant in the mines and Indians in the plantation. There were Malay rubber tappers, some Malay miners, and Malay minor bureaucrats and professionals. Partly the multi-ethnic society was skewed from the classic Furnivall model because of the special position the British, from the beginning of the "connection," granted to the Malays. The British gave protection to Malay custom and culture (and later reserve land), and a special place to the Sultans and the Malay nobility (unlike the decapitation of the Burmese monarchy and the indifference to the nobility.) In this arrangement, both peasant and noble were shielded (or blocked, depending on historical perspective and values) from the impact of modern commercial and capitalist activity. The Malays were largely indifferent to the influx of Chinese, who in some real sense came to an economic and geographic frontier in which the padi farming peasant and the malay aristocrat had little interest. The three major populations did not compete economically, did not mingle socially, and in the colonial setup did not compete for political power. The British and the Malays (when they thought about it) expected the Chinese to leave once their economic needs were met. Indians lived largely self contained lives in the near total institutions of the rubber plantations, and it was unclear whether or not they intended to return to India. So the historical circumstances of the spread of capitalistic enterprise to the Malay peninsula, hardly involved the "indigenous" populations in the new economy, emerging on the West Coast and using largely immigrant labor. One basis for difference in economic performance among communal groups is always historical, as it was in Malaya, and the ineluctable causality of historical events makes any explanation, anywhere at any time, in part descriptive and extensive, beyond the bounds and hopes of deductive theory.

After the 1920s there were sizeable increases in both the Chinese and Indian populations, but the relations of the groups to each other and to the colonial regime remained the same during the depression years. The depression slowed world demand for Malay produce and slowed the influx of foreign labor. This period also saw the first stirring of a Malay nationalism. More historical work on this period will no doubt show the interplay of class, political, and ethnic consciousness, and how the communal factor came to encompass, more and more of the other social and cultural bases of group formation and concerted political action.

The years just prior to World War II and up to independence in 1957 are marked by crucial shifts in relations among the different populations and underlie the formation of the contemporary communal life and politics of Malaysia. It became clear that the bulk of the Chinese were not going to return to an unstable and war torn mainland. Furthermore, there were significant numbers of Malaya born Chinese, raising problems of the application of jus soli for citizenship status. Also the Chinese continued their economic diversification, filling most of the middle echelons and above of the commercial economy, as well as continuing as professionals and workers. Due to the post war emergency (as the 12 year insurrection was locally called) the Chinese were urbanized to isolate them from the rebels. Chinese also became politically active. Just as the Malays began to realize that they were under represented in the commercial and industrial sectors of the economy (where wealth and income were generated at much higher levels than in padi farming, fishing, or artisan activities), the Chinese began to be aware of their lack of power and organization in the realm of politics. Indians also began to recognize that they also were under represented in the political sphere. The major communal perceptions, aided by competitive politics and politicians, began to crystallize in the form that has dominated Malaysian social life since the middle 1950s. The Malays came to see themselves as rightfully politically dominant, but economically disadvantaged in their "own" land; Chinese viewed themselves as the modern economic sector with the dynamic for growth if they could hold their own in the political arena and get full rights; while Indians moved from the plantation frontier into SE Asia's largest labor union and also sought political power and citizenship protection.

The demographics of peninsular Malaysia (1980 census) show:

Malays	55%
Chinese	34%
Indians	10%
Others	2%

as the visible cleavages to which people respond and census takers enumerate, but this lumping masks important distributional facts about the 12 million or so people of the peninsula. The Chinese are heavily settled in the West Coast of the peninsula, are majority populations in Kuala Lumpur, Ipoh and Penang, and on the whole are urban or town based.

So that even on the East Coast, where the Chinese are small populations, under 6% in Kelantan, they reside in urban conglomerates like Kota Bharu, or Kuantan in Pahang. Indians tend to cluster on the West Coast, but beside cities they still occupy the rubber estates of the region. In the middle of the West Coast Chinese are stretches of padi farm Malays like those in the Krian district, but on the whole Malays are clustered in the rice growing regions of the East Coast — Trennganau and Kelantan deltas — and the rice areas of the North — Kedah, Perlis and Perak — and in Johore and Negri Sembilan. There is no neat, clean or easy way to shuffle the populations into separate compartments, even if someone thought that desirable (as no responsible policy maker in Malaysia does).

This is, then, the setting for the modern period of ethnic, political, and economic relations. The modern period is conventionally divided into two sub-periods, based on climactic political events which restructured communal relations. The first sub-period is from 1952-1969, beginning with the "bargain" of the Alliance, which combined the communal parties for a single national government, and ending with the riots of 13 Malay in Kuala Lumpur. The second period is from 1969 to 1983 (and apparently still continues in large measure) from the reconstitution of the parliamentary system to a new ascendancy of Malay rights and culture. Broadly characterizing the sub-periods, the first period was marked by inter-communal cooperation with periods of confrontation and a breakdown of accommodation in 1969. Since 1969 there is again a time of ethnic cooperation and accommodation, but upon the new basis of accepting greater Malay cultural dominance and at least a willingness to level up the poor, paying special attention to the majority of the poor who are rural farming, fishing and artisan Malays.

The economic facts about the distribution of income (and the assets that lie behind income both tangible capital and what has come to be called "human" capital) are not in much debate. All the reliable sources (cited in the articles in this volume, freeing this preface from footnotes and other forms of scholarly apparatus) agree on the gross facts of the economic and occupational structure of peninsular Malaysia, whatever the discord is on the more trying problems of accounting for the distribution, or trying by policy initiatives to change it in more egalitarian directions.

Defining poverty at $25 (ringgit, Malay dollars) per capita per month (a reasonable level based upon several dimensions of customary expenditure for minimal levels of subsistence — this is a census estimate and it accords with my ethnographic experience in Kelantan, and reports of other recent ethnographers in other parts of the peninsula) about 40% of all households fall below this poverty line. In estimates of number of persons by communal category, Malays are 56%, Chinese are 18%, and Indians are 33% of the poor. Chinese income on the average is about 2.44 times that of the Malays, while Indians earn 1.77 times that of Malays. The poverty profiles in peninsular Malaysia can be summarized under seven topics (the interpretation of this summary is of course the social science problem and the stuff of policy, politics, and ideology and has serious implications for ethnic harmony or communal strife):

1. Of the poor households 78% are Malay. The Malays are over-represented in poverty by a 1:41 ratio.

2. Poverty is rural. More than 87% of poor households are rural.

3. Farmers as household heads are 62% in poverty.

4. The agricultural sector holds 75% of the poor.

5. Persons whose schooling does not extend beyond primary school are 93% of the poor households.

6. The poor are in Kelantan, Trengganu, Perlis and Kedah, the rice bowls of delta padi production, a rural Malay occupation.

7. The rich are in Johore, Penang, Perak, and Selangor (where the modern economic sector is found, as are the cities, the Chinese and the middle and upper echelons of Malays and Indians).

These distributional facts are obvious. How they came about is partly explained by the historical tale recounted earlier. Why they persist is far from obvious, and how amenable they are to public policy that is politically feasible is also highly problematic for theory and for practice. Economic theory does not get far beyond the obvious: those who hold the assets (capi-

tal in all of its forms) have the wealth and income. This near
tautology does not come close to saying how the asset structure
came to be, and how, over time it is perpetuated. There are two
kinds of explanations that try to penetrate the economic sur-
faces: sociological and anthropological, or more elegantly, a
structural or a cultural rationale for the origin and perpetuation
of differences in wealth and income (both the structural and the
cultural accounts have psychological implications, sometimes
spelled out as variants of schools of psychology, like Freud, or
learning theory, and often left implicit or self-evident to common sense).

The structural explanation holds that there are barriers
facing the poor. The barriers may be legal, they may be customary discrimination, or they may stem from deficiencies in information. What the empirical test of the structural explanation
consists of is to control social variables (like education, place of
residence, occupation of father, etc.) and see if there is discrimination when all these variables are controlled. In the
Malay case, it turns out that controlling for "face sheet" and
"background" variables, there are no structural blocks to social
and economic attainments and mobility. This is, in part, leger-
demain. All the qualified Malays or Indians or Chinese are
where theory expects them to be—there is, as in economic
theory, nothing much to be explained. If the pool of Malays and
Indians had the social characteristics of the Chinese, then they
would be distributed like the Chinese and vice-versa.

If economic theory fails to frame the important questions
and sociology makes the questions do a disappearing act, then
one falls back on the anthropological staples of values, taboos,
and culture for an in-depth explanation. Specific values are
often invoked—like a preference for leisure or work, or an un-
willingness to display wealth, or a notion of the limited good, or
a desire to seek salvation or approbation rather than wealth and
power. Sometimes these "values" are dressed up in elegant garb
like the differences in the "need to achieve" among different
cultures or populations, or the child rearing practices promot-
ing or inhibiting risk taking, even deeper motivations like sup-
pressed anxiety stemming from badly resolved Oedipal conflicts
may be cited as well. These values are first too specific, secondly too static, and thirdly not helpful in accounting for those

creatures or carriers and creators of the cultural values who manage to be economically successful.

Explanation, as far as it can go in cases like Malaysia and other similar societies of the multi-ethnic variety, needs to be less fragmented, less empirically muscle-bound, and less devoted to a scientific view of what an adequate account of economic differentials may look like. I do not want to, nor did any of the authors of the papers want to, offer a general and comprehensive theory, I merely want to stress what is diagnostic, in understanding dynamic social and cultural systems and hence, most likely to be both relatively true and useful.

Culture, in the sense of symbols and meanings used to orient and define action, is of first importance in understanding differences among populations (or societies, or communal groups, or other more or less bounded social entities exhibiting cultural variation). But culture taken in this sense is not a series of traits, or items with direct behavioral or social consequences. Culture is seen as defining and shaping a world view, an orientation toward action, and an interpretation of on-going and past actions. The axis of this orientation or world view (or implicit dominant ontology as it has elsewhere been called) informs people about possibilities, suggests means toward hierarchial ends, and assigns meaning to what happens, or will happen in the world. Such cultural meanings can be found in the "kampong ideology" among many Malays. The ideology (in necessarily brief and near caricature terms here) holds that "halus" behavior, refined and elegant as against "kasar" rough and crude is to be preferred. The ideology also holds that living in a society of peers, on one's own land, in some earthbound activity, and working for a common good among one's co-religionists are the highest goods. This ideology is widespread among, for example, padi rice farmers. It does not dictate behavior, political adherence, or occupational choice, rather it offers a view of the ideal life, and suggests where honor, virtue, and piety lie. It forms an implicit background where the traditional Islamic parties had their strength. Sometimes it enters directly into choice and behavior, but when it does it needs to be specified at a lower level of cultural norms and where they are socially and structurally relevant. For example, the ideal that social equals live in a kampong means that at a funeral each household must send at least one representative to the house of the deceased, or else hostility is implied, or that at a kenduri (festive meal) neighbors must all be invited, or again a hostile gesture is publicly announced. The kampong ideology, along with notions of time, space, piety, learning, and civil virtue must be woven into a coherent pattern from a host of observations, then broken down into normative rules, and then social context specified, and finally behavioral possibilities adumbrated, and finally the probable economic and political consequences, both aimed at and unintended, described. This is a large order. It is time consuming; it is fraught with grave potential for error, and it merely triangulates probabilities rather than makes predictions. For example, there is an Islamic prohibition on taking interest (this is at the level of normative rule and it derives from a cultural axiom about legitimate income coming from earned sources). But there are Islamic banks and bankers. The rule against riba (interest, as unearned) is over-ridden by the rule that when payment by banks to depositors is faeda (yield) which comes from taking on risk, and hence is, like profit, a result of effort and therefore earned.

Of course town dwelling Malays, members of the salariat have modified their world views away from the "kampong ideology" example I have used. And even some town Malays may quit successful modern careers to implement more religious and traditional views of the proper and worthwhile life. The family is the chief locale along with the kampong for the learning of and transmittal of orientations, world views, and the full ontology of the cultural template. But it currently also competes with the school, where more "central" or "modern" world views are expounded, and often absorbed by the students exposed to more cosmopolitan views. The families of even padi farmers send their children to school (about 90% of the eligible cohort is enrolled in primary school), so even in the kampong strongholds, urban, central values are shared between generations, and generally admired in Malaysia.

From culture, to structure requires judging by actors, when and what norms are applicable and can be effectively acted upon. For Malays interested, as they are, in economic advancement, the best road is through the professions, or the civil service, or politics. Business is cluttered with Chinese and Indians, requires networks, languages, relations of trust, capital and other ingredients of which there is a dearth in the Malay communal groups as compared to Chinese, or even Indians just as there is a shortage of trance doctors, Bomohs and Pawangs, among Chinese and Indians who consult Malay experts when they need these services. (And they need them because of the Malay definition of the world). So within the structures open to them Malays follow the most promising routes to wealth and power, given the opportunities they face.

Of course, the greatest opportunity is to enlist the resources of the national government in providing assets, income and jobs to the Malays. This they have done, and so far successfully, in the New Economic Plans following the Third Malaysian Plan. This political route of levelling up the poorest and most deprived culturally depends upon the acquiesence of the rest of the polity, who must be convinced both of its fairness and of its legitimacy and reassured that such policies will not harm them, or merely substitute them for the formerly deprived.

At least a growing economy is required to implement even the smallest socially meaningful redistribution, and a growing economy often depends on the dynamic minority who is being asked to pay for the transformation of the economy and the income and wealth structure. It is a difficult path to tread, and the political, economic and moral dimensions of this path are all problematic, and not easily solved by current wisdom.

I do not want to continue expounding or giving examples of the kind of "creative eclectism" I favor over grand theorizing, for I do not know whether the authors of these papers agree with my views. I mean here only to stress that culture, social structure, and history are the necessary ingredients for understanding and giving a coherent account of why there are different patterns of economic performance among different communal groups. This must be done so that the economist's "rational choice" models have cultural, social and historical content built into them, rather than mere assumption of the conditions under which so called rational choices takes place. The integrated use of the diagnostic concepts of culture, norm, social structure, opportunity for social action, and unintended consequences of purposeful action as applied to real societies in real time and space is what I mean by the slightly oxymoronic idea of "creative eclectism."

Proscription for policy, I have abjured, although there are attractive and reasonable proposals scattered throughout the papers in this book. I have avoided policy recommendations on two grounds: on the one hand, anthropology is not a policy science and my knowledge is too meager and fragmentary to offer detailed policy, and, on the other, the fact that the people who will be most affected by the policy should have a large hand in the making of it. This, I suppose, shows my preference for democratic means and a bias toward an open society, as against experts and elites.

A final, but not least, aspect of these papers is the closing of the "hermeneutic circle." This interpretative problem of social science often takes in anthropology under the guise of "insider versus outsider views," or put more technically, the "emic" versus the "etic" description (the local meanings in all their richness as against an abstract scientific bare bones account). In part this hermeneutic circle is closed (or squared, if you like metaphors) by having scholars of the subject under study to speak for, as well as about themselves. Here, not a group of Euro-American experts or (Japanese, Australian, Indian, or other outsider) social scientists create, analyze and generalize about Malaysian economic, cultural and social life, but rather a group of Malaysians (Malay, Chinese, and Indian) write about these matters. For a variety of logistic reasons no members or spokesperson for the Orang Asli or other groups came to the two conferences. Logistics, the inevitable juggling of time, place, and seminar also kept some of the finest Malaysian scholars from being part of the proceedings. This did not diminish the stellar quality of these papers presented by leading intellectual and scholars of Malaysia. This view of Malaysian economic activity over time replaces the usual bifocal view of insider-outsider with the reflexive arc of self-analysis. Here the papers are not only multi-disciplinary, but multi-cultural within a stream of shared historical events. That such an enterprise could be launched and completed is a measure of the maturity of social inquiry in Malaysia and a tribute to the trans-cultural aspects of social science.

1

Development of the Rice Sub-sector in Peninsular Malaysia: Relative Economic Efficiency

Mokhtar Tamin

The Importance of Rice Production in West Malaysia

West Malaysia, unlike the major rice producers in Southeast Asia, particularly Thailand, Burma and the Indo-Chinese countries, is not well endowed with great alluvial plains suitable for rice production. The only exceptions are the Kedah-Perlis plain in the northwest and, to a lesser degree, the Kelantan River delta in the northeast, the latter's rice-growing potential being somewhat limited by its rolling topography and periodic exposure to severe monsoon conditions. Other areas of less significance are Seberang Prai, Krian, and Sungai Manik in Perak, Tanjung Karang in Selangor, and some narrow inland river basins. These areas, totalling 913,000 acres, constitute the entire rice-producing land in West Malaysia (see Map 1).

Despite the fact that rice occupies only about 12% of the total cultivated land in West Malaysia, it holds a unique position in the socio-economic framework of the country. Rice production accounts for approximately 20% of total employment. Few countries, even among the major rice consumers, depend so heavily on a single staple food crop as does West Malaysia. Only Thailand and Burma exceeded Malaysia's level.

For a long period of time, spanning the colonial era to more recent times, West Malaysia has relied rather heavily on

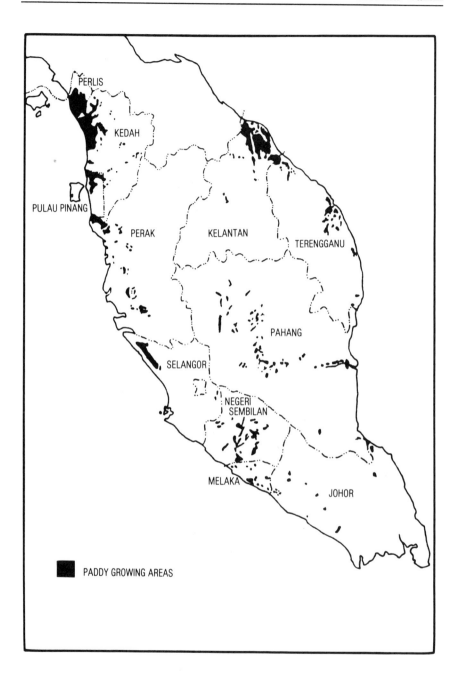

Map 1. Paddy Growing Areas in West Malaysia

imports, as can be seen in Table 1. Thus, by 1957, when West Malaysia attained her independence from the British, 44% of domestic requirements came from imports, particularly from Thailand, Burma, and more recently, from the People's Republic of China. Despite this seemingly unfavorable position, and the concern it engendered, few attempts were made to expand domestic rice production. The reason, no doubt, was the basic strength of the West Malaysian economy, with its comparative advantage derived from the production of tradable primary commodities such as rubber and tin. As a result of her over dependence on rice imports to meet per capita requirements, West Malaysia was particularly vulnerable to deficits during uncertain periods of world shortages. At such times, the government was confronted with difficult decisions in the face of rising import prices and the high cost of intervention in the form of consumer subsidies.

Table 1
Growth Of Double Cropping And Rate Of Self-sufficiency*

Year	Acres		Production		Level of Self-Sufficiency (%)
	Main Season (1,000) Ha.	Off Season (1,000) Ha.	Main Season (1,000) Tons	Off Season (1,000) Tons	
1955-56	344	43	443	3	56
1960-61	364	9	585	15	63
1965-66	360	42	612	75	72
1970-71	373	159	670	245	78
1975-76	348	222	599	476	90
1980-81	319	210	667	472	85

Source: Some Monthly Statistical Bulletin, Peninsular Malaysia and Buku Maklumat Perangkaan Pertainian.

Note: * Excludes smuggled rice from Thailand.

The colonial administration produced a great deal of debate and rhetoric regarding the need for public investments to provide drainage and irrigation. The record not only showed a meager commitment, but also cultivation restrictions, as pointed out by Goldman (1975). Immediately after achieving independence in 1957, priorities were reordered and the new administration embarked on a comprehensive policy of self-sufficiency in rice production, even at the expense of considerations of comparative advantage. In addition to the target of self-sufficiency, this new policy took on the goals of equity and distribution of income and saving foreign exchange. The new policy necessarily entailed an income transfer in favor of the rice farmers. Thus within the framework of the post-independence policy of self-sufficiency, the new administration conceived a four-pronged program which included (1) heavy infrastructure investment, (2) manipulation of input and output prices, (3) research, and (4) agricultural extension and institution building. The specific objectives were as follows:

1. Increase the welfare of the Malay rice farmers
2. Save foreign exchange
3. Reduce the risk attached to over dependence on foreign sources of rice.

Infrastructure Investment

In keeping with this costly policy of self-sufficiency, the government committed $515,000.00 for the construction of drainage and irrigation infrastructures during the first three

Table 2
Development Expenditures for Drainage and Irrigation

Plan Period	Plan Allocation M$ Million	Expenditure as % of Total for Agricultural Development
1956-60	96.0	17
1961-65	100.0	23
1966-70	319.0	36
1971-75	314.2	13
1976-80	575.8	17

Source: First and Second Malaya Plans; First, Second, Third and Fourth Malaysia Plans.

five-year development plans between 1956 and 1970, as can be seen in Table 2.

This represented approximately 30% of total public expenditures in the agricultural sector. As a result, the main season acreage increased from 334,000 ha. in 1956 to 370,000 ha. in 1973 while the corresponding figures for the off season rice acreage increased from 3,000 ha. in 1956 to 217,000 ha. in 1975. The reliance on double cropping for production increase of the required magnitude was justified by the very sluggish rate of increase in yields, 1.6% and 2.8% annually for the first and second seasons, respectively, between 1953 and 1976.

This massive commitment provided a sound base for the rapid adoption of new short-term rice varieties required for double cropping. Although economic arguments may be made against this bold policy, its role in setting technological preconditions for double cropping has been amply justified.

Output Price Supports and Input Price Subsidies

The package of incentives was made more attractive by a system of rice price control, which provided a guaranteed minimum price (GMP) predicated on an import mixing regulation and import licensing. This system entails a requirement for importers to purchase a certain proportion of government stockpile rice for every unit of rice they import. Essentially, the end result of this policy has been the maintenance of domestic rice price at a level higher than world prices. The tying of imports to domestic purchase provides a way for importers to off-set a loss on the domestic account by high premium prices the cheaper imports command in the market. The market margin between Thai No. 1 wholesale and the CIF (cost, insurance, and freight) price has ranged from 14% in 1961 to 42% in 1973.

The mechanism of the mixing scheme is best represented in Figure 1. The supply curve for domestically produced rice is given by S_dS_d, the total demand curve, i.e., the combined demand for domestic and imported rice is given by D_tD_t, and the supply curve for free trade imports is given by SS. These schedules set the CIF price for imports at OS per unit, the amount of rice produced domestically at OA, and the quantity imported at AB. Under the mixing scheme, the fixed proportion of domestic purchase to imports is given by OA'/A'B', which sets the domestic purchase price at OP per unit. The price that consumers face is market determined for the various grades and may be anywhere between OS and OP, say at an average of OC. The mechanism operates very much like a self-financing subsidy scheme in which a tariff of magnitude SC is imposed, the revenue (IJKL) from which is used to finance a producer support at OP, the cost of which amounts to CPML. Increasing the ratio of minimum domestic purchase to imports raises both the quantity domestically purchased and consumer prices.

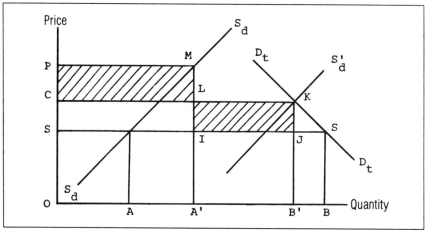

Figure 1
Rice Import Mixing Regulation

If self-sufficiency requires a total quantity of OB' and if all the programs to increase production succeed in shifting the domestic supply curve to S'dS'd, it becomes clear that the domestic purchase price, in the absence of direct government support through the fiscal process, would fall to OC.[1] The question of what farmers would to in the prospect of falling producer prices becomes very pertinent. It can also be seen that the price elasticity of the farmer supply curve is crucial to the formulation of any producer price policy.

The government stockpile or buffer stock, which is the underpinning of the price support system, operates by supporting a floor price (GMP) through direct purchase and sale to arrest falling and rising prices respectively. The GMP levels for the 1952-1976 period have been quite stable ($15-17) and later increased to its current level of $38-40 per pikul. The mandatory rice import ratios have manifested wide variations over the years. These variations indicate the extent of government market intervention through its stockpile operations.

Besides output price support, prices of certain inputs were distorted from time to time and some still are to promote their use. Fertilizers were subsidized in a somewhat disorganized fashion between 1957 and 1960. The Second Malaya Plan (1961-65) and the subsequent two Malaysia Plans (1966-75) provided for varying levels of subsidy ranging between 10-50% of fertilizer price. Besides fertilizers, irrigation water rates have ranged between M$6.00 and M$8.00 per acre per year compared to the Drainage and Irrigation Department's estimate of administrative and maintenance costs of M$24.00 per 0.4 ha. per year.

Rice Research: Improvement of Varieties

The availability of genetically improved varieties to the farmers constituted an important part of the total effort to increase output, particularly the breeding of short duration varieties and, to a lesser degree, high-yield varieties. A major milestone in rice research was the release of the first hybrid Malinja in 1964 followed by Mahsuri in 1965. These were short-term hybrids with fair grain quality and have been credited with the rapid expansion of double cropping. In association with the International Rice Research Institute, IR8 renamed Ria was adopted in 1966. All these varieties had their own defects, particularly their cooking qualities, and because of these drawbacks were replaced by the variety Bahagia in 1968. Numerous other varieties have been developed. Other areas of research pursued included breeding for fertilizer responsiveness and for disease and pest resistance.

Institutional Development

Finally, to complete the package of incentives, a systematic consolidation of inefficient credit and marketing institutions was undertaken. At the end of 1970 there were 1,050 rural thrift and loan cooperative societies compared to 1,640 in 1966. To provide much needed short-term production credit as well as medium and long-term loans, the Agricultural Bank was formed with the infusion of government funding while commercial banks were encouraged to extend credit to the paddy farmers. To streamline the marketing system, the National Rice Board (LPN) was formed to promote stability in both producer and consumer prices through its various functions, such as the control of imports in conjunction with the maintenance of the guaranteed minimum price, licensing rice purchase and sale, direct trading, artificial drying and storage as well as the provision of some extension service. Prior to this, these functions had been the responsibility of the Padi and Rice Marketing Board of the Federal Agricultural Marketing Authority. In an effort to make the extension service of the Department of Agriculture more effective, a comprehensive reorganization along the lines of the immensely successful Taiwan Farmers' Association was undertaken. This farmers' organization was designed to provide an integrated service, including marketing, credit and savings, agricultural and home economics extension.

The impact of these has been the remarkable increase in the rate of self-sufficiency from 56% in 1955-56 to an all time high of 93% in 1974-75, as shown in Table 1, above. This was made possible mainly by a dramatic increase in off season production, which accounted for 40% of the total. The rapid increase in production took such dimensions that the prospect of overshooting self-sufficiency in a good year arose. Since West Malaysia is a relatively high cost producer, commercial export prospects must realistically be written off. Hence, the second Malaysian five-year development plan (1970-1975) called for only 90% self-sufficiency, which was justified by increasing world supplies and falling prices in the late sixties and early seventies. Falcon (1975) estimates that between 1968 and mid-1972 prices declined by as much as 30% in each succeeding year. Thus, the price of Thai white rice (15% brokens) fell from

US$220 per ton in February 1968 to only US$90 in March 1972.

The favorable trend of excess supplies and falling prices was suddenly arrested in 1972-73 as a result of unfavorable weather conditions, especially in the Far East. The situation of strong demand and short supply raised prices considerably. As a result, the country went through an agonizing experience in 1973 and 1974, with the amount of stockpiled rice so low as to be ineffective in stabilizing prices. the wholesale price of Kedah No. 1 rice rose from M$26.70 per pikul (133 lbs.) in 1972 to M$69.70 in February 1974. The severe problems this generated began to take on political dimensions when legal price ceilings were imposed at twice the 1972 level in mid-1974. This action entailed large government intervention which amounted to direct expenditures of US$46.7 million to subsidize the import of 358,000 tons of rice between January 1973 and October 1974.

The 1973-74 episode called for a revision of policy goals based on a more realistic overall world rice perspective. One reality in the world rice situation has been the extremely low proportion of exports to total production. Between 1965 and 1976, the total exports averaged only around 7 million tons annually, representing less than 3% of total production, as can be seen in Table 3. This feature in and of itself causes far-reaching repercussions in the export price swings as a result of even relatively small changes in levels of production. Thus, the decline in the export price indices in the late sixties and early seventies (see Table 3) can be attributed to production increases resulting from the so-called green revolution. A 9.4% increase in production between 1967 and 1971 resulted in a 41% fall in the export price index, while a 4% decrease in production between 1971 and 1972 generated extreme successive increases in export price indices - 138%, 281%, 187%, and 95% in 1973, 1974, 1975, and 1976, respectively, in spite of the fact that total production had more than recovered. The lesson to be learned, is that while the sensitivity of export prices to long-run yield-increasing technology, as reflected in downward movement in the export price indices in the late sixties and early seventies, is very welcome in importing countries, the opposite is clearly disastrous. Hence, Malaysia reverted to the policy of self-sufficiency under the Third Malaysia Plan (1976-1980). However, the most recent pronouncements had reversed this policy.

Under these changing conditions the rice sector of West Malaysian agriculture has assumed an increasingly important role economically, socially, and politically. With this in mind, the important question centers on the microeconomic implications of macropolicies, since the latter trigger input-output price changes which, in turn, would affect input demand and output supply. Hence, how farmers respond becomes pertinent since it would help explain differential economic performance. This paper focuses on the findings of past studies of micro farm households to ascertain farmers' response to development projects. The farmers' response determines their economic performance which in the final analysis translates into income differentials between categories of farms be they inter-ethnic or intra-ethnic. At this juncture it is pertinent to point out that the rice sub-sector of the Malaysian economy is overwhelmingly Malay with only two regions in which Chinese and Indian farmers exist, namely Tanjung Karang and Seberange Prai. Thus, a major portion of the analysis pertains to the intra-ethnic differentials between different categories of operators in the Malay padi farming community.

Approaches to the Problem of Differential Economic Achievement

High and low economic achievement have long been the concern of economists, sociologists, anthropologists, historians and others. The sixties had been called the development decade while the seventies witnessed a concentration of research into the income and employment distributional effects of economic growth. Quite naturally there exist at least as many methodological approaches to the analysis of relative economic efficiency and income distribution as there are disciplines. While it is not within the scope of this paper to review the literature exhaustively, it is pertinent to highlight a number of theories that have applicability to the Malaysian context. Although economic literature is replete with studies that purport to explain differential economic performance, a general theory that explains this economic phenomenon does not exist. What does exist, however, is an array of inconclusively contending

Table 3
World Rice Production, Exports, And Export Price Indices, 1965-1982

Year	Production (million tons)	Exports (million tons)	Exports as % of Production	Export Price Index 1957 - 59 = 100
1965	254.6	7.3	2.9	105
1966	255.2	7.0	2.7	118
1967	282.3	6.5	2.3	141
1968	285.1	6.3	2.2	147
1969	295.6	6.5	2.2	129
1970	309.3	7.2	2.3	104
1971	308.8	7.7	2.5	86
1972	296.7	7.3	2.5	99
1973	321.5	7.2	2.2	236
1974	321.7	7.4	2.3	377
1975	348.2	7.1	2.0	284
1976	345.2	8.2	2.4	193
1977	370.3	10.2	2.7	211
1978	383.5	8.8	2.2	274
1979	373.5	11.5	3.0	255
1980	397.3	11.9	3.0	317
1981	412.1	12.5	3.0	345
1982	406.6	11.3	2.8	256

Source: Commodity Review and Outlook (FAO, 1967-1983).

general and special theories which have varying degrees of applicability to specific developing country contexts. It is therefore evident that the analytical approach to differential economic achievement and subsequently income distribution issues is essentially an eclectic one. In the sociological and anthropological arena, the cultural hypothesis which seeks to explain differential economic performance in terms of the underlying cultural differences in values, holds currency. A great number of researches in the economic sphere on the other hand is predicated upon the structural hypothesis which attempts to explain income differentials in terms of differences in opportunities. The marginalist revolution led Marshall, for example, to generalized marginal productivity as the basis of payment of all factors. This system requires the assumption of constant returns to scale to avoid the adding up problem. The neoclassical view is especially appealing because it gives a ready answer to the question of how income distribution is determined. Thus each individual has at his disposal an endowment of factors and his income is merely the sum of the product of those factors and their respective marginal products. The evolution of factor shares over time depends on changes in relative factor quantities, elasticity of substitution between factors, changes in demand pattern and the capital or labor saving bias in technological change. Certain useful conclusions about the patterns and trends in income distribution flow from this theoretical approach. It can be argued that one approach to equalizing income distribution is precisely to accept the neoclassical assumption that factor ownership or control affects relative economic efficiency which in turn causes the distribution and seeking ways to transfer resources over to the impoverished classes, Ahluwalia and Chenery (1973), which would enhance equity. This of course requires effective instruments for redistribution. In this respect land and human resources as well as their quality are particularly important in explaining differential economic performance and finally income differentials between groups of operators.

The analysis in this paper is predicated upon the neoclassical structural approach. Particular emphasis is given to the evaluation of the various policy instruments that have been used to develop the padi sub-sector at the microhousehold level.

At the outset, it can be claimed that the various policy instruments employed have been remarkably successful in achieving the macro objectives of increasing aggregate output to reduce the level of dependence on imports and subsequently to save foreign exchange as can be discerned in Table 1. The transfer of the green revolution technology of the sixties and early seventies has been very rapid. In areas where adequate irrigation and drainage facilities have been provided, the rate of adoption of high yield short maturing varieties has been rapid. Thus, the entire 100,000 ha. of the Muda Irrigation Project successfully adopted double cropping in four seasons or about two years. Most farms in all size and tenureship categories were equally receptive to the new technology.

On the other hand, the objective of increasing the welfare of padi farmers has not met with the same success as the macro-objectives as can be seen in Table 4 which shows that more than half of padi farm households remain below the poverty income level in 1983. This reflects a significant income differential across farm households. An evaluation of the effectiveness of the various policy instruments would explain some of the income differential.

Table 4
Incidence Of Poverty^2 Among Padi Farmers

	1970	1975	1980	1983
Total households ('000)	140.0	148.5	151.0	138.9
Total Poverty Households ('000)	23.4	114.3	83.2	75.0
Poverty rate (%)	88.1	77.0	55.1	54.0

Source: Third and Fourth Malaysia Plans.

2.Poverty is defined in an absolute sense as monthly household income of less than M$ 300

Farm Supply Response

Various hypotheses about the responsiveness of output supply and factor demand to price changes have been put forward and tested in the past. First, there is the hypothesis that farmers in developing countries respond normally, quickly, and efficiently to relative price changes. A major proponent of this hypothesis is T.W. Schultz (1964) who repeatedly and emphatically maintained that after considering risks and uncertainty, profitability is the farmer's main criterion for the adoption of a new factor of production. Further, he asserts that price policies predicated on the notion that the farmer is either indifferent or responds perversely to price changes must necessarily impair the productivity of agriculture.

A number of economists agree with Schultz. W.P. Falcon (1963), for example, emphasizes that the composition of output responds to relative price changes. J.W. Mellor (1966) suggests that short-run responses may be greater in underdeveloped

agricultural regions than in advanced agricultural regions because of the greater flexibility in respect to factor inputs and
distribution channels. P.T. Bauer and B.S. Yamey (1959) cite as
evidence the response of Nigerian cocoa and oil palm
producers to increased price differentials for various grades of
the produce. C.R.Wharton (1962) suggests that the expansion
of world coffee production after the high prices in the early
1950s is a case in point. In a specific reference to Thailand, L.R.
Brown (1963) attributes the expansion of corn and kenaf to a
remarkable price response.

Second, there is the hypothesis that the marketed production of small farmers is inversely related to price. This
hypothesis also has an impressive line of advocates. S.D.
Neumark (1959), P.N. Mathur and H. Ezekiel (1961), and S.
Enke (1963) all argue that small farmers may have fixed or relatively fixed monetary obligations and, therefore, only sell as
much of their production as is necessary to obtain a desired
money income. Put differently, R.D. Olson (1960) and R.
Krishna (1962) argue that an increase in price for a subsistence
crop may increase the producer's real income sufficiently so
that the income effect on his demand for consumption of this
crop outweighs the price effects on production and consumption. The marketed surplus may, therefore, vary inversely with
the market price.

Third, there is the hypothesis that traditional constraints
are so limiting that any price response is insignificant. This
viewpoint appears repeatedly in the literature and in policy dis-
cussions. An extreme position is the "social dualism" contention of J.H. Boeke (1953), who maintains that the social systems
that prevail in many underdeveloped countries are different
from those in developed countries not in degree, but in kind,
and thus require economic theories that are different in kind
from those applicable to more developed economies.

Be that as it may, even if we accept the validity of these
hypotheses, it is obvious that conflicting policy recommendations are implied by each of them. In light of these considerations, it can be argued that the degree of the responsiveness,
particularly the magnitude and signs of the elasticity coefficients, overshadow any simple generalization about farmer behavior.

The Farm Input Demand Response

The demand for an input generally depends on its own price, the prices of all other inputs, and the price of output. The demand for an input is also a derived demand, since it depends upon the price of the product and is thus derived indirectly from the demand for the product. To the extent that changes in the price of the product result in changes in the input-product relative prices, the nature of farm input demand response becomes of crucial importance in formulating policies designed to encourage the use of certain factors, particularly for fertilizers, since new improved high-yielding varieties which are normally fertilizer responsive are bound to play an ever increasing role in the total effort to increase production. This effect is especially important on account of the fact that after converting all possible areas into double cropping regions, yields must necessarily take on greater significance. The prices of related goods are the second determinant of the supply of output and the demand for input. Hence, a comprehensive output and input price policy must necessarily take cross-price elasticities into consideration.

The Economic Efficiency Versus Equity Issue

One of the implicit objectives of the rice self-sufficiency program is the improvement of the welfare of poor rice farmers in general, and the poorer groups among them in particular. The income transfer that the policy entails has seldom been explicitly expounded, but tenant and small farmers have been singled out for special consideration. Thus, in the past, there have been discriminatory credit and input subsidy programs which favored these groups. As Goldman (1975) has pointed out, 33% of the farmers own about 60% of the land, and about 47% of them are either pure tenants or rent a major part of the land they operate. Furthermore, about 40% of the farmers belong to the small farm category operating less than 1.2 ha. Programs to help disadvantaged farmers have often been alleged to favor income equity at the expense of economic efficiency. To address this issue in its proper perspective, the questions of relative economic efficiency between small and large farms, owner and tenant and also between ethnic groups where they prevail, have been explored.

Table 5
Size Distribution of Rice Farms in Muda 1975 – 1976

Size Category (Ha.)	Owners				Operations			
	Holdings		Area		Holdings		Area	
	%	Cum %	%	Cum %	%	Cum %	%	Cum %
< 0.30	21.4	21.4	2.3	2.3	6.7	6.7	0.7	0.7
0.31 - 1.14	40.4	61.8	19.4	21.7	40.0	46.7	16.4	17.1
1.15 - 2.82	27.1	88.9	36.3	58.0	38.8	85.5	43.0	60.1
2.83	11.1	100.0	42.0	100.0	14.5	100.0	39.9	100.0

Source: Lim et al. (1981).

Empirical Evidence

(1) MUDA Irrigation Region

Lim *et al.* (1981) estimated that there were 78,000 legal owners of approximately 60,000 lots on which some rice was grown while there were about 61,000 operators in the MUDA area in 1976. The relative distribution is summarized in Table 5.

It is evident from Table 5 that the distribution is somewhat less inequitable amongst operators than owners with a Gini Index[3] of distribution of 0.44 and 0.54 respectively. Even so, there is a high concentration of small farms in the distribution. Thus on the basis of ownership, 61.8% of the farms were below 1.14 ha. accounting for only 17.1% of the area compared to 46.7% accounting for 17.1% of the area for the operators. About 11.1% of the holdings amongst the owners were larger than 2.83 ha. accounting for 42.0% of the area compared to 14.5% accounting for 39.9% of the area amongst operators.

With regards to farmers' response to factor and product prices, Barnum and Squire (1976), and Tamin (1978) showed that rice farms across size and tenurial categories were economically efficient in resource allocation in that they equated marginal factor costs with their respective marginal revenues. In the main, the results of these studies provided compelling evidence that padi farmers in the MUDA irrigation region respond normally, efficiently and significantly to economic incentives as shown in Table 7. The results also showed that output supply was rather inelastic with respect to both output and input prices. The output elasticity with respect to output price was only 0.42 and only -0.25, -0.02, -0.06 with respect to prices of labor, animal services, and mechanical services respectively. The results of efficiency tests between small and large owners, small and large tenants, large owners and large tenants, small owners and small tenants showed no significant difference with regard to both technical and price components of the efficiency measure. Every group therefore succeeded in maximizing profit. This clearly indicates that given the quantities of fixed inputs, namely land, and fixed assets and the price regimes of the variable factors as well as output, all categories of farms are equally efficient in the overall analysis.

Another significant empirical finding of both these independent studies conclusively established the existence of constant returns to scale as shown in Table 6.

Table 6
Input-output Elasticities Of The Production Function

Variables	Parameters	Tamin (1978) Elasticities	Barnum & Squire (1976) Parameters	Elasticities
Labor	n_1	0.1796	a_1	0.29
Animal services	n_2	0.0173		
Mechanical services	n_3	0.0440		
Fertilizer	n_4	0.0535		
Land	v_1	0.6542	b_1	0.62
Fixed assets	v_2	0.0514		
Other variable inputs			a_2	0.08
Capital			b_2	0.01
$n_1 + n_2 + n_3 + n_4$ $+ v_1 + v_2 =$		1.000		
$a_1 + a_2 + b_1 + b_2 =$				1.00

Table 7
Indirect Estimates Of Input Elasticities And Related Statistics (per Acre) [1]

Variable	Production Elasticity	Mean Value	Price (M$)	Marginal Revenue Product (M$)
Value of Output (M$)		318.40	235.80	
Labor (man-days)	0.1796	18.18	3.15	3.14
Fertilizer (nutrient lb.)	0.0535	66.00	0.24	0.25
Animal (day)	0.0173	0.80	6.08	6.88
Mechanical services (hour)	0.0440	2.30	6.00	6.09

Source: Tamin (1978).

[1]Mean farm size = 3.8 acres.

The prevalence of constant returns to scale in all inputs is an important finding which has relevance to land redistribution in that it precludes the concept of an optimum farm size. Coupled with the dominance of the output elasticity with respect to land (0.65) it means that the expansion of hectarage would be the quickest way to achieve a substantial production increase on the macro and micro farm household level.

The constant returns to scale in all inputs coupled with the absence of any relative economic advantage between small and large farms and the fact that land is the highest productivity resource (output coefficient of 0.6542), can have income inequity implications. So long as income depends overwhelmingly on hectarage rather than farmers' acumen, the successful introduction of income increasing technology such as double cropping, and the introduction of high yielding varieties may be destabilizing in the long run. This derives from the fact that larger farms have larger incomes and therefore larger savings which need to find more investment outlet. In agrarian societies, land constitutes a most attractive investment proposition with the result that as large farmers seek to become larger, land values would increase, with larger farmers standing to gain the most at the expense of their small counterparts. Thus the Gini index of distribution of the price support scheme has been estimated to be

0.62 which is rather skewed in favor of larger farmers, Tamin (1986).

A vicious circle exists among small farmers since with their meager income, savings will be very low such that investments on resource acquisitions are most difficult if not impossible. Carried to its ultimate as Falcon (1970) has forcefully argued, these windfall gains trigger certain mechanization of the type that displaces labor thus increasing the number of people out of agriculture particularly landless laborers. This of course, is desirable if the non-agricultural sectors can absorb the marginalized manpower. It is very clear that under the prevailing conditions with regard to both technical and price efficiencies, any proposal of land redistribution would have to be predicated largely upon welfare considerations.

The finding that both owner and tenant farmers cutting across size categories are equally efficient economically provides empirical evidence that in some cases tenancy systems can exist in a manner that is not detrimental to economic efficiency. A fixed cash rental system is a good case in point. Again, this has some relevant implications on land reforms. In this case, it may be argued that the mere prevalence of a sizeable proportion of tenants in the distribution provides insufficient condition for the often touted land reform which favors ownership, since on pure economic grounds, a well enforced commensurate fixed rental is equally efficient. On this score, as with the farm size issue, some persuasive socio-political basis must be found if farm ownership is desirable.

(2) Tanjung Karang

Situated north-west of the State of Selangor is Tanjung Karang, a much smaller rice bowl in West Malaysia covering only about 19,600 ha. compared to the 100,000 ha. of the MUDA irrigation region. This padi growing region was drained and developed in the thirties and forties under the British colonial administration. Fears of communist insurrection spurred the colonial administration to settle the Chinese farmers in one particular district, which is surrounded by Malay settlements. Both ethnic groupings were largely padi farmers. Although the region has been subjected to numerous studies, few have been empirically rigorous. Snodgrass (1980) cites Huang (1981), (1974); as only one of two studies that attempt to explain the cultural basis of differentials in economic performance across ethnic boundaries.

Huang noted that it took five to seven years to convince farmers to adopt double cropping which was initiated in the early sixties. At the time the study was conducted double cropping had been complete over the entire region.

Huang's study contrasts the economic behavior of a group of Chinese padi farmers with their indigenous Malay counterparts. The major findings of the study are reproduced in Tables 8, 9, and 10 below.

Table 8
General Economic Indicators

	Malay Farms	Chinese Farms
Area Cultivated (acres)	8.72	7.08
Production (gantangs)	3,960	4,103
Yield (gantangs/acre)	443[1]	567[1]
Other Income (M$)	442[1]	719[1]

1.These mean values are statistically significantly different at the 99% level, see Freund (1960, pp. 266-69).
All data are annual figures. For definitions, see section on data.

Tables 8 and 9 show statistically significant differences in productivity and levels of input use with the Chinese registering higher productivity and income levels as well as the use of variable inputs and hired labor. However, in an attempt to determine inter-ethnic differences in technological expertise by fitting double logarithmic Cobb-Douglas production function after standardization for input usage, Huang failed to establish the existence of a significant difference. Huang's estimation is reproduced below:

$$\log Q = 5.071 + 0.856 \log X_1 + 0.047 \log X_2 + 0.116 \log X_3$$
$$\quad\quad (20.71) \quad (11.47) \quad\quad\quad (4.48) \quad\quad\quad\quad (3.09)$$

$$+ 0.068 \log X_4 + 0.080 \log X_5$$
$$\quad\quad (2.45) \quad\quad\quad\quad (1.27)$$

$$R^2 = 0.87$$

where Q = output; X_1 = hired labor; X_2 = family labor; X_3 = variable inputs; X_4 and X_5 = dummy variables with the value of 1 for Chinese and 0 for Malays.

Table 9
Input Usage

	Malay Farms	Chinese
Family labor per acre (manhours per acre)	282.0	270.0
Variable inputs per acre (M$ per acre)	4.32[1]	14.58[1]
Hired labor per acre (M$ per acre)	34.92[1]	87.10[1]

1.These mean values are statistically significantly different at the 99% level, see Freund (1960, pp. 266-69).

The coefficient of the dummy variables although positive, is not statistically significant. Thus the perceived inter-ethnic yield and income difference cannot be attributed to differences in technological expertise. Huang subsequently argues that both groups' production functions differ as opposed to the implicit assumption of similar shaped production function in the Cobb-Douglas estimation. He analyzed inter-ethnic allocative efficiencies by separate functional estimations. His results are summarized in Table 10.

The above results clearly show that the Malay farmers have significantly misallocated all resources compared to only one, namely land amongst the Chinese. However economic literature is replete with qualifications on this technique, the main one being the simultaneous equation bias.

One important empirical finding of the study is the existence of constant return to scale among both the Malay and Chinese farmers. The sum of the input elasticity coefficients of the Cobb-Douglas production function is not significantly different from unity, 1.078 and 1.080 for the Malays and Chinese respectively. This entails that doubling all inputs will double output for both groups.

Table 10
Allocative Efficiency: Ratio Of VMP To Opportunity Costs

	Malay	Chinese
Area	2.66^1	2.32^3
Hired labor	1.61^3	1.24
Family labor	0.54^1	1.00
Variable inputs	7.33^2	1.73

1.Significantly different from unity at .05 level.
2.Significantly different from unity at .10 level.
3.Significantly different from unity at .20 level.
The significance of the ratios were calculated from the formula in Carter and Hartley (1958).

Huang's analysis stresses the importance of cultural factors in explaining differential economic performance. Thus implicit in his arguments is that there exist cultural values, different between the Chinese and Malays, that finally translate into higher efficiency of the Chinese farmers. The study did not consider important factors such as soil fertility, infrastructural facilities, and in particular, the efficiency of water supply. Based on communication with soil scientists and agronomists, there were indeed differences in soil fertility and infrastructural facilities, but these have been systematically bridged by improvement of the irrigation system. A Department of Agriculture Report (1985)[4] gives strong evidence that yield gaps have been substantially bridged. This is further validated by preliminary empirical results by Anuwar (1986).

While there might have been differences in relative efficiencies across ethnic lines in the past, more recent findings show that as a result of technology transfer over time these differences have been minimized, at least as far as padi production is concerned. However, as padi farm households also carry out non padi farming activities it is a matter for conjecture that inter-ethnic differences in relative efficiencies may indeed exist in a diversified farming system.

References

Ahluwalia, M. and Chenery, H. (1973), "A Conceptual Framework for Economic Analysis," in H. Chenery *et al.*

Barnum, H.N., and Squire, L. 1976. "Aggregation, Labor Heterogeneity and Agricultural Production Functions," *Studies in Employment and Rural Development No. 34.* Washington, D.C.: U.S. Government Printing Office.

Bauer, P.T., and Yamey, B.S. 1959. "A Case Study of Response to Price in Underdeveloped Countries." *The Economic Journal,* 69:300-305.

Boecke, J.H. 1953 *The Economics and Economic Policy of Dual Societies.* New York:

Brown, L.R. 1963. "Agricultural Diversification and Economic Development: A Case Study." *Foreign Agricultural Economic Report #8.* Economic Research Service, U.S.D.A. Washington, D.C.: U.S. Government Printing Office.

Enke, S. 1963. *Economics for Development.* Englewood Cliffs, N.J.: Prentice-Hall, Inc.

Falcon, W.P. 1963. "Real Effect of Foreign Surplus Disposal in Underdeveloped Economies: Further Comment." *The Quarterly Journal of Economics,* 77:323-326.

----------- 1970. "The Green Revolution: Generation of Problems." *American Journal of Agricultural Economics,* 52, no. 5:709.

Goldman, R.H. 1975. "Staple Food Self-Sufficiency and the Distributive Impact of Malaysian Rice Policy." Food Research Institute Studies, 14, No. 3.

Huang, Y. 1971, "The Economics of Padi Production in Malaysia: an Economy in Transition", Ph.D. dissertation, Princeton University.

----------- 1974, "The Behavior of Indigenous and Non-Indigenous Farmers: A Case Study, Economic Development and Cultural Change 23:4 (July 703-18.)

Krishna, R. 1962. "The Marketable Surplus Function of a Subsistence Crop: An Analysis with Indian Data." *The Economic Weekly,* 17:79-84.

Mellor, J.W. 1966. *The Economics of Agricultural Development.* New York: Cornell University Press.

Mathur, P.N., and Ezekiel, H. 1961. "The Marketable Surplus of Food and Price Fluctuations in a Developing Economy." *Kylos,* 14:396-406.

M. Amin, M.A., The Padi Subsidy: Economic Impact, Ph.D. preliminary findings, dissertation, University of Malaya 1986 supervised by Tamin, M.

Neumark, S.D. 1959. "Some Economic Problems of African Agriculture." *Journal of Farm Economics,* 41.

Olson, R.D. 1962. "The Impact and Implications of Foreign Surplus Disposal in Underdeveloped Economies." *Journal of Farm Economics,* 42:1042-1045.

Schultz, T.W. 1964. *Transforming Traditional Agriculture.* New Haven: Yale University Press.

Snodgrass, D.R. 1980, *Inequality and Economic Development in Malaysia* Oxford University Press, Kuala Lumpur.

Tamin, M. (1979), "Microeconomic Analysis of Production Behavior of Malaysian Farms: Lessons from MUDA." *Food Research Institute Studies,* Vol. XVII, No. 1, Stanford University.

Wharton, C.R., Jr. 1962. "The Inelasticity of South East Asian Agriculture: Problems of Monocultural Perennial Export Dominance." Paper read at the meeting of the Thailand Agricultural Economics Society, Bangkok, November 1.

Notes

1. The National Rice Board estimated a fall in prices form $16.00 to $12.00 per pikul according to the minutes of its policy meeting, January 1, 1973.
2. Poverty is defined in an absolute sense as monthly household income of less the M$300.
3. Gini Index of distribution gives an indication of concentration in a given distribution. It ranges from 0-1.0. Thus the lower the index the more equitable the distribution. An index of 1.0 means that one person owns everything.
4. Project Completion Report of West Selangor Development, Department of Agriculture, Malaysia 1985.

The New Economic Policy and the Differential Economic Performance of the Races in West Malaysia, 1970-1985

G. Sivalingam

Introduction

The New Economic Policy (NEP) was promulgated in 1970 to accommodate the conflicting economic interests of the three major racial groups in Malaysia. The NEP was promulgated in the wake of the May 13, 1969 racial riots, which followed the May 10, 1969 general elections. UMNO had fared badly in the elections and in Selangor the possibility of a non-Malay assuming the post of Mentri Besar was imminent. The government interpreted the loss of Malay majority seats to PAS in the northern and eastern states as a rejection of UMNO by the Malay voters. The thesis was if UMNO had delivered the economic and social goods then most Malays would have voted for UMNO. UMNO's inability to uplift the Malay masses from poverty was the offical diagnosis of the riots. The non-Malay parties of the ruling Alliance Party agreed with the official diagnosis of the problem. The Malays felt strongly that since Malay and Malaysia was Tanah Melayu they were entitled to "special rights" and were bitter that these "special rights" enshrined in the Constitution had not been implemented effectively. The non-Malays, who voted for the opposition were resentful of the "special rights" and felt a keen sense of discrimination. The Alliance, however, felt that the Malays had a genuine case whereas the non-Malays had not kept to the spirit of the 1957 communal compromise. The compromise was that in exchange for citizenship for the non-Malays, the Malays will enjoy "special rights." The post-1969 Alliance government was bent on honouring this compromise. The strategy chosen was the New Economic Policy. To curb the growth of non-Malay based opposition parties, which threatened the political legitimacy of the Alliance, new "rules of the political game" were drafted, legislated and implemented.

Our concern in this paper is to trace the effect of this massive social engineering program called the NEP on the economic performance of the various racial groups. In the discussion emphasis will be given to inter-racial employment trends; access to education; progress in acquiring and accumulating ownership of corporate share capital and trends in racial income differentials. The social, economic and political consequences of the NEP will be discussed briefly in the conclusion. First a brief description of the NEP and the political environment in which it was to operate will be discussed.

The New Political Model and the NEP

Tun Razak, the Director of the National Operations Council (NOC), which was formed on May 16, 1969, after a state of emergency was declared, was not keen to restore democracy. Parliamentary democracy was suspended and a moratorium on politics was declared. The Malay political elite was disenchanted with parliamentary democracy and the electoral outcomes. Dr. Mahathir Mohamed declared that the NOC should continue under Tun Razak until the "aspirations of the Malay race" were fulfilled.[1] Tun Razak himself declared that "Democracy cannot work in Malaysia in terms of political equality alone. The Democratic process must be spelt out also in terms of more equitable distribution of wealth and opportunity."[2] He went on to argue that "unless the have-nots are assured a better position in the economic life and unless the benefits are justly distributed, there is no possiblility of the country returning to normal."[3]

UMNO was not keen on democracy as it was practised

before May 13, 1969 because of the abuse of fundamental liberties by opposition political parties. The then Home Minister, Tun Dr. Ismail was reported to have said that unlimited freedom would lead to "the frequent questioning of Malay 'special rights' by non-Malays and the Malays' fear that the Malay rights will be taken away."[4]

Tun Razak and his men were eager to change the political system from one that vacillated because of communal pressures to one that was centrally directed. Planning would be done at the top with as little "politicking" as possible. Malay supremacy in policy making was to be underlined. Policies were to be implemented to enhance the economic status of the Malays without hurting the non-Malays as well as policies to eradicate poverty regardless of race. As Ghazali Shafie argued:

> "...the politics of this country has been and must remain for the foreseeable future, native-based ... It must be a native base which believes not in tube promises but in cooperation with all the other races in the country."[5]

To reduce "politicking" and to enhance the Government's powers to improve the economic status of the Malays, the Constitutional (Amendment) Bill was passed in 1971. The Amendments were to facilitate the removal of certain sensitive issues form the realm of public discussion to reinforce the "special rights" clauses and to facilitate the entry of Malays into institutions of higher learning. Article 10 of the Constitution was amended to give Parliament the right to pass laws that make it an offence to question the "special privileges" of the Malays, the National Language, the special position of the Malay Rulers and the citizenship laws. Articles 63 and 72 were also amended to make it seditious even for MPs and State Assemblymen to question these provisions during debate.

The suppression of specific fundamental liberties was to Tun Razak and UMNO a necessary precondition for the restoration of parliamentary democracy. He called them the new ground rules in order to create a united and prosperous Malaysia and more importantly to further Malay economic interests without hurting the non-Malays. Although he had the support of UMNO, the civilian bureaucracy, the armed forces, and the police, Tun Razak was hesistant to push new Malay economic programs unilaterally or in a draconian manner. He did not want Parliamentary scrutiny for his programs but broad based multi-racial support for the policies he had enunciated as Director of the NOC. In exchange for the restoration of Parliamentary Democracy Tun Razak wanted the support of the leaders of the various racial groups, opposition parties, intellectuals, and the commercial and aristocratic elites. This he obtained by appointing representatives of these groups into the National Consultative Council (NCC). The NCC was set up in January 1970, with representatives from all the parties except the DAP. Partai Rakyat (now PSRM) withdrew soon after the NCC was set up. Other members coopted were drawn from the federal and state governments, professional bodies, religious groups, the public services, the universities, trade unions, employers' associations, journalists, women's associations, teachers and minority groups. The NCC, which held its meetings in secret and had broad based representation, was given the task of discussing freely a new strategy for racial unity and the growth of a national identity. Decisions were made on the basis of consensus and not by majority vote.[6]

The NCC was apparently successful under Tun Razak. At the NCC it was established that the opposition parties present were willing to cooperate with the UMNO-led government. The NCC also supported the NEP, the Rukun Negara and the proposed ammendments to the Constitution that were to be tabled in Parliament in 1971.[7]

Once the Constitution Amendment Bill was passed Tun Razak actively sought coalition partners from amongst the opposition parties to reduce "politicking" to facilitate the smooth implementation of the NEP. Between 1970 and 1972 the Alliance formed coalitions with four major political parties in Malaysia; three at the national level and one at the state level. The state level coalition was between the Sarawak Alliance and the SUPP, a Chinese based party. The three coalition partners at the national level were Gerakan, the PP, and PAS. This increased the majority of the Alliance in Parliament and reduced the feelings of insecurity of the Malays and non-Malays.

The NEP, which was an offspring of the NCC deliberations, was promulgated in 1970. The main focus of the NEP was to increase the proportion of corporate wealth owned by the Malays from less than 3% in 1970 to 30% in 1990. This was to be done, however, within the context of an expanding national pie and not at the expense of the non-Malays. The non-Malay share of corporate wealth was planned to be increased to 40% by 1990. The NEP was also targeted at eradicating poverty regardless of race or creed. The explicit policy was "to eradicate poverty among all Malaysians and to restructure Malaysian society so that the identification of race with economic function and geographical location is reduced and eventually limited, both objectives being realized through the rapid expansion of the economy over time."[8]

It was the global emphasis of the NEP that attracted the GRM, PPP, and SUPP to join the Alliance. It was understood that Malays, Chinese, and Indians would participate in proportion to their population at all levels of economic activity and the poor of all races would receive public support to increase their income and wealth positions.[9]

Employment Distribution by Sector and Race

The Malay political and administrative elite had agitated for an increased participation of Malays in the secondary and tertiary sectors of the economy. In 1970 61.06% of all employed Malays found employment in the primary or agricultural sector. Only 14.59% and 24.34% of all employed Malays found jobs in the secondary (mining, manufacturing, construction, and transport) and tertiary (wholesale and retail trade, banking, public administration, education, health, defense, and utilities). The Malays had wanted to migrate out of the agricultural sector or as the leading Malay intellectuals put it "out of the viscious circle of poverty"[10] where they suffered from low incomes and lack of nutrition, especially proteins.

Tun Razak's plan or strategy to move the Malays out of the rural sector into the modern sector coincided with the theoretical underpinnings of the Lewis Dual Sector Model,[11] the World Bank's concern with growth and redistribution[12], and International Agricultural Agency's concern with increasing agricultural productivity[13] through technological innovations.

Malaysian development plans were predicated in the Lewis Model, that is, the plans explicitly recognised that there was surplus labor in the agricultural sector, whose marginal product is zero, and which could be moved to the modern sector without sacrificing total output in the agricultural sector. A positive wage differential of about 40% would be able to induce this out migration and at the same time provide cheap labor to fuel industrialization and capital accumulation in the modern sector. As capital accumulation proceeded in the modern sector with infinitely elastic supplies of labor at a constant low wage, more and more of the surplus labour would be induced to migrate until equilibrium wages in the modern and rural sectors acted as a deterrent. Malaysian development planning was also predicated on the need to increase total agricultural productivity. To achieve this goal technological innovations were introduced in the agricultural sector. These innovations had the effect of inducing the evolution of large farms, increasing land, labour, and capital productivity in the agricultural sector. The labour displaced as a consequence could be used in the modern sector at a low price. The World Bank's concern with redistribution in the 1970s could also be satisfied by depopulating the agricultural sector, increasing the output per capita, and by providing incentives to spur the growth of employment creating industries in the modern sector.

The employment objectives of the NEP must, therefore, be seen within the context of the global strategy of Malaysian development planning after 1970. The strategy to increase modern sector jobs, enrich the agricultural sector, and induce rural-urban migration was not designed to restrict mobility. No racial group was to be positively discriminated against but the Malays were to be given preferential treatment.

Total employment in West Malaysia increased by 49.61% or 1.414 million between 1970 and 1980. This was due to the commodities boom, which triggered a high annual average GNP growth rate in the decade 1970 to 1980. One consequence of the high growth rate was structural change in the employment pattern. Over time the proportion employed in the primary sector declined from 46.82% in 1970 to 36.09% in 1980. By 1980, the tertiary sector was contributing as much to employment as the primary sector. The unemployment rate fell from 7.99% in 1970 to 6.69% in 1975 to 5.48% in 1980. The total labor force increased by 1.414 million and most of the new entrants into the labor market found jobs. The total unemployed remained constant.

Of the 1.414 million new jobs created between 1970 and 1980, the primary sector contributed 204,500 or 14.46% of the new jobs, the secondary sector 573,000 or 40.52%, and the tertiary sector 45.02%. The large increase in secondary and tertiary sector employment was caused by modern sector enlargement due to rapid industrialization and increased government involvment in traditional private sector activities.

Table 1
Employment By Sector (Total), 1970-1980 (000)

	1970		1975		1980		% Change		
							1970-75	1975-80	1970-80
Primary	1334.6	46.82	1476.5	41.39	1539.1	36.09	-5.43	-5.30	-10.73
Secondary	671.7	23.56	932.8	26.14	1244.7	29.18	2.58	+3.04	+5.62
Tertiary	844.0	29.61	1157.9	32.45	1480.6	34.72	2.84	+2.27	+5.11
Total	2850.3		3567.2		4264.4		25.15	19.54	+49.61
Unemployed	247.7	7.99	255.9	6.69	247.7	5.48			
Labor Force	3098.0		3823		4512.7				

Source: Government of Malaysia, Fourth Malaysia Plan, 1980-85, (Kuala Lumpur Government Printer) p. 59.

As a result of the huge public sector impact in the agricultural and modern sector, the share of Malay employment in the new employment created was larger than the Malay share in the total population of West Malaysia. Total Malay employment between 1970 to 1980 increased by 733,900 jobs, whereas total Malay labor force increased by 723,100. Total Malay employment growth outpaced total Malay labor force growth by 1.49%. Most of the Malays, however, continued to be employed in the primary sector. Total Malay employment in the primary sector increased by 117,900 between 1970 and 1980. However, the total amount of Malay job creation in the agricultural sector declined tremendously from 1975 to 1980, when only 11,000 new Malay jobs were created in the primary sector. This was

Table 2
Employment By Sector (Malays), 1970-1980 (000s)

	1970		1975		1980		% Change		
							1970-75	1975-80	1970-80
Primary	902.3	61.06	1009.2	54.39	1020.2	46.12	-6.67	-8.27	-14.94
Secondary	215.6	14.59	336.7	18.14	495.4	22.40	+3.55	4.26	7.81
Tertiary	359.7	24.34	509.5	27.46	695.9	31.46	3.12	4.0	7.12
Total	1477.6		1855.4		2211.5		25.56	19.19	49.68
Unemployed	130.7	8.12	120.3	6.08	119.9	3.14			
Labor Force	1608.3	8.12	1975.7	6.08	2331.4	5.14			

Source: See Table 1.

Table 3
Total Job Creation (Malays), 1970-1980

	New Jobs 1970-75	%	New Jobs 1975-80	%	New Jobs 1970-80	%
Primary	106.9	28.29	11.0	3.08	117.9	35.06
Secondary	121.1	32.05	158.8	44.56	279.8	38.12
Tertiary	149.8	39.65	186.4	52.34	336.2	45.81
Total	377.8		356.1		733.9	
Change in Labor Force	367.4		355.7		723.1	

Source:　See Table 1.

Table 4
Changes in Employment by Sectors (Malays), 1970-1980　(000s)

	1970-75	1975-80	1970-80
Primary	106.9	11.0	117.9
Secondary	121.1	158.7	279.8
Tertiary	149.8	186.4	336.2

Source:　Derived from Table 1.

only 10.28% of the total new Malay primary sector jobs created in 1970 to 1975. As a result the ratio of Malays employed in the primary sector to all Malays employed fell from 61.06% in 1970 to 46.12% in 1980. In contrast the rate of new Malay jobs creation in the secondary and tertiary sectors was accelerated. The total number of new Malay jobs in the tertiary sector increased by 121,100 from 1970 to 1975 and 158,700 from 1975 to 1980. In all, the tertiary sector created 336,200 new jobs for Malays between 1970 and 1980; this helped increase the proportion of all Malays employed in the tertiary sector from 24.34% to 31.46% between 1970 and 1980.

The net impact of these structural changes was that the Malays were now being increasingly absorbed into the modern sector instead of the primary sector. In 1970 only about 35% of all Malays were employed in the modern sector; by 1980 more than 53% of all Malays were employed in the modern sector. The movement of Malays from the traditional to the modern sector meant that Malay incomes would increase because the value added per worker in the modern sector is much higher than in the traditional primary sector.

The average value added per worker in the secondary and tertiary sectors in 1980 was approximately 3.23 and 4.825 times the average value added per worker in the primary sector.

Between 1970 and 1980, the total Chinese labor force increased by 46.59%, that is, from 1,122,400 in 1970 to 1,645,400 in 1980. A total of 515,000 new jobs were created. This meant that a substantial proportion of the 522,600 new Chinese entrants into the labor market were absorbed into productive activity. 7.91% of the new Chinese jobs were created in the primary sector. The secondary and tertiary sectors created 46.98% and 45.10% of the 515,000 new Chinese jobs. Half of the Chinese new jobs, that is, 259,000 or 30.29% were created in 1970 to 1975; the other 49.71% were created between 1975 and 1980. The unemployment rate among the Chinese fell from 7.55% in 1970 to 4.48% in 1980 but the total number unemployed increased by 8,200. This increase in absolute unemployment was about 1.6% of the total increase in the Chinese labor force.

The pattern of Chinese employment by sector did not change drastically between 1970 and 1980. More than 74% of

Table 5
Value Added Per Worker by Sector, 1970-1980
($ in 1970 prices)

Sectors	1970 (000s)	1975 (000s)	1980 (000s)	Average Annual Growth Rate (1971-1980)
Primary				
Agriculture, Forestry Fishing	2215	2498	2810	2.4%
Secondary				
Mining & Quarrying	8781	8969	13549	4.4%
Manufacturing	4269	4983	6692	4.6%
Construction	3475	3482	4513	2.7%
Transport, Storage, Communications	5048	6471	8778	5.7%
Electricity, Gas, Water	8642	10994	11960	3.3%
Tertiary				
Wholesale & Retail Trade	4400	4408	508	1.5%
Banking, Finance, Real Estate, Insurance	32889	36069	41363	2.3%
Public Administration Education, Health Defence & Utilities Other Services	3447	3976	4785	3.3%
Total	3624	4089	5141	3.6%

Source: Government of Malaysia, Fourth Malaysia Plan, 1980 -1985 (Kuala Lumpur: Government Printers), p. 86.

all employed Chinese continued to find employment in the modern sectors, in fact, this pattern was reinforced in 1980, when more than 78% of the Chinese found work in the second-ary sector. The trend was for a declining proportion of the Chinese to work in the primary sector. The percentages of all Chinese employed in the primary sector declined from 25.43% to 18.60% between 1970 and 1980 or by 6.83%.

The absolute number of Chinese working in the primary sector, however, increased by 40,700. This is 7.9% of the total increase in Chinese employment between 1970 and 1980. This absolute increase in Chinese employment in the agricultural sector was insignificant compared to the increase in the secondary (241,700) and tertiary sectors (232,000).

Between 1970 and 1980, total Indian labor force increased by 159,400. Total Indian employment increased by 159,300. The Indian unemployment rate fell from 11.01% to 8.11%. The absolute number unemployed increased by 100. The largest proportion of Indians continued to find employment in the primary sector. In 1970, 51.0% of all employed Indians worked in the primary sector; in 1980 the proportion was 43.28%. The proportion in the other two sectors increased over time. The proportion employed in the secondary and tertiary sectors increased from 18.94% to 22.96% to 33.75%, respectively between 1970 and 1980.

Of the total 139,300 new Indian jobs created; 40.92% were created in the tertiary sector; 30.57% in the secondary sector and 28.49% in the primary sector. The modern sector created more than 70% of the all new Indian jobs which helps explain why a declining proportion of Indians are employed in the primary sector. With modern sector enlargement a large number of Indian plantation workers migrated out of low wage employment to work in industries and the service sector. The absolute number of Indians working in the primary sector has, however, increased over time.

Table 6
Employment by Sector (Chinese), 1970-80 (000s)

	1970		1975		1980		1970-80
Primary	265.4	25.43	287.3	22.05	306.1	18.60	
Secondary	394.3	37.78	500.0	38.38	636.0	40.82	
Tertiary	383.9	36.78	515.3	39.55	615.9	37.43	
Total	1043.6		1302.6		1558.0		49.29
Unemployed	78.8	7.55	88.1	6.76	87.0	5.58	10.40
Labor Force	1122.4		1390.7		1645.4		46.59

Source: See Table 1.

Table 7
New Job Creation (Chinese) 1970-1980

	1970-75 (000s)	1975-80 (000s)	1970-80 (000s)	1970-75 (%)	1975-80 (%)	1970-80 (%)
Primary	21.9	18.8	40.7	8.45	7.36	7.91
Secondary	105.7	136.0	241.7	40.81	53.24	46.98
Tertiary	131.4	100.6	232.0	50.73	39.38	45.10
Total	259.0	255.4	514.4			

Source: See Table 1.

Table 8
Employment by Sector (Indians), 1970-80 (000s)

	1970	1975	1980	1970-75	1975-80	1970-80
Primary	154.0	167.3	199.4	51.09	44.31	43.28
Secondary	57.1	88.6	105.8	18.94	23.74	22.96
Tertiary	90.3	121.6	155.5	29.96	32.21	33.75
Total Employed	301.4	377.5	460.7			
Unemployed	37.38	44.3	37.4	11.01	10.30	0.02
Labor Force	338.7	421.8	498.1			

Source: See Table 1.

Table 9
New Indian Jobs, 1970-1980

	000s % of all Jobs					
	1970-75	1975-80	1970-80	1970-75	1975-80	1970-80
Primary	13.3	32.1	45.4	17.47	38.58	28.49
Secondary	31.5	17.2	48.7	41.39	20.67	30.37
Tertiary	31.3	33.9	65.2	41.13	40.74	40.92
Total	76.1	83.2	159.3			

Source: See Table 1.

Between 1970 and 1980, the Malays continued to dominate the agricultural sector. In 1980 66.3% of all primary sector jobs were held by Malays. Their share of primary sector employment only fell by 1.3%. In the secondary sector the Chinese continued their dominance holding 51.1% of all jobs. The Chinese share of secondary sector jobs, however, fell from 58.7% in 1970 to 51.1% in 1980. The Malay share in the secondary sector increased by 7.7%. The Indian share remained constant. In the tertiary sector, the Malays increased their share of jobs by 4.4% and in 1980 held the most number of jobs. The Chinese share of tertiary sector employment fell by 3.9%. The Indian share of tertiary sector employment remained constant between 1970 and 1980 but their share of primary sector jobs increased by 1.5%.

The NEP in its first 10 years had helped change the racial distribution of employment by sectors. The Malay share of modern sector employment increased by 4.65%, whereas the Chinese share fell by 5.41%. The Indian share of modern sector employment fell by 0.17%. The Malay share of primary sector employment fell by 1.4%, whereas the Indian share increased by 1.5%. The Chinese share of primary sector employment has remained constant.

In terms of unemployment the Chinese and Indians suffered more than the Malays.

Table 10
Employment by Sector and Race, 1970-1980 (Percentage)

Sectors	1970 Malays	Chinese	Indians	Total	1980 Malays	Chinese	Indian	Total
Primary	67.6	19.9	11.5	1334.6	66.3	19.9	13.0	1539.1
Secondary	32.1	58.7	8.5	671.7	39.8	51.1	8.5	1244.7
Tertiary	42.6	45.5	10.7	844.0	47.0	41.6	10.7	1480.6
Modern	38.0	51.3	9.8	1515.7	42.6	45.9	9.6	2725.3

Source: See Table 1.

In 1970 and 1980, the unemployment rate among the Indians was the highest. In 1970, the Malay unemployment rate was 1.1% higher than the Chinese but in 1980 it was 0.2% lower than the Chinese. In absolute terms, the Chinese and Indian unemployment figures were worse than the Malay unemployment figures. Total Malay unemployment fell by 10,800 between 1970 and 1980; Chinese unemployment increased by 8,600; and Indian unemployment increased by 100.

None of the communities suffered a loss in absolute terms. The total number of Chinese, Indians and Malays employed did not decline. In a relative sense the Malays benefitted. The number of Chinese and Indians unemployed, however, did increase by a miniscule amount.

Between 1980 and 1985, total employment went up by 8.205% or by 249,900 jobs. Total unemployment increased by 57,600 jobs. The unemployment rate increased by 0.72%. Of the 520,900 new jobs 71,000 jobs were created by the secondary sector, and 349,900 jobs were created by the tertiary sector. Primary sector jobs contracted by 103.100.

Table 11
Unemployment by Race 1970-1980 (000s)

	1970			1980		
	Malay	Chinese	Indian	Malay	Chinese	Indian
Total Labor Force	1608.3	1122.4	338.7	2331.4	1645.4	498.1
Total Employment	1477.6	1043.6	301.4	2211.5	1558.0	460.7
Total Unemployment	130.7	78.8	37.3	119.9	87.4	37.4
Unemployment Rate	8.1	7.0	11.0	5.1	5.3	7.5

Source: See Table 1

The sectoral allocation of employment that emerged was similar to that of between 1970 and 1980, that is, primary sector compaction and modern sector enlargement. In 1985, the primary sector accounted for less than a third of total jobs — a fall of 4.97% from 1980 and a fall of 15.7% from 1970. The secondary and tertiary sectors accounted for more than two-thirds of all jobs. The secondary sector now accounted for 30.68% of all jobs, an increase of 1.3% from 1980 and 7.12% from 1970. The tertiary sector accounted for 38.18% of all jobs in 1983, an increase of 3.46% from 1980 and an increase of 12.04% from 1970.

However, what is significant is that total employment fell in the agricultural sector by 103,100 or 6.6% between 1980 and 1985. This was due to out migration.

Total Malay primary sector employment declined by 70,700, whereas total Chinese primary sector employment declined by 36,600. Indian primary sector employment increased by 3,400. The Malays and Chinese who gave up jobs in the primary sector probably migrated into the modern sector, which was enlarged.

Total modern sector jobs increased by 453,000 or 16.62% between 1980 and 1985 or by 75,500 jobs a year. Between 1970 and 1980, modern sector jobs increased at an average rate of 70,609 jobs a year. Most of these new modern sector jobs created between 1980 and 1985 were created in the tertiary sector (62.16%). The Malays captured 70.88% of the new tertiary sector jobs and 49.00% of the secondary sector jobs. In all the Malays captured 62.26% of all new modern sector jobs. The Chinese and Indians captured 25.12% and 13.02% respectively of all new modern sector jobs. The Chinese were able to capture 34.36% of all new secondary and 19.49% of all new tertiary sector jobs, whereas the Indians captured 16.36% of all new secondary sector and 10.65% of all new tertiary sector jobs.

Table 12
Malay Share of Modern Sector Jobs 1980-85

	Total	%
Secondary	84,000	49.00
Tertiary	199,600	70.88

Source: Government of Malaysia; Mid-Term Review of the Fourth Malaysia Plan, (Kuala Lumpur Government Printers, p. 108).

Table 13
Chinese Share of Modern Sector Jobs 1980-85

	Total	%
Secondary	58,900	34.36
Tertiary	54,900	19.49

Source: See Table 12.

Table 14
Indian Share of Modern Sector Jobs 1980-85

	Total	%
Secondary	29,000	16.36
Modern	30,000	10.65

Source: See Table 12.

Although most of the new modern sector jobs went to the Malays it was not sufficient to reduce Malay representation in the primary sector. In 1980 66.3% of all primary sector employees were Malays; in 1985 66.1% of all primary sector employees were Malays; in 1970 the proportion was 67.6%. The net effect of the NEP till 1985 has been to reduce the Malay participation rate in the primary sector by 1.3%. The absolute number of Malays employed in the agricultural sector has, in fact, increased by 47,200 jobs.

On the other hand, Chinese participation in the primary sector has declined by more the 1.1% between 1970 and 1985. The Indian participation rate has increased by 2.6% over the same period. Notwithstanding this setback, the Malays have made impressive inroads into the modern sector; the Malay share of modern sector jobs has increased from 37.96% in 1970 to 42.61% 1980 to 46.66% in 1985. The Chinese share has in fact declined from 51.34% in 1970 to 43.93% in 1980 to 43.2% in 1986. The Indian share has increased from 9.75 to 9.58 to 10.13 over the same three time periods.

Table 15
Employment by Sector and Race 1980-1985 (000s)

	1970			1980			1988		
	M	C	I	M	C	I	M	C	I
Primary	67.60	19.90	11.50	66.30	19.90	13.00	66.10	18.8	14.10
Secondary	32.10	58.70	8.50	39.80	51.10	8.50	40.90	49.1	9.50
Tertiary	37.96	51.34	9.75	42.61	45.93	9.58	46.66	43.2	10.13

Source: See Table 12.

Table 16
Employment By Sector and Race, 1985

	Malays		Chinese		Indians	
	No.	%	No.	%	No.	%
Primary	949.30	39.16	269.50	16.48	202.80	38.77
Secondary	579.40	23.89	694.90	42.49	134.80	25.77
Tertiary	895.50	36.93	670.80	41.02	183.40	35.44
Total	2424.40		1635.20		521.00	
Unemployed	198.70		69.70		35.60	
Labor Force	2623.10		1704.90		558.60	
Unemployment Rate	7.57		4.08		6.37	

Source: See Table 12

When racial comparisons are made, the Malays show the best rate of progress. Among the Malays the proportion employed in the primary sector has declined secularly from 61.06% in 1970 to 39.16% in 1985. The proportions employed in the secondary and tertiary sectors has increased secularly from 14.59% to 23.89% and 24.34% to 36.93% respectively. Among the Chinese the proportions employed in the primary sector has declined from 25.43% to 16.48%; in the secondary and tertiary sectors it has increased from 37.78% to 42.49% and 36.78% to 41.02%. Among the Indians, the proportion employed in the primary sector has declined secularly from

51.09% to 38.77%; the proportion employed in the secondary and tertiary sectors has increased from 18.94% to 25.77% and 29.96% to 35.44%.

The Chinese have made remarkable progress in reducing their unemployment rate to 4.08% in 1985. The Malay unemployment rate fell secularly from 8.12% in 1970 to 5.14% in 1980 but increased to 7.5% in 1985. The Indian unemployment rate fell secularly from 11.01% in 1970 to 6.4% in 1985. The Chinese unemployment rate fell secularly from 7.55% to 4.08% between 1970 and 1985.

Whatever may be said about the NEP and its employment target, one fact stands out quite clearly, that is, the Malays benefitted from the NEP in the sense they obtained the lions' share of the modern sector jobs but were not able to reduce significantly their share of total primary sector jobs. Although the Chinese and Indians had their share of tertiary sector jobs reduced by 7.4% and 2.4% respectively between 1970 and 1985, the absolute number of Chinese and Indians in the secondary sector increased by 286,900 or 74.73% and 95,100 or 105.31% respectively. In the secondary sector the Chinese lost 9.6% of their share but gained 300,000 new jobs; an increase of 16.23% between 1970 and 1985. The Indians gained 1% of the share of secondary jobs or total 77,700 new jobs; an increase of 136% between 1970 and 1985.

Occupational Distribution by Race

A source of great discontentment among the Malays before the implementation of the NEP was that a large number of Malays were peasants, agricultural laborers, or government servants. Very few Malays were professionals, managers, or businessmen. In comparison a large proportion of the businessmen, managers, and professionals were non-Malays. The NEP intended to change this by financing professional education and by providing business training and soft loans for the Malays.

In 1970, there were 64,200 Malay professional and technical personnel. But this included lawyers, engineers, doctors, administrators, and civil servants, nurses and teachers. The total

number of Malays, who were registered as architects, account-
ants, engineers, dentists, doctors, veterinary surgeons, lawyers,
and surveyors only numbered 225. The number of similarly
registered Chinese and Indian professionals were 2,793 and
1,063 respectively. The number of Malays, who held jobs as administrators and managers was only 7,400. This was low in comparison to the Chinese who held 19,300 similar jobs. The
Malays were dominant as agricultural workers. 72.0% of all
agricultural and service workers in 1970 were Malays. The
Chinese were dominant as private sector administrators and
businessmen, sales, clerical workers and production workers.
The Indians like the Malays were predominantly agricultural
workers. UMNO wanted to change this by public policy. It
wanted 50% Malays; 40% Chinese and 10% Indians in each of
these occupations.

By 1980, UMNO had done splendidly well because the
number of registered Malay professionals (architects, account-
ants, engineers, dentists, doctors, verterinary surgeons, surveyors and lawyers) had increased to 1,237 or by 449.7%. The
number of Chinese registered professionals had increased to
7,154 or 186.14%. The number of Indian professionals had increased to 2,375 or by 123.42%.

Table 18
Registered Professionals, 1970-1980

| | Number | | % | |
	1970	1980	1970	1980
Malays	225	1237	5.51	11.48
Chinese	2793	7154	68.43	66.44
Indians	1063	2375	26.04	22.06
	4081	10766	100	100

Source: Government of Malaysia, <u>Fourth Malaysia Plan, 1980 - 85</u>, (Kuala Lumpur:
Government Printers) 1980, p.60.

However, up to 1980 the inter-racial distribution of
registered professionals was far below the expectations of
UMNO. In 1970 5.51% of all known registered professionals

were Malays; by 1980 the Malay share had increased to 11.45%. This was because of the long gestation period in human capital formation and the emphasis placed on professional education by non-Malays. Although the Malay share had more than doubled; the Chinese share had only contracted by 1.99%. The Indian share fell much more, that is, by 3.98%.

Between 1980 and 1983, the number of Malay registered professionals increased by more than 77%.

Table 19
Registered Professionals, 1980 -1983

| | 1980 | | 1983 | |
	Number	%	Number	%
Malay	2534	14.9	4496	18.9
Chinese	10812	63.5	14933	62.8
Indian	2963	15.3	3638	15.3

Source: Government of Malaysia, Mid-Term Review of Fourth Malaysia Plan, 1980 - 85, (Kuala Lumpur: Government Printers) 1984, p. 100.

The number of Chinese and Indian registered professionals increased by 38.1% and 22.7% respectively. These uneven increases helped raise the Malay share of professionals by 4% and reduce the Chinese share by 0.7%. The Indian share remained constant. The "others" category of Malaysians lost 3.3% of their share.

Between 1970 and 1983 the Malay share increased by more than 13.39%; whereas the Chinese and Indian shares declined by 5.63% and 10.74%. The losers in relative terms were the Indians and then the Chinese. The expectation is that the Chinese and Indian share will be eroded further if the Malay rate of increase between 1980 and 1983 is indicative of future trends. The Indian share of the professional cake will probably shrink the most because its rate of growth is only 29% of the Malay rate and 59.76% of the Chinese rate. Continued generous state sponsorship of Malay professional education is expected because the 19.9% Malay share is far below the goal of 52%.

Between 1970 and 1983, the total number of professional and technical workers increased by 176,800 or 129%. Of these, 107,500 new jobs or 60.80% of all new jobs went to the Malays. Of these 107,500, 4,271 or 3.9% were registered Malay professionals. The rest were Malay teachers and nurses. The number of Chinese and Indian professional and technical workers increased by 43,500 or by 80.55% and 24,400 or by 164.86% respectively. Of the 43,500 additional Chinese in this occupational group 12,140 or 27.90% were registered professionals. Among the 24,400 new Indians in this group 1,263 or 5.17% were registered professionals.

The Malays increased their share in the professional and technical occupational group from 47.0% to 54.8% from 1970 to 1983. The Chinese and Indian share declined by 8.4% and 2.3% respectively.

In the administrative and managerial group the Malay share increased from 24.1% in 1970 to 27.4% in 1983. The Chinese share increased by 3.1% but the Indian share fell by 2.5%. The workers in this category include legislative officals, government administrators, and managers. The Chinese share of this occupation has been large (62.9% in 1970 and 66.0% in 1983) because of the large number of Chinese managers in the private sector. The Malay share has been small because only top government administrators and legislators are included in this occupational category. If all government executive officers (who are now included in the clerical category) are counted as administrators and managers, the Malay share would increase. In 1980, for example, there were 20,609 Malay government executive officers and 3,025 Malay top legislative officers and government administrators. If the category of government executive officers was included in the Administrative and Managerial group, the Malay share of this group would be 47.89 in 1980 instead of 28.7%. The non-Malay share would be 52.11% instead of 68.6%.

Using the present classification the total number of jobs in this category increased by 16,300 between 1970 and 1983. Of this the Malays captured 5,500 or 33.74%; the Chinese took 11,700 or 71.77%; and the Indians took 100 or 0.061%. The present distribution of jobs in this category by race is skewed in favour of the Chinese, who now command 66.0% of all

administrative and managerial jobs. The prospects of increasing
the Malay share appeared bright between 1970 and 1980 when
its share increased from 24.1% to 28.1%; but thereafter it
declined to 27.4% in 1983 and 26.7% in 1985. The Chinese
share increased to 67.7% in 1985 indicating the resilience of the
Chinese in the private sector. The Indian share has, however,
been secularly rising from 2.4% in 1970 to 3.1% in 1980 to 6.1%
in 1983 before falling to 4.8% in 1985. However, the Malays and
Indians have not lost in an absolute sense because the total
number of Malay administrative and managerial workers has
increased by 6,000 or 81% and the total number of Indians in
this category has remained constant between 1970 and 1985.

The Malay share of employment in the clerical and related
services has increased from 35.4% in 1970 to 55% in 1985. This
tremendous increase was possible because of the vast expansion
of the public services. Out of a total of 207,600 new clerical jobs
created, 142,400 or 68.59% were captured by the Malays. 59,200
or 28.51% were captured by the Chinese and 6,900, or 3.25%
were captured by the Indians. As a result of these dramatic
changes, the Malay share increased by 19.6%; whereas the
Chinese and Indian shares fell by 10.3% and 8.2% respectively
over the period 1970 to 1985. This occupational category
includes clerical supervisors, government executive officials,
typists, bookkeepers, cashiers, telephone operators, and
telegraph operators. The vast expansion of the government
increased the demand for this category of workers.

In the sales and sales related occupational category the
Chinese maintained their dominance although their relative
share of jobs diminished. In 1970, 61.7% of all jobs in this
occupational category was held by the Chinese, by 1985 the
Chinese share fell to 55.9%. The real erosion came after 1980
due to the stricter enforcement of racial employment quotas in
retail outlets. The Chinese share had actually increased from
61.7% in 1970 to 65.7% in 1975 to 69.2% in 1980 before it fell
to 60.1% in 1983 and 55.9% in 1985. The Malay share on the
other hand increased from 26.7% in 1970 to 37.8% in 1985. The
real increase came in 1980, when the Malay share increased by
9%. The Indian share, on the other hand, declined from 11.1%
to 6.3% between 1970 and 1985. The slide was gradual but
persistent.

A total of 158,400 new sales and related jobs were created between 1970 and 1985. Of these the Malays took 88,600 or 55.93%; the Chinese took 73,400 or 46.33%; and the Indians lost 2,600 jobs or 1.64%. The "others" lost 1,000 jobs or 0.6%.

The Malays also made substantial inroads as service workers. The percentage of Malay service workers as a percentage of all service workers increased from 44.3% to 57.6% between 1970 and 1985. Out of a total of 241,700 new service jobs the Malays were successful in obtaining 169,400 or 70.08% of the new jobs. These new jobs were in catering and lodging services, working proprietorships, housekeeping and related services, cooking and related work. The demand for these services rose as average incomes increased and also because the government and public enterprises invested in hotels and restaurants. Malay rural-urban migrants were also easily absorbed as house servants and service operators.

The Chinese took 56,900 or 23.54% of the new service jobs. The Indians gained 15,600 or 6.45% of the service jobs between 1970 and 1985. The Malay gains were at the expense of both the Indians and the Chinese. The Chinese and Indians lost 8.3% and 4.2% respectively of their share of service jobs. The Malays gained an extra 13.3% of all service jobs between 1970 and 1985.

The Malays continued to decline as agricultural workers between 1970 and 1985. In 1970, they had 72.0% of the agricultural jobs and in 1985 they had 65.9% of the agricultural jobs. The Chinese gained 3.2% and the Indians gained 2.7% of agricultural jobs between 1970 and 1985. A total of 18,900 new jobs were created. The Chinese took 44,900 new agricultural jobs; the Indians took 36,800 new agricultural jobs; and the Malays lost 64,900 jobs between 1970 and 1985. It is possible that Chinese and Indians went to work as planters and farmers because of the primary commodity boom after 1979.

A total of 918,700 new production and transport jobs were created between 1970 and 1985. These jobs accounted for 52.07% of all new jobs created between 1970 and 1985. This category of jobs included production supervisors and general foremen, miners, quarrymen, well drillers, motor-vehicle drivers, and related workers. The Malays took 482,800 or 52.55% of these jobs. The Chinese and Indians took 32.11%

and 14.92% respectively of these jobs. The Malay and Indian share of these jobs increased by 9.9% and 2.9% respectively. The Chinese share decreased by 12.9%.

Table 20

Changes in Occupational Structure 1970 - 1985 %

	1970			1985		
	M	**C**	**I**	**M**	**C**	**I**
Professional & Technical Workers	47.0	39.5	10.8	55.5	30.2	12.7
Administrative & Managerial Workers	24.1	62.9	7.8	26.7	67.7	4.8
Clerical & Related Workers	35.4	45.9	17.2	55.0	35.6	9.0
Sales & Related Workers	26.7	61.7	11.1	37.8	55.9	6.3
Service Workers	44.3	39.6	14.6	57.6	31.3	10.4
Agricultural Workers	72.0	17.3	9.7	65.9	20.5	12.4
Production, Transport, & Other Workers	34.2	55.9	9.6	44.1	43.0	12.5
Total	51.8	36.6	10.6	52.5	35.5	11.3

Source: Government of Malaysia, Fourth Malaysia Plan, 1980 - 85, (Kuala Lumpur: Government Printers) 1980, p. 59. Government of Malaysia, Mid-Term Review of Fourth Malaysia Plan, p. 109.

The Malay share in all occupations increased from 1970 to 1985. In 1970, the Malays were only dominant in one occupation, that is, as agricultural workers. In 1985, they were dominant in four occupations, that is, agricultural workers, professional and technical workers, clerical and related workers, and service workers. They also held the largest share of jobs in the occupational category production, transport and other workers. Although the Malays moved mainly into public employment the NEP managed to shift the Malays from being predominantly agricultural workers.

The Chinese share in all occupations declined except in the occupations agricultural workers and administrative and managerial workers. The Chinese continued to dominate as administrators, managers, and sales workers. The Indian share declined in four occupations, that is, administrative and managerial, clerical, sales, and service. The Indian share, however, increased in three occupations, that is, professional and technical workers, agricultural, production, transport and related workers. The Indians have never been the dominant race in any occupation.

Education

Education and language have been a persistent source of racial tension in Malaysia. The development of human capital is the main avenue of social mobility and hence the denial of access to education creates intense inter-racial distrust. In Malaysia, racial quotas are enforced for entry into public universities. Chinese attempts to set up private universities to increase the supply of local Chinese graduates has been prohibited by legislation.

The quotas had their origins in the Constitution Amendment Bill, 1971, whose main force was to halt non-Malay human capital formation until the Malays caught up. This "catching up" was to be done by ensuring that the majority of university places were allocated to Malays.

To vastly expand the supply of Malay graduates from institutions of higher learning the government enforced quotas and created more institutions of higher learning. After 1970 the number of universities increased five fold. Public development expenditure for education and training programmes increased by more than 121% between 1971-1975 and 1976-1980.

The trends in the enrollment in tertiary education between 1970 and 1980 are clear. In 1970, all Malaysians enrolled for certificate, diploma, and degree courses were enrolled in public institutions. By 1980 local and foreign private institutions became the preferred institutions among the non-Malays because of blocked access to public funded tertiary education in Malaysia. In 1980, only 8,369 Chinese students were enrolled in public tertiary institutions in Malaysia. 25,366 Chinese were enrolled overseas and 7,387 were enrolled in local private institutions. Public institutions could only satisfy 20.35% of the

Table 21
Enrollment in Tertiary Education by Race and Levels of Education
1970 -1980 (000s)

	1970			1985		
	M	C	I	M	C	I
Certificate Local PTE				554	3029	455
Overseas				194	4351	654
Local Public	151	209	9	1612	850	96
Diploma Courses						
Local PTE				577	4358	943
Overseas				1811	2563	515
Local Public	2871	393	32	12494	2069	184
Degree Courses						
Local Public	3084	3752	559	13857	5450	1248
Overseas				5194	11538	2676

Source: Fourth Malaysia Plan, p. 351.

Table 22
Share of Local Public Tertiary Education by Race 1970 -1980
(000s - figures in brackets are percentages)

	1970				1980			
	M	C	I	Total	M	C	I	Total
Certificate	151	209	9	369	1612	850	96	2585
	(40.92)	(36.63)	(2.43)		(62.35)	(32.88)	(3.71)	
Diploma	2871	393	32	3318	12494	2069	184	14776
	(86.52)	(11.84)	(0.096)		(84.55)	(14.0)	(1.24)	
Degree	3084	3752	559	7677	13857	5450	1248	20766
	(40.17)	(48.87)	(7.28)		(66.73)	(26.24)	(6.01)	
Total	6106	4354	600	11364	27963	8369	1528	38125
	(53.73)	(38.31)	(5.27)		(73.34)	(21.95)	(4.00)	

Source: See Table 21.

effective demand for tertiary education from the Chinese population. More than 61% of the effective demand was met by overseas institutions. It cannot be said that more expensive overseas institutions were preferred by the Chinese because a choice of a place in a local public institution was not always available.

Among the Indians, 3,845 or 56.78% had to enroll for tertiary education overseas. 1,528 or 22.57% were absorbed by local public institutions and 1,398 or 20.64% were absorbed by local private institutions.

The Malay demand for tertiary education was mainly satisfied by local public institutions. Out of 36,293 Malays enrolled in tertiary education in Malaysia and overseas in 1980, more than 77% or 27,963 were enrolled in local public institutions in Malaysia. In fact, local public tertiary institutions by 1980 catered largely to the training needs of the Malays. In 1970, Malays as a percentage of students enrolled in all public tertiary institutions was only 53.73% but by 1980 the Malay percentage had risen to 73.34%. The Chinese and Indian enrollment fell from 38.31% to 21.95% and 5.276% to 4.00% respectively.

In certificate courses Malay enrollment in public tertiary institutions as a percentage of total enrollment increased from 40.992% to 62.35% between 1970 and 1980; in diploma courses it fell from 86.52% to 84.55%, but in degree courses it increased from 40.17% to 66.73% between 1970 and 1980. The Chinese and Indians suffered the largest reverses in degree courses and here the option was to seek overseas education at private expense.

Of all Malaysian overseas students, in 1980, 62.57% were Chinese, 24.40% were Malays and 13.03% were Indians. Most of the Chinese (62.50%), Malays (72.11%), and Indians (69.59%) were pursuing degree courses. The major difference was that nearly all the non-Malay students were privately sponsored.

Between 1980 and 1983 the enrollment pattern by race did not change drastically. Total enrollment increased by 43,681 and of these 16,891 or 38.66% were Malays; 18,696 or 42.801% were Chinese; 6,401 or 14.65% were Indians. Most of the new Chinese candidates, that is, about 14,785 candidates or 79.08% were private candidates. Of the net increase in Indian can-

Table 23
Changes in Enrollment by Race 1970 -1980 (000s)

| | 1980 | | | 1983 | | |
Certificate Courses	M	C	I	M	C	I
Local Public Institutions	1590	907	96	2480	1628	158
Local Private Institutions	554	3029	455	995	4038	1095
Overseas	194	4351	654	822	5090	1516
Total	2338	8287	1205	4297	10756	2769
Diploma Courses						
Local Public Institutions	11427	1993	161	18570	2479	250
Local Private Institutions	577	4358	943	513	5730	2488
Overseas	1811	2563	315	1484	4585	684
Total	13815	8914	1619	20567	12794	3422
Degree Courses						
Local Public Institutions	13604	5161	1193	19143	7865	1967
Overseas	5194	11538	2676	7835	21181	4936
Total	18798	16697	3869	26978	29046	6903
Grand Total	34591	33900	6693	51842	52596	13094

Source: Mid-Term Review of the Fourth Malaysia Plan, p. 355.

Table 24
Enrollment in Public Institutions by Race 1980 - 1983 (In Percent)

| | 1980 | | | 1983 | | |
	M	C	I	M	C	I
Certificate Courses	61.31	34.97	3.70	38.13	38.16	3.70
Diploma Courses	84.13	14.67	1.18	87.18	11.63	1.17
Degree Courses	68.16	25.85	5.97	66.06	27.14	6.78
Total	26621	8061	1450	40193	11972	221.9
	73.67	22.30	4.01	73.90	22.01	4.08
Total for 1980	36132	Total for 1983		54384		

Source: See Table 23.

didates 5,476 or 85.54% were private candidates. Among the net increase in Malay candidates only 377 or 0.02% were private candidates.

The Malays continued to receive preference in the ratio of 2.7 Malays to 1 non-Malay in public tertiary institutions. The Chinese and Indians continued to be eligible for 22% and 4% of the total places in such institutions. The Malays predominated especially in public institutions offering diploma courses, the percentage of Malays as a percentage of all students in diploma courses increased from 84.13% to 87.18% from 1980 to 1983. The proportion of Malays as a percentage of all students in certificate and degree courses offered by public institutions fell from 61.31% to 58.13% and 68.16% to 66.06% between 1980 and 1983. The Chinese share increased marginally in certificate and degree courses but declined in diploma courses offered by public institutions. The Indian share only increased marginally in degree courses.

Table 25
Enrollment in Private Institutions by Race, 1980 - 1983 (000s)

| | 1980 | | | 1983 | | |
	M	C	I	M	C	I
Certificate Courses	13.71	75.01	11.26	16.23	65.89	17.86
Diploma Courses	9.81	74.14	16.04	5.54	61.98	26.91
Total	1131	7387	1398	1508	9768	3583

Source: See Table 23.

Between 1980 and 1983, the total enrollment in local private institutions increased from 9,916 to 14,859 or by 4,943 or by 49.84%. Most of this increase, about 48.2% was made up of Chinese candidates. The Indians accounted for another 44.2%. The Malays only accounted for 377 or 7.6% of the increase. The Chinese continued to constitute more than 60% of all students in local private institutions. Although the percentage enrolled declined from 74.49% in 1980 to 65.73%, most of this vacant share was taken up by Indians, whose percentage

share increased by more than 10% between 1980 and 1983.
The Malay share declined by more than 1%.

Table 26
Enrollment in Overseas Institutions by Race, 1980 - 1983 (000s)

	1980			1983		
	M	**C**	**I**	**M**	**C**	**I**
Certificate Courses	3.73	83.68	12.57	11.06	68.52	20.40
Diploma Courses	37.04	52.42	10.53	21.97	67.89	10.12
Degree Course	25.21	56.0	12.98	23.07	62.38	14.53
Total	7199	18452	3845	10141	30856	5778

Source: See Table 23.

The number of Malaysian students enrolled in overseas
institutions of higher learning increased by 17,279 or 58.58%
between 1980 and 1983. Most of this increase, about 71.78%,
was due to increased Chinese enrollment. This was
due,17.02% and 11.18%, to increased Malay and Indian enrollment respectively. The Chinese continued to account for
the largest proportion of Malaysian students overseas. Between 1980 and 1983 their share of Malaysian students overseas
increased by more than 3%. The Malay and Indian share
declined by about 3% and about 1% respectively.

The pattern of enrollment by race suggests that the local
public institutions are the domain of the Malays; the local
private institutions the domain of the Chinese; overseas
education is a more expensive substitute for non-Malay
students; and government, not to be left behind, because of
the relatively inelastic supply of university places in the institutions of higher learning in Malaysia.

Ownership of the Corporate Sector

The Malay ownership of the share capital of limited companies in peninsular Malaysia rose from 1.5% to 18.7% between 1969 and 1983. At this rate of growth it is possible that

the Malay share will reach 30% in 1990. The Chinese share increased from 22.8% to 27.9% between 1969 and 1975 and, thereafter, the figures for Chinese ownership is not available. The Indian share also increased from 0.9% between 1969 and 1975 and, thereafter, the figures for Chinese ownership are not available. Data after 1975 lumps the Chinese, Indian and nominee companies and other individuals and locally controlled companies under one category, that is, "Other Malaysian Residents." This category includes foreigners resident in Malaysia. The proportion share capital owned by "Other Malaysian Residents" increased from 37.3% in 1975 to 47.7% in 1983. The losers, in terms of proportions, in this restructuring game have been foreigners whose stake has fallen from 62.1% in 1969 to 33.6% in 1983.

The trends are consistent with the aims of the NEP, that is, to increase Malay ownership of share capital not at the expense of the non-Malays but at the expense of foreigners. However, reports on the changes in share ownership have been misleading.[14] The non-Malay ownership figures may be misleading on several counts; first because nominee companies can be set up by Malays and foreigners. If the 1975 ratios were used for 1978, 1980 and 1983, then the pattern of racial share ownership would be:

Race	1978	1980	1983
Chinese	32.680	33.350	35.670
Indians	1.404	1.431	1.531
Nominee Companies Other Individuals and Locally Controlled Companies	9.606	9.803	10.480

It would appear, therefore, that the Malaysian Plans overstate the proportion of share capital owned by Chinese and Indians in 1983 by more than 10%. The recalculation shows that Chinese ownership of share capital increased by 12.87% between 1969 and 1983 and the Indian share increased by a meager 0.631%. The Malay share increased by more than 17.2%. The Malays, therefore, made the most remarkable progress in acquiring ownership of share capital between 1969 and 1983. This was due to individual enterprise and state sponsorship and subsidy. The government utilized funds allocated from the public budget to buy shares in the open market at subsidized prices. By regulation it required new share issues to be sold to Malay public companies, institutions, private Malay companies and individuals on a quota basis.

Between 1970 and 1980 total share capital in the economy increased by 20,993,800. Of this 3,148,100 or 14.99% was captured by Malay individuals and Malay interests. Foreigners captured 9,128,100 million or 43.47% of the increase. Other Malaysians captured 41.52% of the increase. Using the 1975 proportions this would mean that the Chinese would have captured 31.05% and the Indians would have captured 1.332% of the increase in share capital.

Dramatic changes, however, occurred between 1980 and 1983. The Malay ownership of share capital increased by more than 50%. This was no doubt due to the boom in commodity prices, which enabled the government to pump more funds into acquiring share capital in trust for the indigenous Malays. Individual Malays were also encouraged to buy shares through soft loans. The ASN was also created to encourage Malays to buy shares and a minimum dividend of 10% was assured.[15]

Table 27

Changes in Ownership of Share Capital of Limited Companies in Peninsular Malaysia 1970 - 1983 (in percent)

Race	1969	1975	1978	1980	1983
Malay & Malay Interests	1.5	7.8	10.3	12.5	18.7
Chinese	22.8	27.9			
Indians	0.9	1.2			
Nominee Companies	2.1	8.2			
Other Individuals & Locally Controlled Companies			43.7	44.6	47.7
Federal & State Governments	0.5				
Foreigners	62.1	54.9	46.0	42.9	33.6
Total	100.0	100.0	100.0	100.0	100.0

Source: Parti Gerakan Rakyat Malaysia: The National Economic Policy 1990 and Beyond, (Kuala Lumpur: PGRM) 1984, p. 185.

Table 28
Creation & Acquisition of New Share Capital by Race
1970 to 1980 ($ millions)

	1970	1980	1970-80 Change	1970-80 % of Total Change
Malay & Malay Interests	125.6	3273.7	3148.1	14.99
Malay Individuals	84.4	1128.9	1044.5	4.97
Malay Interests	41.2	2144.8	2103.6	10.02
Other Malaysians	1826.5	10544.1	8717.6	41.52
Foreign	3377.1	12505.2	9128.1	43.47
Total Private Sector	5329.2	26323.0	20993.8	

Source: Fourth Malaysia Plan, p. 62.

Table 29
Creation & Acquisition of New Share Capital by Race
1970 to 1983 ($ millions)

	1970	1983	1970-83 Change	1970-83 % of Total Change
Malay & Malay Interests	125.6	9274.6	9149	20.61
Malay Individuals	84.4	3762.2	3677.8	8.28
Malay Interests	41.2	5512.4	5471.2	12.33
Other Malaysians	1826.5	23735.9	21909.4	49.36
Foreign	3377.1	16697.6	13320.5	30.01
Total Private Sector	5329.2	49708.2	44379.0	

Source: Mid-Term Review of the Fourth Malaysia Plan p. 101.

There has been some public skepticism about the released official figures on Malay ownership of share capital in Malaysia largely because of the tremendous inroads made into the corporate sector by Malay institutions funded out of the public budget. One component party of the ruling BN party has called in to question these figures. The PGRM has asserted that:

"It is our contention that a detailed ownership breakdown by
industry will give further evidence that the Government's efforts in increasing Bumiputra share ownership has been highly
successful and that the overall Bumiputra share has exceeded
18.7% by 1983/84. Our own rough estimates indicate that corporate share ownership far exceeds the 30% target in plantation agriculture (45%), and mining (30%), the two command-
ing sectors of the Malaysian economy, while it is more than
double the target in the banking and finance sector."[16]

The PGRM claims that in finance and banking, Malay
ownership is 70-80%, in manufacturing it is 18%, in construction, and others 10-15%. The weighted average share of share
capital, economy wide, according to PGRAM is 30%.[17] The
Government has not refuted these allegations nor made any effort to ban the publication.

The PGRAM's claim is plausible because of the post 1980
activities of the Permodalan Nasional Berhad (PNB), its associates, Petronas, the MMC and the large injection of public
funds on behalf of the Malays into the banking system. The
PNB has bought into the largest plantation groups.[18] The MMC
is the largest mining corporation. Petronas is flushed with oil
money and deposits its money in Bank Bumiputra.

The PGRAM has, in fact, called upon the government to
release "a more accurate set of figures.... to mitigate demands
for a further continuation of this particular restructuring effort.
This would in turn relieve the government of both the political
pressure and the financial resources which could then be chan-
neled for poverty eradication along non-racial lines."[19]
However, the Government released data up to 1985 do not
show that the Malays have reached the 30% ownership target.

Between 1983 and 1985, the Malay ownership of share
capital increased by more than $4,963.4 million or 53.51%.
Most of this increase (64.65%) was due to the increase in share
capital owned by Malay trust agencies. Total share capital increased by $15,403.1 million or by 30.98%. Of this $15,403.1
million shares, the Malays captured 32.22%; other Malaysian
residents took $784 million or 50.79%; and foreigners took
$2,615.9 million or 16.98%.

As of 1985, the Malay ownership of total share capital
stood at 21.9%; the other Malaysian residents owned 48.4%;

and foreigners owned 29.7%. If the 1975 ratios are used the Chinese share would be 36.19% and the Indian share would be 1.56%. The share of nominee companies would be 10.632%.

Of all the communities the Malay share has shown the most dramatic changes since 1970.

Table 30
Changes in Share Capital Ownership 1983 - 1986

	1983 $M	1985 $M	Absolute change $M	Percentage Change %
Bumi Individuals &Trust Agencies	9274.6	14237.9	4963.3	32.22
Bumiputra Individ.	3762.2	5516.7	1754.5	11.39
Bumiputra Trust Ag	5512.4	8721.2	3208.8	20.83
Other Malaysian Residents	23735.9	31559.9	7824.0	50.79
Foreign Residents	16697.6	19313.5	2615.9	16.98
Total	49708.2	65111.3	15403.1	

Source: Mid-Term Review of the Fourth Malaysia Plan, p. 110.

Table 31
Ownership of Share Capital by Race 1970 - 1985 (In Percent)

	1970	1985	% Change 1970-85
Malay & Malay Interests	2.0	21.90	19.90
Chinese	22.8	36.19	13.39
Indians	0.9	1.56	0.66
Nominee Companies Other Individuals & Locally Controlled Companies	2.1	10.63	8.33
Foreigners	62.1	29.70	32.40
Total	100.0	100.00	

Source: Derived from Tables 27, 28, and 30.

The Malays increased their total share by 19.9%. The Chinese share increased by only 13.39%. The Indian share increased by only 0.66%. The Indian rate of progress has been the most dismal.

Racial Income Differentials

In 1970, the Malays had the lowest mean and median income of all the races in Malaysia. By 1979 the situation had not changed. However, the income differential between the races narrowed between 1970 and 1979.

Table 32
Racial Income Differentials Mean 1970 - 1979 (Constant 1970 prices)

Race	1970	1973	1976	1979	Annual Growth Rate %
Malay	172	209	237	309	6.7
Chinese	394	461	340	639	5.9
Indian	304	352	369	467	4.9
Malay : Chinese	0.436:1	0.453	0.438	0.468:1	
Chinese : Indian	1.29	1.309	1.463	1.411	
Malay : Indian	0.365	0.593	0.6422	0.661	

Source: Government of Malaysia: Fourth Malaysia Plan, 1980 -1985, (Kuala Lumpur: Government Printer), 1980 p. 56.

The Malay mean income grew at a more rapid rate than Chinese or Indian mean income between 1970 and 1979. The slowest rate of growth was achieved by Indian mean income. However, the rapid pace of growth in Malay mean income was unable to narrow significantly the mean income differential between the Malays and Chinese. In 1970, the Malay mean income was 42.6% of the Chinese mean income, whereas in 1979 it was 46.8%. However the differential between Malay and Indian mean income was reduced significantly. In 1970, Malay mean income was 56.3% of Indian mean income, whereas by 1979, the Malay mean income was 66.1% of Indian mean income. This narrowing of the differential was possible because of the much slower annual rate of growth in the Indian mean income.

Table 33
Racial Income Differentials Median 1970 - 1979 (Constant 1970 prices)

Race	1970	1973	1976	1979	Annual Growth Rate %
Malay	120	141	160	200	5.8
Chinese	268	298	329	383	4.1
Indian	194	239	247	314	5.5
Malay : Chinese	0.447	0.473	0.486	0.322	
Chinese : Indian	1.381	1.246	1.331	1.219	
Malay : Indian	0.408	0.588	0.486	0.636	

Source: See Table 32.

The Malay median income has done better than the Malay mean income in the sense that the Malay-Chinese median income differentials have narrowed much more over time. Malay median income as a proportion of Chinese median income has increased from 44.7% in 1970 to 52.2% in 1979. Malay median income as a proportion of Indian median income has also increased from 40.8% to 63.6% from 1970 to 1979.

Conclusion

The New Economic Policy has been extremely successful for the Malays because of the tremendous support the Malays received from the state. It is fortunate that the first dozen years of the NEP coincided with the years of high economic growth. The NEP also coincided with a period of structural change in the Malaysian economy, that is, modern sector enlargement and traditional sector contraction. The Malays, Chinese, and Indians were affected positively by this structural change. Most of the new modern sector jobs were taken by the Malays but

Chinese and Indian modern sector jobs also expanded. Within the modern sector, the tertiary sector expanded more than the secondary sector and most of the tertiary sector jobs were taken by Malays because of large government investments in the tertiary sector.

By occupation too, the NEP helped the Malays increase their share of the highest paying jobs. Under the NEP a large number of Malays obtained jobs as professionals, administrators, and managers. The rural-urban Malay migrants were easily absorbed as clerical, service, and production workers.

In education, the Malays obtained preferential treatment in enrollment in local public institutions. More than 73% of all places in local public institutions were reserved for Malays. The Malays also received generous financial support for local and overseas education.

The state also was active in increasing the Malay share of the corporate wealth of the country. Throughout the 15 years the Malay share had increased at a faster rate than the non-Malay share. The income differential between the non-Malays and Malays was also reduced.

The Chinese, who were left to fight for their survival in a segmented society, did remarkably well too. They held on to what they had before the NEP and managed to increase their human and physical capital at least in an absolute sense. The rate of change of their physical and human assets although positive was not as high as the Malays in many areas of economic activity.

The Indians did the worst among all the races. This is because of their low initial endowments and the lack of state support systems. The Indians did not suffer any absolute loss but lost some of their share of jobs, assets and educational places over time.

The NEP brought to surface many problems not hitherto faced by the Malaysian society. The most alarming and disturbing has been the intra-Malay conflict over wealth and religion. There have been allegations that a select few Malays enriched themselves at the expense of the poor Malay masses. The widening income inequality within the Malay race has created antagonism between the poor and rich. The deprived, it is alleged, are protesting through their overt support of fundamental Islam. They are also demanding that an Islamic state be set up to rid the society of injustice, inequality, corruption, and sin.

The non-Malays are also bitter about the NEP and the three non-Malay based parties within the ruling Barison Nasional have made it known that the NEP is discriminatory.[20] A large number of the younger generation of non-Malays also do not subscribe to the 1957 communal compromise because they were born after 1957 and are just solid citizens. New social justice groups have sprung up among the non-Malays and are speaking on issues of concern to the non-Malays.

The economy is under stress at the moment and it is feared that redistribution without growth or expected negative growth[21] may ruin the long term prospects of the economy. The government has anticipated this by relaxing employment quota requirements in business and the rules on equity ownership; reducing agricultural subsidies; reducing the number of Malay students sent overseas; amending the Industrial Coordination Act to attract investment; reducing taxes and utility rates and encouraging deregulation and privatization.

It appears that the Malaysian economy and society are set for stormy times ahead. With lower or negative growth rates expected the NEP targets may not be achieved. At the same time it appears the NEP should continue in the present form. Obviously a new communal compromise may be necessary to maintain peace, stability, and to generate growth and development.

Notes

1. Goh Cheng Teik, *The May Thirteenth Incident and Democracy in Malaysia*, (Kuala Lumpur: Oxford), 1971, p. 31.
2. *New Straits Times*, 10 November 1969.
3. *New Sunday Times*, 15 March 1970.
4. *Utusan Melayu*, 18 July 1969.
5. Prime Minister's Department, Malaysia, *Development Forum*, Vol. II, No. 2, December 1969, pp. 5-6.
6. D. Mauzy, *Barisan Nasianal*, (Kuala Lumpur: Marican's), 1984, p. 48.
7. *ibid.*
8. Government of Malaysia, *Third Malaysia Plan*, 1976 - 1980, (Kuala Lumpur: Government Printer), 1976, p. 7.

9. *ibid.*
10. Ungku A. Aziz, Facts and Fallacies in the Malayan Economy, *Straits Times*, 28 February 1957 to 5 March 1957.
11. W.A. Lewis, *A Theory of Economic Growth*, London: MacMillan, 1954.
12. H.W. Bhenery *et.al., Growth with Redistribution*, (London: Oxford University Press), 197.
13. T.W.Schultz, *Transforming Traditional Agricultural*, (New Haven: Yale University Press), 1964.
14. Parti Gerakan Rakyat Malaysia (PGRM), *NEP Selepas 1990?*, (Kuala Lumpur PGRM), p. 185.
15. J.M.Gullick and Bruce Gale, *Malaysia: Its Political and Economic Development*, (Kuala Lumpur: Pelanduk), p. 259.
16. *op.cit*, PGRM, p. 186.
17. *ibid*, p. 187.
18. *op.cit*, Gullick and Gale.
19. *op.cit*, PGRM, p. 187
20. *op.cit*, PGRM; MCA, *The Malaysian Chinese: Towards National Unity*, (Kuala Lumpur: Eastern Universities Press), 1982; Datuk Samy Velu in *New Straits Times*. October 4, 1985.
21. *Far Eastern Economic Review*, 20 February 1986, pp. 52-53., 1982;

3

Political Change and Economic Development at the Grassroots in Contemporary Rural Malaysia

Shamsul A. Baharuddin

...The party (UMNO) was held together not because the members had generally identical ideas on politics, but through a system of patronage and disguised coercion based on Government rather than party authority ... As patronage became more and more indirect, as when a village was denied or given development projects, it became more and more difficult to elicit favourable responses ... The advent of patronage as a factor in intra-party politics was significant, for it meant that the leaders were no longer answerable to the ordinary members and the faceless supporters, but were only answerable to themselves. A feeling of power normally grips those who wield patronage, a feeling that they can mould and shape people and opinion any way they please. The leaders of UMNO ... succumbed to this disease, believing that they no longer needed to heed the opinions of the supporters, they disregarded them at every turn...

Mahathir Mohamed,
The Malay Dilemma,
1970, pp. 9-10

I

In the above statement made about 15 years ago, Dr.Mahathir
Mohamed, then an expelled UMNO (United Malays National
Organization) party member and now the party's national
president and Malaysia's Prime Minister, revealed to us two
important trends that were taking place at the grassroots in
rural Malaysia. Firstly, politics at the local, village level was
greatly influenced by "a system of patronage and disguised
coercion." Secondly, and as the consequence of the first, the
distribution of economic development projects at the
grassroots was politicised to such an extent that only the loyal
supporters of the dominant faction (within UMNO, a major
component of the then Alliance ruling party) enjoyed the
benefits and not the supposed beneficiaries, such as the needy
and the poor.

These observations were made by Dr. Mahathir at the eve
of the launching of Malaysia's New Economic Policy (NEP) in
association with the *Second Malaysia Plan of 1971-75*. They
were certainly based not only upon his observations but also
his own experiences as an active UMNO politician at the
grassroots then; hence his observations were both reliable and
significant.

Unfortunately, since the days when Dr. Mahathir made
those observations, the whole of the NEP era—Malaysianists
have not attempted a single serious, detailed empirical study
to examine whether or not the trends mentioned by him continue to exist at the grassroots in contemporary rural Malaysia;
and if they do exist, how they have affected social life at that
micro level and so on. In short, there is not a single study in
English or Malay which has examined in detail the complex interplay, at the grassroots, of political dynamics and economic
development initiatives originating from and generated by circumstances within as well as beyond the local level during the
NEP period. This is despite the fact that there exists now a
considerable body of scholarly publications on Malaysian social studies and especially on Malaysian politics and economic
development.

This brief paper is, therefore, a small and modest attempt
to redress this empirical gap in Malaysian social studies.[1] Most
of the material presented in this paper is drawn from an inten-

sive field research I conducted, throughout 1980 and 1981, in a rural, administrative district of peninsular Malaysia. I will also use empirical data from other related studies conducted by both the academics and government researchers in various regions of Malaysia,[2] not only to complement my own but also to provide some comparisons when and if necessary.

II

Since the advent of the NEP, the national government has made many changes, mostly political, to facilitate the implementation of various economic development programs. The most affected was the all important "administrative machinery"[3] responsible not only for the planning but also the implementation as well as the monitoring of the NEP, at all levels. In order to understand why these changes were effected it is imperative to examine the circumstances and sociological context within which the NEP was introduced.

The NEP was launched as an integral part of and in association with the *Second Malaysia Plan of 1971-75*. This occurred not long after the May 13th, 1969 racial riot which broke out in Kuala Lumpur, Malaysia's capital city. Its expressed overall, long term aim was to help the economically backward *bumiputera* (autochthonous) population, residing mainly in the underdeveloped rural areas of the Peninsula, Sarawak and Sabah.

Although the NEP's two-pronged strategy was outlined in the *Second Malaysia Plan 1971-75* document, a clearer and more specific elaboration of the strategy appeared in the *Mid-Term Review of the Second Malaysia Plan 1971-75*, published in late 1973. The strategy consisted of the following:[4]

(a) eradicating poverty by raising income levels and increasing employment opportunities for all Malaysians, regardless of race. This is to be achieved by programs aimed at raising the productivity and income of those in low productivity occupations, the expansion of opportunities for intersectoral movements from low productivity to higher productivity activities, and the provision of a wide range of social services especially designed to raise the living standards of the low income groups;

(b) accelerating the process of restructuring Malaysian society to correct economic imbalance, in order to reduce and eventually eliminate the identification of race with economic function. Programs for this purpose include the modernization of rural life, the rapid and balanced development of urban activities, the establishment of new growth centres and the creation of a Malay commercial and industrial community in all categories and at all levels of operation. The objective is to ensure that Malays and other indigenous people will become full partners in all aspects of the economic life of the nation.

The overriding objective of the above strategies and substrategies, essentially economic in nature, is to bring about national unity, which is clearly a long term political goal. In short, the NEP is an economic development program for a political end. Therefore, the political changes effected with the introduction of the NEP and its implementation were inevitable when seen in the above context.

However, it is insufficient to understand both these economic and political efforts, as expressed through the NEP, without further locating them in a wider sociological context, from which these efforts found their social roots. It was obvious that the May 13, 1969 incident, its aftermath and the state's subsequent reactions to the traumatic event became the immediate circumstances, which, sociologically, justified the formulation and implementation of the NEP. Nonetheless, by no means were these the only set of circumstances to which the NEP was responding. If one examines closely the detailed contents of the NEP, one easily finds a striking similarity of most of its philosophical ideas and practical policies to those of the proposals and resolutions of the *Kongress Ekonomi Bumiputera* (Economic Congress of the Indigenous People) of 1965 and 1968.[5]

The congresses were organized and sponsored by the dominant component of the ruling party, namely, the elite-based UMNO, as a result of the mounting pressure exerted by the dissatisfied, but extremely influential, Malay entrepreneurial group within the party. The dissatisfaction stemmed from the successive failure of the government's efforts, particularly in the 1950s and 1960s, to place this group on a stronger economic footing in order to compete effectively along with other local and foreign entrepreneurial groups for the nation's wealth.[6] Hence the Congresses reflected the emerging coherence and consolidation of the Malay fraction of the capitalist class.

Sociologically, it was the interests of this class that were embodied and articulated in the NEP. The bloody May 13th incident, ironically, presented these emerging Malay capitalists with a golden opportunity to promote their interests on the economic fronts, by pressuring (and participating in) the UMNO-controlled government to incorporate their demands in the NEP. This was clearly reflected in both the objectives of the NEP and its concomitant practical policies. For example, in its first objective of poverty eradication, this was to be achieved without eliminating class exploitation and without challenging the interest of the propertied class, or, in short, without effecting any fundamental structural changes to the inequality-generating social system which has been responsible for perpetuating the poverty the NEP intended to eradicate.[7] Similarly, the second objective of the NEP, to restructure Malaysian society to correct the racial economic imbalance, and its component strategies presented an even stronger stimulus to the economic interests of the Malay capitalists. The UMNO-controlled government intervened in the free market process to assist the private Malay entrepreneurs. The subsequent setup of various public enterprises and statutory government bodies was part of the strategy.[8]

Since the NEP is also an 'outline perspective plan' for 1970-90, the successive five-year plans after the Second Malaysia Plan of 1971-75 have incorporated the original objectives and policies of the NEP, but, necessarily, with changes to suit the economic, political and social situations of the day. However, these changes have not affected the interests of the Malay capitalists; on the contrary, they have been consolidated and strengthened as the recent 'privatization' policy has demonstrated.[9]

Interesting and revealing studies on the economic, social and political impact of the NEP's implementation at the national, macro level are abundantly available to date.[10] Useful as they are and insightful as they seemed to be, we still learned very little from this ever-growing body of literature about the

NEP's consequences at the grassroots. The few that exist are confined to routine, performance evaluation exercises.[11] However, a meaningful understanding of the consequences of the political change and economic development at the grassroots, brought about by the NEP, still rests largely on the information provided by the macro studies mentioned and particularly the general background described above. Therefore, the subsequent parts of this paper must be located within the broader sociological picture presented in this section.

III

Central to the effective implementation of the NEP is the important development of administrative machinery upon which NEP's success and failure depends to a large extent. Almost a separate administrative organization has been set up to deal with problems of the rural poor under the NEP. The program for the poor is popularly called the rural development projects which are essentially strategies of the NEP's poverty eradication objective.

The existing administrative structure responsible for the implementation of the rural development projects for the poor is by no means a new one. It was in fact constructed during the rural development era of the 1960s, which, in turn, was laid down on the model of the administration that the British, in late colonial Malaya, developed for the successful prosecution of the emergency (1948-1960).[12] Therefore, the highly politicized nature of this administrative structure remains, in fact enhanced after the NEP was introduced.

During the Razak era of the 1960s, the then Ministry of Rural Development was responsible for the over-all planning, coordination, and formation of local committees.[13] This enabled the Ministry to have direct access to the local units despite the problematic federal-state relations. As a result, the composition of the rural development committees from the national down to the district level is almost similar in structure, particularly between the state and district committees. The District Rural Development Committee consisted of district heads of technical departments, state councilors, and members of the parliament from the district. The district officer was designated chairperson of the committee.

Planning was organized around a standardized master plan that came to be known as the *Red Book*. The main task of planning, as required by the Ministry, lay with the district rural development committee. The Minister himself was involved in an extensive series of visits to the state and district committees to explain and oversee the plan's implementation. Thus he brought his political and administrative power to bear upon local officers and politicians to ensure the effective implementation of the rural development programs.

The major component of these development programs were minor rural development projects, small in size and financial cost. They were often called "quick results projects" such as village mosques, *surau* (small prayer house), markets, bicycle paths, small bridges and so on, because these projects were of high political value but not necessarily costly. By the mid and late 1960s these projects were almost scrapped because they were considered wasteful.[14] More attention was given to larger and more expensive projects which were the physical and social infrastructural type, for example, road networks, electricity supply, telephone and postal services, piped-drinking water, and publicly-provided low-cost housing. However, most of these projects were not within the power of the district committee to plan and implement, hence the political infuence of the said committee at the local level was very much reduced at the end of the 1960s.

Then, with the introduction of the NEP, major political changes occurred at the national level which have direct consequences at all levels of the economic sphere. Expectedly, the rationale and content of the rural development programs changed too. The rationale for rural development policies prior to NEP was to increase productivity amongst the peasants and improve the infrastructure and social services for consumption as well as production purposes. However, after 1969, the rationale for rural development policies was affected. The most important consequence was to reduce the overall priority of rural development relative to industrialization and urbanization in policies and education.[15]

The new emphasis was not only meant to improve rural life and economic activity but also to prepare rural Malays for inter-sectoral mobility while the rest wait for further opportunities when and if the NEP takes its full effect by 1990. In other words, the government hopes that the backwash effects of the NEP or bumiputera policy will convey development to the rural economy — that is, to develop the rural area is to modernize and urbanize it.

The change in the rationale consequently changed the development administrative structure at the district level and below, too.[16] Before the NEP, there was only one district rural development committee, but after, a series of development committees were formed at the district level. The largest is the District Action Committee (DAC) which includes not only the district heads of technical departments, state councilors, and members of parliament, who were also in the previous district rural development committee, but also the Penghulus, representatives of semi-government bodies, state governments and other district heads of state and federal non-technical departments. This new committee functions as the highest decision-making body in the district pertaining not only to development matters but other district affairs. It handles public funds on the order of M\$4 to 4.5 million annually and not M\$50,000, which the former district rural development committee was allowed. On top of that, each state councillor and member of parliament (only of the ruling party) was allocated between M\$100,000 to 200,000 "development funds" annually to spend on his/her constituency.

The District Development Committee (DDC) and District Planning Committee (DPC) are the other two new committees created to deal specifically with development matters. The DDC monitors the progress of all development projects throughout the district and the DPC draws up the annual master plan of the district physical and physically-related development. Though the District Land Committee (DLC) is not directly related to the development process at the district level, nonetheless it plays an important role in deciding the use of land for development purposes.

One significant and striking feature of these committees is that the top district politicians (state councilors and members of parliament) are members of all the committees. Their influence and dominance in the decision-making process has certainly increased compared to before the NEP. This dominance is further enhanced by the fact that many local bureaucrats have become partisans who openly belong to the local ruling UMNO party organization. Hence, they are under the control of the top district politicians, not only within their local party organization but also in the development committee itself. As a result, the district development administrative machinery, which controls and monitors every aspect of the implementation of all district economic development projects under the NEP, has now become an integral part of the local ruling party apparatus.

The picture was quite different in the 1960s when the local bureaucrats enjoyed more power and influence than the district politicians in matters pertaining to rural development. So influential were the bureaucrats then that the Minister of Rural Development himself had to make frequent surprise visits to the districts in order to ensure the "proper" implementation of development projects. Despite that, he achieved limited success and often met with strong direct or indirect oppositions from the local bureaucrats.

But in the 1970s and 1980s, that is during the NEP era, the situation has almost reversed. The hegemony of the local district politicians has been so overpowering that, according to a government report, the district office has been facing some problems as a result of the politicians bypassing government financial procedures in the implementation of development projects.[17] For example, often a politician chooses a contractor and awards him a contract instead of going through the normal procedure of choosing a contract or through the calling of quotations, or decides on a site of a project and commences construction without first investigating if the site is available and technically viable, and so on.

Usually, the District Officer (DO) must do as the politicians direct; the latter feel they are in a stronger position, with more power which they are quite willing to demonstrate by transferring a particular bureaucrat from the district to some remote area of Malaysia. Besides, the DO believes, and is often correct, that the district politicians have the final authority for approval at the state level by virtue of being members of either the all powerful state cabinet, popularly known as State EXCO, or the State Action Committee.

The political and economic implications of this pattern for the whole process of development of benefit distribution at different levels of the grassroots in contemporary rural Malaysia has been far reaching and wide ranging. Therefore, in the next section of this paper some of these implications are discussed.

IV

The development "goods" which have been delivered and distributed by the district development administrative machinery are, by official definition, economic in nature. However, the process of the distribution of these "goods" has been highly politicized. Therefore, the "goods" are perceived at the grassroots as economic and political at the same time.

Similarly, both objectives of the NEP are perceived as one by local politicians, bureaucrats and the rural folks. Whatever programs implemented under the NEP are simply called development projects or *projek pembangunan,* irrespective of whether they are for "poverty eradication" or to "restructure Malaysian society." The significance of such perceptions vis-a-vis the implementation of the *projek pembangunan* will emerge as we examine the distribution of such projects, their ultimate beneficiaries, and the resultant political configurations that followed.

Firstly, as funds allocated for rural development projects have generally been biased toward basic amenitites, mainly involving construction jobs, the biggest beneficiaries in the district have been the politicians, namely, the *wakil rakyat,* and their Malay and Chinese associates. They have managed to turn rural development projects, initially aimed at eradicating poverty, into rich financial resources for themselves, by establishing their own companies and then awarding them lucrative government contracts. These efforts are interpreted by them as fulfilling the 30 per cent quota of *bumiputera* ownership in business and management, as outlined in the NEP. In other words, they believe that they have fulfilled to some degree the societal "restructuring" objective of the NEP, but, ironically and on their own admission, it was by exploiting the poverty eradication objective. This is a very different strategy from that pursued by the Malay national bourgeoisie, who generally involve themselves in the stockmarket or in large-scale business ventures in the national industrial sector. Nonetheless, the emerging local nouveaux riches comprising top district UMNO politicians, cannot be described simply as petty Malay entrepreneurs because their operating capital ranges from M$50,000 to M$250,000.

Secondly, the *wakil rakyat* through their successful business activities, have managed to foster a new locally-based Malay business class, not of petty commodity traders, but full-fledged capital-based entrepreneurs. The existence of such a class, which is far from small at the village and *mukim* level was unknown prior to the NEP. In this sense, the NEP has been successful, especially, in creating new Malay entrepreneurs but at the expense of the impoverished peasants in each locality.

Thirdly, although there exist numerous other development projects at the *mukim* and district level which are relatively small in material value, the distribution of these projects is based on personal links of patronage within the political arena, as many cases have shown.[18] As a result, at the village and *mukim* level, the beneficiaries have been small, select groups of peasants, not necessarily the poorest, although the projects are supposedly for them. It is also important to note that low-ranking bureaucrats (Malays and non-Malays) and favoured local UMNO leaders also benefit materially from the distribution of this pool of *ikan bilis* projects. Those closely-associated with the centre of power at the local level stand to benefit most from the implementation of the development programs under the NEP.

Fourthly, there have been significant changes in the operation of local politics, especially with UMNO. Since the introduction of the NEP, the general position of the ruling party *wakil rakyat* at the grassroots has undergone substantial change. Prior to the NEP, a *wakil rakyat* was seen more as a political patron than as an economic one. The NEP has transformed not only the image but also the objective position of the *wakil rakyat* within the district. Their political power has been greatly increased by their control of the district development machinery, which, in turn, places them in an unassailable position in distributing development benefits. This situation has not only brought them very substantial personal gain but also, by virtue of their new-found wealth, has given them the ability to buy continued political support with hard cash. Consequently, the nature of internal politics within local UMNO organizations has been reshaped. Bitter factional struggles have increased within local UMNO over the coveted postion of *wakil rakyat*, especially during the preselection period before a general election, since the contending leaders reqard the position as providing the passport to riches and power. This has resulted, in many cases, in the directing of development benefits away from disfavoured groups of people within the ruling party ranks. Sometimes whole villages have been denied such benefits on the basis of belonging to the "wrong camp" within the local UMNO organizations or of supporting an opposition party, such as PAS. The intense internal political strife within local UMNO organizations has reached new heights as recent events in Selangor and elsewhere in Malaysia show.[19] Outbreaks of violence at UMNO branch and divisional meetings both in Selangor and in other parts of Malaysia have been on the rise.[20] In fact, in one particular UMNO division, in Negeri Sembilan, a protracted vehement factional conflict ended in what has been widely referred to as a "political" murder.[21]

It is also significant that the leadership struggle within local UMNO organizations is not only for the *wakil rakyat* postion but also for other offices at the branch and divisional levels.[22] The latter is usually a stepping stone to the former. Failing that, such an office gives one the opportunity to be involved in the financially lucrative "business of development" at the local level. Yet another route to being a *wakil rakyat* or a potentially successful Malay entrepreneur is to be elected as one of the divisional representatives to the all-important UMNO Annual General Assembly and to participate in the election of the UMNO national supreme council members. Before or during this meeting a divisional representative has the chance to get to know or to be known to the various canidates of the UMNO national leadership, or at least, to the latter's lieutenants. This opens up another opportunity for one to be considered as a potential *wakil rakyat* candidate or to receive patronage in the form of material benefits. Given these benefits, it is not uncommon, in the contest for official positions within local UMNO organizations, for the contending leaders to use money to achieve their goal. Such a practice is by no means a local level phenomenon. The Prime Minister and the present President of UMNO Malaysia, Dr. Mahathir Mohamed, has stated that "with more Malays becoming rich, the contests for the posts (in the UMNO Supreme Council) are carried out by using large amounts of money".[23] Thus the rise of "money politics," at all levels, within UMNO, is closely related, if not the direct result, of the NEP itself.

At the local level, it is now clear that since the advent of the NEP, local politicians, especially the *wakil rakyat*, have become influential not only in deciding the allocation of rural development benefits, but more importantly, in determining the future course of district-level development. Such a situation has, in turn, transformed the basis of local politics within the ruling party organization into a fierce internal competition for the *wakil rakyat* position because it promises the opportunity for more wealth and power. This vicious circle of political behavior has gathered considerable momentum, and the social consequences must be weighed if they are not to go beyond the level of party politics.

Notes

1. This paper is an extract from a larger study on politics and planning in Malaysia in *From British to Bumiputera Rule: Local Politics and Rural Development in Peninsular Malaysia* (Singapore: Institute of Southeast Asian Studies, 1986).

2. The research findings of the academics are found in unpublished MA and PhD theses. I have also referred to the rich collections of BA theses in the various departments of the social science, arts and economics faculties at Universiti Malaya and Universiti Kebangsaan Malaysia. Specific studies referred to for this paper will be cited in detail in subsequent notes. Two sets of government reports have been extensively used to inform this study, namely *Kajian Mendalam Pentadbiran Daerah - Daerah Jelebu, Sereban das Kuala Pilah, Negeri Sembilan*, 5 volumes (1979) and *An In-Depth Study of District and Local Government in the State of Selangor*, 4 volumes (1979) both produced by the Prime Minister's Department of Malaysia. For a detailed bibliography of the above materials see *From British to Bumiputera Rule*.

3. The term "administrative machinery" hasbeen used by the government to describe the development administration organization in Malaysia; see *Second Malaysia Plan 1971-75* (Kuala Lumpur: Government Printer, 1971) pp. 112-119. The subsequent use of this term in the paper subscribes to the meaning spelled out in the document cited above.

4. See *Mid-Term Review of the Second Malaysia Plan 1971-75* (Kuala Lumpur: Government Printer, 1973), pp. 1.
5. See *Lapuran Seminal Kongres Ekonomi Bumiputera Pertama* (Kuala Lumpur: 1966) and *Lapuran Seminar Kongres Ekonomi Bumiputera Kedua* (Kuala Lumpur: 1969). See, also J. H. Beaglehole, "Malay Participation in Commerce and Industry, the Role of RIDA and MARA," *Journal of Commonwealth and Political Studies*, 7:3 (1969), pp. 316-45; Tham Seong Chee, "Ideology, Politics and Economic Modernization: The Case of the Malays in Malaysia", *Southeast Asian Journal of Social Science*, 1:1 (1973), pp. 41-59; R.S. Milne and D.K. Mauzy, *Politics and Government in Malaysia* (Kuala Lumpur: Federal Publications, 1978), pp. 321-6; and R.S. Milne, "The politics of Malaysia's New Economic Policy," *Pacific Affairs*, 49:2 (1976), pp. 235-62.
6. See Beaglehole, ibid and Tham Seong Chee, ibid.
7. I have examined the economic, political and social implication of the NEP in greater detail in my own published study, *RMK, Tujuan dan Pelaksanaannya: Suatu Penilaian Teoretis* (Kuala Lumpur: Dewan Bahasa dan Pustaka, 1977).
8. See, Milne, "The Politics of Malaysia's New Economic Policy" and also the excellent study by Bruce Gale, *Politics and Public Enterprise in Malaysia* (Kuala Lumpur: Eastern Universities Press, 1981). Also worth noting is an interesting essay by Lim Mah Hui and William Canak, "The Political Economy of State Policies in Malaysia," *Journal of Contemporary Asia*, 11:2 (1981), pp. 208-24.
9. See, M. Puthucheary, "How to Privatise? The Crucial Questions," *Ilmu Masyarakat*, 9 (1985), pp. 48-54.
10. A useful list of such studies is found in D.R. Snodgrass, *Inequality and Economic Development in Malaysia* (Kuala Lumpur: Oxford University Press, 1980). The literature survey on the social science of Malaysia by Tham Seong Chee is also helpful, see Tham Seong Chee, *Social Science Research in Malaysia*, (Singapore: Graham Brash, 1981).
11. See, for example, Stephen Chee, *Rural Local Government and Rural Development in Malaysia* (Cornell University: Special Series on Rural Local Government No. 9, 1974); G.S. Cheema, et al. *Rural Organisations and Rural Development in Selected Malaysian Villages* (Kuala Lumpur: Asian and Pacific Development Administration Centre, 1978).
12. See. G.D. Ness, *Bureaucracy and Rural Development in Malaysia* (Berkeley and Los Angeles: University of California Press, 1967); C.G. Ferguson., "The Story of Development in Malaya (Now Malays Some Aspects", *Journal of Local Administration Overseas*, 4:3 (1965), pp. 149-64; and M.J. Esman, *Administration and Development in Malaysia* (Ithaca: Cornell University Press, 1972).
13. See, Ferguson, ibid and, M. Puthucheary "The Operations Room in Malaysia as a Technique in Administation Reform", in Hahn-Been Lee and A.G. Samonte, eds., *Administative Reform in Asia* (Manila: E.R.O.P.A., 1970), pp. 165-98.

14. See, Snodgrass, *Inequality and Economic Development in Malaysia*, p. 193.
15. See *Second Malaysia Plan*, pp. 4-7, 66-75, 120-146, and comments by Snodgrass, ibid, pp. 165-203.
16. See the excellent detailed study by Abdullah Sanusi Ahmad, "The District Office as an Institution of Development," PhD Diss., University of Southern California, 1977. He was the research consultant and resource person for both the district-level studies carried out by the Prime Minister's Department, the details of which are cited in note 2.
17. See, the Prime Minister's Department report, *An In-Depth Study of District and Local Government in the State of Selangor* (1979), pp. 235-6.
18. See, for, Mansur Yusof "Peranan Ketua Kampung dalam Pembangunan Negara", Ba diss., Faculty of Economics and Administation, Universiti Malay (FEA, UM), 1971; Shahar Abdullah,"Perhubungan antara Pentadbir dan Ahli Politik di Peringkat Daerah: Kajian Kes Mersing", BA diss., FEA, UM, 1975; J. H. Beaglehole, "The District: Some Aspects of Administration and Politics in West Malaysia," *Journal of Administration Overseas,* 12:4 (1973), pp. 184-98; Jailani Md. Dom, "Sistem Patronage di Kampung Bagan Johor: Satu Kajian Kes," BA diss., Dept. of Anthropology and Sociology, Universiti Kebangsaan Malaysia, 1979; Mohamed Khatib Ismail, "Pola Hubungan Patron-Client: Satu Kajian Kes di Kampung Serengkam, Maran, Pahang," BA diss., Dept. of Anthropology and Sociology, Universiti Kebangsaan Malaysia, 1979.
19. On the various incidents in Selangor see for example, the *Star* 4 January 1984, *Berita Harian*, 2, 3, and 4 Janauary 1984 for news on the "Port Klang Shooting and Free-for-all Incident"; the *Star*, 4 and 5 January 1984 and *Berita Harian*, 3, 4, and 5 January 1984 for the "Tanjung Karang demonstrations"; and the *Star*, 6, 12, 19, 22 and 23 March 1984, and 17, 18 and 19 April 1984 for reports on the "Petaling UMNO controversy." For reports on other states, see the *Star*, 23 January, 12 March, 3 April, and 23 May 1984 on the "Penang UMNO power struggle". In fact all Malaysian newspapers for the months of December 1983, January, February, March, April, and May 1984 covered in detail the UMNO meetings at the branch, divisional, and national levels. For comments by Musa Hitam, the Deputy Premier and Deputy President UMNO Malaysia on "the violent trends in UMNO local level meetings," see the *Star*, 9 March 1984. See, also Chandra Muzafar's comments on the above issues in *Far Eastern Economic Review*, 19 July 1984, pp. 24-25. It is also important to note that for the first time in UMNO's history, an unresolved divisional conflict was brought to the court of law for a decision, see the *Star*, 22, 23 and 25 May 1984. In an effort to control this so-called negative tendency UMNO is to amend its constitution to prevent members from bringing their political problems and differences to court (*New Sunday Times*, 7 July 1985). However, resorting to the court of law to resolve internal party disagreements is common amongst other National Front component parties, such as the MCA and, particularly, the MIC.

20. *ibid*
21. On 14 April 1982, eight days before the 1982 Malaysian general elec-
    tions, the speaker of the state legislative assembly of Negeri Sembilan
    was murdered (see *New Straits Times*, 15 April 1982). A few months
    later, a federal cabinet minster and four of his loyal supporters were
    arrested and charged with the murder. The trial began in November
    1982. Evidence presented at the trial showed the existence of an in-
    tense power struggle within the UMNO division over two closely re-
    lated issues: the pre-selection of candidates and the distribution of
    development benefits under the NEP (see *New Straits Times*, 5, 9, 10
    and 11 November 1982 and 21, 22, 23 and 24 Decmber 1982). The
    minister was finally convicted and sentenced to death but not his four
    supporters. It is interesting to note some of the statements made by
    the presiding judge who said, "the prosecution (has) proven beyond
    reasonable doubt that the murder weapon belonged to Datuk Mokhtar
    (the minister) and was in his possession at the time of killing ....He
    plotted to shoot Datuk Taha Talib (the deceased) because of political
    antagonism... (This has) been a grim and gruesome tale of political in-
    trigue, sorcery, conspiracy, and murder involving a minsiter of the
    crown." To date, that is the extent to which intra-party conflict in
    Malaysia could develop; it is not unrelated to circumstances en-
    gendered by the implementation of the NEP. In the latest develop-
    ment of the case, the ex-minister was given a royal pardon and his
    death sentence commuted to life imprisonment. See *New Straits Times*,
    3 March 1984. For a detailed description of the trial see Alias
    Mohamed, *The Trial of Mokhtar Hashim* (Kuala Lumpur, 1983).
22. The struggle for executive positions at all levels of UMNO reached a
    new height recently when UMNO Youth and Wanita proposed an
    amendment to the UMNO constitution to open all executive positions
    (except at the UMNO Supreme Council) for contest. At present, an
    UMNO branch leader is empowered to appoint two persons to the
    branch executive committee in addition to the five elected during its
    general meeting. At the divisional level, the divisional head is em-
    powered to appoint three in addition to the seven elected ones., At
    the natinoal level, an UMNO Youth leader is empowered to appoint
    five to its executive council in addition to the ten elected during its
    general assembly. Similarly, UMNO Wanita leader is empowered to
    appoint five to its executive council in addition to the ten elected ones.
    New Straits Times, 27 July 1985.
23. See Dr. Mahathir Mohamed's presidential address to the 35th UMNO
    general assembly, *New Straits Times*, 26 May 1984 and to the 36th
    UMNO general assembly, *New Straits Times*, 28 September 1985. See
    also comments by Musa Hitam on the issue of money politics within
    UMNO in the *Star*, 14 April 1984 and by Rais Yatim, another cabinet
    minister, in the *Star*, 21 April 1984. Also a recent analysis of the issue
    by Zainal Epi *Changes to Check Money Politics*, in the *Star*, 23 Sept.
    1985.

Value Systems of Malay and Chinese Managers
A Comparative Study

Nik A. Rashid Ismail

Introduction

In a multiracial society like Malaysia, employees bring into the organization differing systems of values. Extremely heterogeneous value profiles may result in conflicts that threaten organizational stability, harmony, and growth.

Objective Of Study

This is a study of the work related value systems of Malay and Chinese managers in Malaysia. The study seeks answers to the following questions:

1. Are the work related value systems of Malaysian managers different across racial origin?
2. What are the value system patterns of the Malay and Chinese managers?

Values and Value Systems

Despite the variety of definitions, some theoretical consensus regarding the conception of values can be seen to be developing (Kahl, 1968; Coleman, 1969; Kolasa, 1969; Elbing dan Elbing, 1967; Steiner, 1971; Brown, 1976; Taylor and Thompson, 1976). Values imply a code or a standard which persists through time, or which organizes systems of actions. Values place things, acts, ways of behaving, goals or actions on the approval-disapproval continuum. Values, according to Graves (1970), change in a regressive-progressive fashion when each set of existential problems are solved and presage movement to a higher level of the psychological system. The pressure of changing conditions will first produce a regression and disorganization of values. Disorganization is not however, decay, but rather a stage in preparation for a higher level organization. When man's old values are no longer appropriate to his new state of existence they break down as he searches for more congruent values.

The term value system suggests hierarchy, and implies some kind of rank-ordering of values along a single continuum (Rokeach, 1973). One writer defines value systems as "a set of individual values which exist in a scale or a hierarchy that reveals their degree of relative importance" (Sikula, 1971).

Methodology

This study is based on a sample of 391 managers from 112 companies operating in Malaysia. The sample was selected by types of companies, racial groups, and public or private sectors, i.e., government owned corporations (public sector) or privately-owned firms (private sector). Sole proprietorship and government institutions not directly dealing with any business activity were excluded from the sample.

The present study compares the value systems of Malay managers (N = 180), Chinese managers (N = 164), and "Others" (N = 47). Malaysian Indian managers, who are classified under "Others" are deliberately left out of the analysis, because the total of 47 respondents, of which 25 were

Malaysian Indians, offer a sample size too small for significant results.

Two sets of questionnaires were used, the "Value for Working Questionnaire" (VWQ), and the "Personal Information Questionnaire" (PIQ). The VWQ instrument was adapted from Flowers et. al. (1974) study. Since the original VWQ instrument was designed for American managers, the instrument's terminology was revised by the translation-retranslation procedures to adapt to the Malaysian situation.

Using Grave's theoretical framework, Flowers (1975) developed seven systems of values for working, i.e., the reactive, tribalistic, egocentric, conformist, manipulative, sociocentric and existential. The description of each value system is given in Figure 1. Eight items were used to measure each value system. The items relate to the topics of company loyalty, the boss, money, profits, work itself, job freedom, big companies and company rules. A total of 48 items were then used to measure six value systems. The first level of the value systems, the reactive level as shown in Figure 1, was excluded from the study since it is theoretically impossible to find managers at this level on organizational payrolls.

In light of the a priori expectation that Malays are fatalistic, animismic, "segan" and "malu", and Chinese are diligent, aggressive and wealth-seeking (Smith and Bastin, 1967; Wilson, 1967; Parkinson, 1967; Charlesworth, 1974), one would expect Malay managers to have dominant value systems in the lower end of Flower's value system hierarchy. Malay managers can be expected to be more tribalistic, more conformist, and more sociocentric.

Results and Discussions

A series of one way analyses of variance (ANOVA) for tribalistic, egocentric, conformist, manipulative, sociocentric, and existential value systems by racial origin of Malaysian managers were used to test the hypothesis. One way ANOVA for each of the eight dimensions measuring each value system of managers by racial origin was also used to test whether Malay, Chinese, and "Other" managers differed in their views toward eight dimensions: company loyalty, boss, money, profit, work, job freedom, big companies, and company rules.

Figure 1
Managerial Value Systems of Malaysian Managers

Existential (7)
High degree of tolerance for ambiguity and people with differing values. Likes to do jobs in his own way without constraints of authority or bureaucracy. Goal oriented but toward a broader arena and longer time perspective.

(6) Sociocentric
Has affiliation needs. Dislikes violence, conformity, materialism, and manipulative management. Concerned with social issues and the dignity of man.

Manipulative
(5) Ambitious to achieve higher status and recognition. Strives to manipulate people and things. May achieve goals through gamesmanship, persuasion, bribery of official authority.

(4) Conformist
Low tolerance for ambiguity and for people whose values differ from his own. Attached to rigidly defined roles in accounting, engineering, and military and tends to perpetuate the status quo. Motivated by a cause, philosophy or religion.

Egocentric
(3) Rugged individualism selfish, thoughtless, unscrupulous, dishonest. Has not learned to function within the constraints imposed by society. Responds primarily to power.

(2) Tribalistic
Found mostly in primitive societies and ghettos. Lives in a world of magic, witchcraft, and superstition. Strongly influenced by tradition and the power exerted by the boss, tribal chieftain, policeman, school teacher, politician and other authority figures.

Reactive
(1) Not aware of self or others as individuals or human beings. React to basic physiological needs. Mostly restricted to infants.

Tribalistic Value System and Race

The ANOVA results show that Malay, Chinese, and "Other" managers in Malaysia, all view the tribalistic value system in a similar manner as evidenced by the fact that no significant difference is found in the test. Similarly, when separate ANOVA for the eight dimensions purported to measure the tribalistic value system of Malaysian managers across race, Malay, Chinese, and "Other" managers are found to have similar views about company loyalty, boss, money, company profit, work, job freedom, big company, and company rules.

Egocentric Value System and Race

The egocentric value system of Malaysian managers is found to differ by racial origin. The overall F ratio of 5.45 shown in Table 1 is significant at the 0.05 level implying that Malays, Chinese, and "Other" managers possess the egocentric value system in different degrees.

Further tests involving individual racial group comparisons as shown in Table 2, imply that Malay managers are more egocentric than Chinese managers.

Table 1
Anova For Egocentric Value System: Managers By Racial Origin

Source	Degrees of Freedom	Sum of Square	Mean Squares	F Ratio	F Prob.
Between Groups	2	124.56	62.28	3.11	0.05
Within Groups	388	7792.02	20.06		
Total	390	7706.57			

Group	Count	Mean
Malay	180	6.04
Chinese	164	4.85
Others	47	5.21

Table 2
Multiple Comparisons Between Egocentric Means:
Managers By Racial Origin

Contrast	F Ratio for Contrast	Critical F Value
1. $M_1 - M_2$	2.45	$N = 391, K = 3, .95 = 3.00$
2. $M_1 - M_3$	1.13	
3. $M_2 - M_3$	-0.48	$\sqrt{(K-1)\,(.95\,_{2,00})}$
4. $[M_1 + M_2/2 - M_3$	0.38	$= \sqrt{(2)\,(3.00)}$
5. $[M_2 + M_3/2 - M_1$	-2.03	$= 2.45$
6. $[M_1 + M_3/2 - M_2$	1.53	

M_1 - mean values for Malays; M_2 - mean values for Chinese; M_3 - mean values for "Others."

Malay managers have been found to be more egocentric than the Chinese or "Other" managers in their views toward importance of money and job freedom. This tendency is evidenced by the fact that the overall importance of money ($F = 6.62$) and job freedom ($F = 3.59$) dimensions of egocentric value system are found to be significant at the 0.05 level (Table 3). Malay, Chinese, and "Other" managers, however, have been found not to differ in their views toward company loyalty, boss, company profit, work, job freedom, big company, and company rules of the egocentric value system.

Wilson and Charlesworth have found Malays to be shy ("segan" and "malu") or an easily embarassed group of people. The present study, however does not find Malays to be so, for the egocentrics are the most unscrupulous, selfish, impulsive, and in general not willing to live within the constraints of the society's norm. The question now is, why are the Malay managers different from the Malay society as a whole? One possible explanation could be due to the recent entry into the business sector among the Malays. The Malays who have chosen employment in the business sector have learned that survival means to be hardened, selfish and aggressive and thus to do away with the characteristics of "segan" and "malu". As a result of the experience of being rejected from entry in business organization, a Malay manager could have developed a feeling of suspicion, a need to foster his individual survival in an organization which he felt was only legally forced to accept him[1]. These feelings could have driven the Malay managers.

Conformist Value System and Race

Malay, Chinese and "Other" managers are found to differ in their values respecting conformity. The overall F ratio of the ANOVA among conformist value system means of Malaysian managers by racial origin is 7.136, very significant at the 0.05 level as shown in Table 4.

When the multiple comparison tests were used to test if individual racial group means differ, Chinese managers were found to be more conformist than Malay managers though Chinese managers were not significantly different from "Other" managers. Similarly the degree of the conformist value system possessed by Malay managers have not been found to differ significantly from "Other" managers. The results in Table 5 address these findings.

The finding that Chinese managers are more conformist than Malay managers is contradictory to the a priori expectation that Chinese managers would be less conformist than Malay managers. The contradiction could be due to either one or all of the following reasons:

1. That the observation about the Malay values as viewed by some people is an oversimplification.

2. That Malay managers are the deviants of the Malay society.

3. That the contradiction is due to the results of the New Economic Policy 2 which calls for the restructuring of society through strategies such as:

   - eradicating poverty through redistribution of income and ownership, restructuring employment patterns in the various organizations according to racial origins;

   - developing a Malay industrial and commercial society;

   - developing the non-growing region; and

   - providing better educational opportunities for the population. [2]

The joint effect of the above policies and efforts could have changed the value system of the Malays to be less conformist, more confident in their views toward work as a whole; or those policies and efforts could have psychologically threatened the employment security of the Chinese and "Other" managers in order to make them more conformist. As shown in Table 4, which displays the result of analyses of variance among the dimensions measuring conformist value system by racial origin, company loyalty and company rules are found to be viewed significantly differently by the various racial groups of managers. The results indicate that Chinese managers are highly conformist relative to the Malay or "Other" managers, in their views toward loyalty and company rules. Similarly, the scores of Chinese managers are also higher for most of the other dimensions, although they are not found to be significantly different.

Table 3

ANOVA For Eight Dimensions Of Egocentric Value System:
Managers By Racial Origin

Group	N	Means							
		Company Rules	Boss	Money	Company Project	My Work	Job Freedom	Big Company	Company Rules
Malays	180	0.06	1.10	1.13	0.49	0.50	2.16	0.25	0.36
Chinese	164	0.16	0.88	0.65	0.44	0.55	1.66	0.19	0.36
Others	47	0.21	1.15	0.94	0.53	0.34	1.32	0.43	0.49
Total	391	1.02	0.91	0.48	0.50	1.85	0.25	0.37	5.45
F Ratio		0.61	1.19	6.62	0.16	0.70	3.59	1.15	0.33
F Prob.		0.55	0.31	0.002	0.85	0.50	0.03	0.32	0.72

A fourth reason which could explain the high conformity characteristic of the Chinese managers relative to the Malay or "Other" managers is the clannish nature of the Chinese society itself. Socially, the Chinese tend to remain separated from the rest of the Malaysian society, and to remain a closely-knit structure of discrete clans, dialect associations and mutual aid groups bound together by a common culture and heritage that

Table 4
Anova For Conformist Value System: Managers By Racial Origin

Source	Degree of Freedom	Sum of Squares	Mean Squares	F Ratio	F Prob.
Between Groups	2	989.31	494.66	7.14	0.001
Within Groups	388	26896.25	69.32		
Total	390	27885.56			

Group	Count	Mean
Malay	180	18.38
Chinese	164	21.74
Others	47	19.34

Table 5
Multiple Comparisons Between Conformist Means:
Managers By Racial Origin

Contrast	F Ratio for Contrast	Critical F Value
1. $M_1 - M_2$	-3.74	$N = 391, K = 3, .95 = 3.00\ _2\,_{100}$
2. $M_1 - M_3$	-0.70	
3. $M_2 - M_3$	1.75	$\sqrt{(K-1)(.95\ _2\,_{100})}$
4. $[M_1 + M_2/2 - M_3$	0.56	$= \sqrt{(2)(3.00)}$
5. $[M_2 + M_3/2 - M_1$	2.29	$= 2.45$
6. $[M_1 + M_3/2 - M_2$	-3.06	

is an amalgam of Confucian, Taoist, and Mahayana Bhuddist elements. The Malaysian Chinese regard themselves as part of the larger Chinese society and therefore aim at conforming to the values which they believe hold the wider Chinese society together. Since business organizations and their activities have for many years been regarded as the main differing institutional and employment factor between them and the Malays, the conformist value system which is apparent in the Chinese society is carried over into the managerial world.

Table 6

Anova For Eight Dimensions Of Conformist Value System: Managers By Racial Origin

Group	N	Company Rules	Boss	Money	Company Project	My Work	Job Freedom	Big Company	Company Rules
Malays	180	2.97	2.07	3.14	3.14	1.49	1.31	1.54	3.230
Chinese	164	3.84	2.16	3.30	2.90	1.84	1.53	1.88	4.290
Others	47	2.87	2.38	3.15	2.45	1.72	1.49	1.85	3.430
Total	391	3.32	2.14	3.21	2.72	1.66	1.42	1.72	3.700
F Ratio		4.72	0.43	0.19	0.99	1.37	0.62	1.61	6.050
F Prob.		0.01	0.66	0.83	0.38	0.26	0.54	0.20	0.003

Manipulative Value System and Race

Overall the degree of the manipulative value system of the Malay, Chinese, and "Other" managers has not been found to differ significantly. Malay, Chinese, and "Other" managers, however, are found to differ in at least three of the eight dimensions that are purported to measure manipulative value system, that is company profit, big companies, and company rules. On two of the three dimensions found to be significantly different across racial origin (company rules and big companies), the mean scores of Chinese managers are found to be higher than the mean scores for Malay managers. These results confirm the expectation that Chinese managers are more manipulative than their Malay counterparts when viewing company profits and big companies. Malay managers, however, are found to be more manipulative in their views toward company rules. A possible cause for the highly manipulative nature of the Malay managers in viewing company rules could also be related to their recent entry into the managerial world. Historically, native business has been predominantly Chinese, Malays have felt that occupational entry into business was socially closed to them. To survive and succeed in businesses owned or controlled by the Chinese would mean to manipulate the company rules.

Sociocentric Value System and Race

The degree to which Malay, Chinese, and "Other" managers possess the dominant sociocentric value system differs significantly. Overall, Malay managers appear to be more sociocentric than Chinese or "Other" managers. Malay managers are more sociocentric than Chinese and/or "Other" managers in their preferences for types of superiors and in their views toward company profits. Malaysian managers from all ethnic groups, however, viewed company loyalty, money, work, job freedom, big company, and company rules indicative of sociocentric value system in similar fashion (see Table 7).

Existential Value System and Race

The degree of dominance in existential value systems has not been found to differ between Malay, Chinese and "Other" managers. Table 8 indicates that further analyses involving effects of race on each of the eight dimensions measuring existential value systems reveal significant differences only for the company loyalty dimension. Malay managers appeared more existential than Chinese or "Other" managers in their views toward company loyalty.

Table 7
Anova For Eight Dimensions Of Sociocentric Value System:
Managers By Racial Origin

Group	N	Means							
		Company Loyalty	Boss	Money	Company Project	My Work	Job Freedom	Big Company	Company Rules
Malays	180	2.03	2.89	1.36	1.79	2.74	1.31	3.39	2.69
Chinese	164	2.05	2.70	1.15	1.49	2.65	1.20	2.77	2.02
Others	47	2.60	1.77	0.94	0.83	2.30	1.49	2.89	2.21
Total	391	2.11	2.68	1.22	1.55	2.65	1.28	3.07	2.35
F Ratio		1.4	5.05	1.69	4.46	0.52	0.47	2.37	2.84
F Prob		0.23	0.01	0.18	0.01	0.60	0.63	0.09	0.06

Table 8
ANOVA For Eight Dimensions Of Existential Value System:
Managers By Racial Origin

Group	N	Means							
		Company Loyalty	Boss	Money	Company Project	My Work	Job Freedom	Big Company	Company Rules
Malays	180	3.91	2.79	2.39	2.32	3.43	3.68	2.33	1.76
Chinese	164	3.18	3.31	2.75	2.93	3.16	3.35	2.35	1.71
Others	47	3.55	3.45	2.62	3.34	3.62	4.19	1.60	2.32
Total	391	3.56	3.09	2.57	3.16	3.34	3.60	2.25	1.80
F Ratio		3.55	2.90	0.82	1.17	0.58	1.44	1.95	1.24
F Prob		0.03	0.06	0.45	0.31	0.57	0.24	0.14	0.29

Conclusion

Evidently, the existing literature on human values of Malaysians indicates that the studies are far from conclusive, and they have not added significantly to the current state of knowledge on the behavior of Malaysian managers. Those studies do not provide substantial empirical evidence on the area under investigation, partly due to the general lack of work in this particular area.

Values of Malaysians as a nationality have never been described as extensively as one has found in literature on human values that relate to Americans. Most studies about Malaysians have been historical, subjective descriptions and non-empirical in nature profiling them in passing rather than delving deeply into the subjects that relate to values, attitudes, or beliefs. The a priori expectation that Malays are fatalistic, animismic, "segan" and "malu", and Chinese are diligent, aggressive and wealth-seeking, as stated earlier, are found to be unnecessarily true, at least among the managerial groups. Scott (1968) using an in-depth interview technique studied the political beliefs of seventeen Malaysian civil servants in Kuala Lumpur. Using the value orientation framework of Florence Kluckhohn, Scott profiles Malaysian civil servants as tradition-oriented, taking the view that human actions are prompted by egoism that is controllable only through external authorities, whether government or the supernatural; that Malaysian civil servants are fatalistic men subjugated by nature, who see nature as too hostile and threatening to be approached; that Malaysians see life as a struggle for a "constant pie" — a struggle for a fixed scarcity of desired material goods.

The findings of this study so far have established that the value systems of Malay, Chinese, and "Other" managers are similar in certain aspects and different in others. Malay managers are found to be more egocentric and sociocentric than Chinese managers, and Chinese managers on the other hand are more conformist than Malay managers. Both Malay and Chinese managers have similar tribalistic, manipulative and existential value systems. Figure 2 exhibits the value profile of Malay, Chinese, and "Other" managers in graphic form.

Malay managers are different from their Chinese counterparts in their view toward leadership style. Malay managers seem to prefer a sociocentric leadership style — a leader that gets them working together in close harmony being more a friend than a boss, — or what is sometimes referred to as the "subordinate-centered" leader. Chinese managers on the other hand prefer the existential leadership style — the kind of leader who "trusts" people and gives them access to the information they need and lets them do their job in their own way. Malay and Chinese managers do not seem to prefer the manipulative, tribalistic or the egocentric type of leadership style or the leader that tells exactly what to do and how to do a particular job or the leader who is tough but allowing them to be tough too. These types of leadership styles are sometimes known as the "boss-centered" or the "authoritative" leadership style.

To a Malay manager job freedom means, an opportunity to do interesting and challenging work and to be able to express opinions openly which is typical of an existential manager. Chinese managers, however, view job freedom very highly as the opportunity to stand on their own two feet and to pursue success without too much interference from supervisors or anything else. This view is the typical expression of an entrepreneur — a manipulative manager.

Malay managers seem to favour big companies playing a role that would support the cause of social and economic justice, provide a pleasant work climate, share profits with employees, and become selective in choosing their products and customers. This view is indicative of a sociocentric-leader, or similar to what England (1974) calls the moralistic-oriented leader. Chinese managers however, are more pragmatic-oriented in their views concerning the role of big companies. They feel strongly that big companies should play a role dedicated to maximising profits—a view that is descriptive of a manipulative manager.

Malay managers also differ from Chinese managers in their views about company loyalty. Loyalty to a Chinese manager means sacrificing for the good of the organization, while to a Malay manager, loyalty has a limit, i.e., for as long as the goals of the organization do not go against his principles. My view is that these principles are usually those associated with religious beliefs and practices.

From the results of the study, it is evidenced that Malaysian managers and particularly Malay managers are not fatalistic, animismic, or man subjugated to nature as many Western scholars assert. Malay managers are no more tribalistic than Chinese or "Other" managers. If there should be any difference, the difference could only be in the degree of sophistication and not in kind.

Figure 2
Mean Score Of Value Systems for Malaysian, Malay, And Chinese

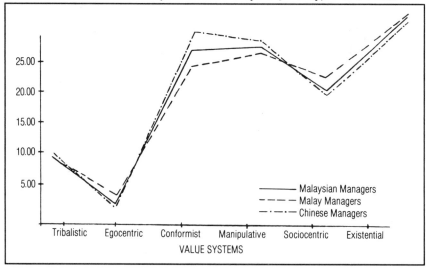

References

Brown, Martha A., "Values - A Necessary but Neglected Ingredient of Motivation on the Job." *The Academy of Management Review*, Vol. i, No. 4, October 1976, pp 15 - 23.

Charlesworth, H. K., "Role Strain in Bumiputral Entrepreneurs - Can it be Overcome?", Unpublished paper submitted to MARA Institute of Technology, Malaysia, 1974.

Coleman, J. C., *Psychology and Effective Behavior*. Chicago, Ill.; Scott, Foresman and Company, 1969.

Elbing, A. O., Jr. and Carol J. Elbing, *The Value Issue of Business*. New York: McGraw-Hill, 1967.

England, George W. and R. Lee. "The Relationship Between Managerial Values and Managerial Success in the United States, Japan, India and Australia." *Journal of Applied Psychology*. Vol. 59(4), 1974, pp. 419 - 441.

Flowers, Vincent S., Charles L. Hughes, M. Scott Myers, and Susan S. Myers. *Managerial Values for Working, An AMA Survey Report*. New York; AMACOM, 1975.

Graves, Clare W. "Levels of Existence: An Open System of Values." *Journal of Humanistic Psychology*, Vol. 10, No. 2, Fall 1970, pp. 131 - 155.

Kahl, Joseph A. *The Measurement of Modernism: A Study of Values in Brazil and Mexico*. Austin, Texas: The University of Texas Press, 1968.

Kolasa, B. J. *Introduction to Behavioral Science for Business*. New York: John Wiley and Sons, Inc. 1969

Parkinson, B. K. "Non-Economic Factors in Economic Development of the Rural Malays." *Modern Asian Studies*, Vol. 1, No. 1, 1967, pp 31 - 46.

Rokeach, Milton. *The Nature of Human Values*. New York: The Free Press, 1973.

Scott, James C. *Political Ideology in Malaysia: Reality and the Beliefs of an Elite*. New Haven: Yale University Press, 1968.

Sikula, Andrew F. "Values and Value Systems: Relationship to Personal Goals." *Personnel Journal*, Vol. 50, 1971, pp. 310 - 312.

Smith, T. E. and John Bastin, *Malaysia*. New York: Oxford University Press, 1967.

Steiner, George A., *Business and Society*. New York: Random House, 1971.

Taylor, Ronald N., and Mark Thompson. "Work Value Systems of Young Workers." *Academy of Management Journal*, Vol. 19, No. 4, December 1976, pp. 536 - 52.

Wilson, P. J. A *Malay Village in Malaysia: Social Values and Rural Development*. New Haven, Connecticut: HRAF Press, 1967.

Notes

1. One underlying policy of the Malaysian government, as laid out in the Second, Third and Fourth Malaysia Plans is to "persuade" organizations in the private sector to restructure their personnel make up at all levels of operations and management so that the ratio of Malay, Chinese, and "Other" employees employed in their organization is consistent with the racial composition of the Malaysian population.
2. The Malaysian New Economic Policy (NEP) was initiated in 1970 after the racial riot incidence of May 13, 1969. This policy was laid out in the *Second Malaysia Plan (1971-75)*, and is continued in the *Third Malaysia Plan (1976-1980)*, and the *Fourth Malaysia Plan (1981-1985)*.

5

Women's Economic Role in Malaysia

Fatimah Daud

Introduction

In recent years there has been a growing awareness of the role and status of women. The considerable increase in the number of working women which can be seen in many countries reflects their changing role. In Malaysia, there has been a sustained and growing interest in matters related to them.

Studies conducted by Shreiner (1911), Clark (1919), Pinchbeck (1969), and Shorter (1976) indicate that industrialization has changed the female economic role, but none of them analyzed the problems faced by females when they ventured into occupations that had been previously filled by men. This is the gap in our information on women's employment and one which I shall examine in my study of women's economic role in Malaysia. A comparative analysis of female labor force participation during the colonial period and after Independence is relevant for this purpose, particularly from 1870s to 1970s.

Women's Role in Economic Development before Independence

In 1874, Britain began direct intervention in Malaysia. The structural conditions of Malayan society during colonial times and the place of women's labor in it set the pattern for later developments which have determined the contemporary structure of women's economic role.

In the nineteenth century, there was little specialization in the Malay economy where people concentrated in a few occupations only. Individual productivity was then low. The basic economic unit was the family engaged in subsistence agriculture. Literally every member of the family took part in contributing to the family's wealth. Although the family unit also engaged in barter trade, for the most part, their production was for family consumption. The woman's work role in this type of productive unit was not only confined to direct laboring in the fields alone, but the woman also produced children whose labor later was necessary to the success of the unit. There was a division of labor between the men on the one hand, and the women and children on the other. In the padi growing society, the men usually carried out the heavy jobs like ploughing and harrowing, while the women and children undertook light 'duties' such as winnowing, and cleaning the padi. But certain other work like weeding, manuring and harvesting were shared by both men and women. The clear picture is indicated in Table 1. Table 1 shows the proportion of males and females in padi cultivation in Malaya during the period 1901-1957. However, these figures do not reflect the true contribution of women in the field because, while all available and able men worked in the padi field, especially during the peak period of harvesting, not all women did so. In most families, the old and the very young females, who were unable to do heavy farming work, assisted in running the household so that the more able women could go out into the fields. In addition, the women supplemented farm income by producing and selling works of crafts like batik, mats, and domestic goods such as eggs and vegetables, and also to a certain extent by involving themselves in cottage industries.

In a fishing society, a great deal, if not most, of the peripheral work related to the fishing industry was done by women. However, they also helped to bring in the catch as indicated by Table 2. After their husbands brought in the catch, it was mainly the women who dried the fish and processed it into various fish products such as belecan (prawn-paste) and budu (fish-sauce). This constituted a considerable amount of the

Table 1

Population Engaged in Padi Cultivation in Malaya: 1901-1957

Year	Males		Females	
	Total	%	Total	%
1901[1]	53,856	53.9	46,131	46.1
1911	66,420	54.4	55,679	45.6
1921	262,960	55.7	209,057	44.3
1931	242,436	64.3	134,368	35.7
1947	333,261	70.8	137,378	29.2
1957[2]	264,895	66.5	133,400	33.5

Source: The Census of British Malaya - Straits Settlements 1901-1957.

1.Federated Malay States only
2.Excluding Brunei

fishermen's family income. Additionally, women ran various small enterprises such as petty-trading and attap-making to supplement the family income.

The growing importance of the western flank of the Malay Peninsula as a tin producer and the subsequent establishment of British protectorates over the Western Malay States produced striking changes within the Malay economy. Before merchant and industrial capitalism was introduced in the country, all members of the family labored together to produce those things (use values) necessary for their basic needs. While the kind of work they performed differed according to the social division of labor, the definition of their labor in relation to production was the same — they both produced use values.[1]

As a result of colonialism and capital accumulation in Malaya, the productive conditions of the pre-capitalist society were gradually transformed, creating the basis for a new type of society, capitalist society. Labor became a marketable commodity and foreign Chinese and Indian workers, both male and female, were imported in large numbers to work in the tin mines and rubber plantations. Initially, the Malays were not drawn into the capitalist fold. However, they soon began to enter the market economy as rubber smallholders.[2]

The British occupation resulted in a division of labor that led not only to the formation of a new class division but also af-

Table 2
Population Engaged in Fishing in Malaya: 1901-1957

| Year | Males | | Females | |
	Total	%	Total	%
1901[1]	2,362	69.6	1,032	30.4
1911[1]	3,025	71.2	1,277	28.8
1921	48,720	95.2	2,488	4.8
1931	48,435	97.5	1,225	2.5
1947	59,357	98.5	931	1.5
1957[2]	60,669	98.8	762	1.2

Source: The Census of British Malaya - Straits Settlements 1901-1957.

1.Federated Malay States only
2.Excluding Singapore

fected relations between men and women. The laboring part of the population now worked under the control of the capitalists to whom their labor power and the product of their labor belonged. More and more Malays were unable to produce the use values necessary to meet their changing needs. In order to survive, they were forced to sell the only thing they owned, their labor power. At the same time that it became necessary for some family members to sell their labor power, it was also essential that certain things with only use values continued to be produced such as the reproduction of labor, the rearing of children, and the maintenance of the home. Because of the existing division of labor between males and females, women continued to be chiefly responsible for selling their labor power to the capitalist. With the advent of colonialism and industrial capitalism, the general labor process was split into two separate spheres; commodity production done mainly by men and domestic labor done by women.

Women immigrants, especially Chinese and Indians, who had undergone this transformation process earlier, sold their labor power to the capitalist. Chinese women predominated in the tin-mining industry. They were employed in concentrating tin-ore in large sluice boxes using dulang. They led a very hard life, standing in water all day long washing for tin ore. Their daily wages, depending upon their terms of employment, ranged from 30-45 cents. During depressed conditions, they earned even less. They lived in huge dormitories, shacks of attap (palm leaf). Since no child-care centers were provided, they had to go to work with their babies strapped to their backs. Table 3 shows that during the period 1901-1957 female (principally Chinese) labor formed between 5 and 19 percent of the total mining force in Malaya. In absolute numbers, there was no major decline in female employment. Two reasons could be given for the percentage decline in female employment:

(i) an increasing use of modern technology in the tin industry;

(ii) a general decline in the industry as a whole with the closing of several mines.

About 60 percent of Indian females were employed as either indentured or free labor in commercial crop cultivation, especially rubber. Their rate of participation in the capitalist labor market was proportionately higher than that of the numerically superior Malay or Chinese women. This was a consequence of particular features associated with the locality and type of economic activity they performed rather than their attitudes or inherent ethnic values. Wages paid to plantation workers were low and it was the norm for almost all working-age members, including females of families to seek employ-

Table 3
Population Engaged in Mining in Malaya 1901-1957

	Males			Females	
Year	Total	%		Total	%
1901[1]	157,334	99.0		1,500	1.0
1911[1]	156,327	95.5		7,353	4.5
1921	74,062	88.5		9,613	11.5
1931	79,450	88.6		10,168	11.4
1947	39,432	80.6		8,258	19.4
1957[2]	49,026	83.8		9,473	12.2

Source: Compiled from Malaya: A Report on the 1901-1957 Census of Population.

1.Federated Malay States only
2.Excluding Singapore.

ment. Plantation owners provided child-care facilities of some sort, which encouraged women to go to work. The women's (principally Indian) participation in commercial crop cultivation in Malay during the period 1901-1957 is clearly indicated in Table 4.

Table 4

Population Engaged in Commercial Crop Cultivation in Malaya: 1901-1957

| | Males | | | Females | |
Year	Total	%	Total	%
1901*	114,661	83.6	22,470	16.4
1911*	127,144	79.6	32,494	20.4
1921	370,407	79.5	95,801	20.5
1931	428,615	78.6	116,547	21.4
1947	369,558	78.0	174,294	32.0
1957[a]	428,134	64.1	289,318	35.9

Source: Compiled from: Malaya, Reports of Population Census 1901-1957.

Notes: *Federated Malay States only
          [a]Excluding Singapore

It was mentioned above that plantation workers worked for very low wages. There was also a wage differential between male and female labor. Prior to the Second World War, an adult male Indian worker earned an average monthly wage of $10.00 - $15.00. However, an adult female Indian worker earned only $3.00 - $10.00.[3] Although wage differentials were based on the specific tasks performed, like rubber tapping and transporting of rubber product to factories, women consistently earned less than their male counterparts. The statistics also include Chinese females who worked in pepper and gambier farms as contract workers.[4]

Malays also participated in the commercial economy as rubber smallholders. But this mainly involved the men. The women's role was rather complementary in nature; be it in the field of rubber and coconut cultivation, or as petty-traders, earning returns which lent support to the family's main source of income.

During the British rule, therefore, apart from Indian female immigrant workers who sold their labor power to the capitalists, women had essentially been defined out of the capitalist labor market. At the time of independence, women as a group (both Malays and non-Malays) had become an available source of labor power for the capitalist system. In effect, they became an institutionalized inactive labor reserve.

In the following section, I will discuss the participation of women in various occupations and show how the Malaysian government created and provided employment opportunities to tap this unused and abundant reserve.

Women's Role in Economic Development after Independence

After examining the data on the economically active rate for Malaysian females over the years, only a very gradual increase of between 1-2 percent before 1957 is revealed. After 1957, however, women were increasingly drawn into the work force at a considerably greater rate of 6 percent per annum between 1957 and 1970 and 7 percent per annum between 1970 and 1976.[5] By 1980, the proportion of female workers in the labor force had reached 35 percent compared to only 20 percent in 1931.[6] The rise in female economic activity rate in recent years is largely due to two reasons. Firstly, during the fifties, sixties and seventies, the Malaysian economy achieved credible rates of growth. For example, the Gross Domestic Product (at constant price) has risen at an average rate of 6.1 percent per annum in real terms during the period 1957-1978. Over the years, the average annual rate of growth has accelerated from 4.1 percent in the second half of the 1950s to 7.6 and 7.9 percent for the period 1974 and 1980.[7]

Secondly, there was an increase in the proportion of the population participating in wage labor. This is due to a significant increase in women working for wages over the traditional "home production." This statement is supported by the data in Table 5 which indicates the proportion of employees to have increased from 48 percent in 1947 to 57 percent in 1980; and the proportion of own account worker to have dropped from 43 percent to 27 percent over the same period.

Table 5
Percentage Distribution of the Work-Force Aged 10 and over by
Employment Status (selected years)

Employment Status	1947	1957	1970	1980
Employer	1	3	4	4
Employees	48	57	45	57
Own Account Worker	43	35	27	27
Unpaid Family Worker	7	3	20	11
Seeking First Job	1	2	4	2
Total	100	100	100	100

Sources: Compiled from Census Reports of 1947, 1957, 1970, and 1980, pp. 111, 54, 78, 127

The data from the 1980 census indicates that women represented half of the total population between the age of fifteen
and sixty-four years (termed the working-age population).
However, in terms of actual labor-force participation, women
made up 35 percent of the group defined as "economically-
active." The rest was being taken up by men. In effect, this
means for various reasons most of the women capable of paid
labor have been excluded from the labor force. Of the 30
percent of men found outside the labor force, 71 percent are
students. Compared to this, housewives are the major
proportion of women outside the labor force, i.e. 81 percent.

Besides family helpers and petty traders, female wage-
workers form the largest category of the economically active.
Where in 1979 family farm-workers constituted half of the
rural female labor force, the other half consisted of wage
workers. In 1980, 70 percent of the urban female labor force
were wage employees.[8]

In general, women are employed in two types of
occupations, professional and non-professional. Professionally,
they are employed as science and technical workers,
medical, educational and legal workers, administrators,
politicians, journalists, artists, economists, and librarians.
Women in the non-professional category consist of clerical
workers, telephone operators, drivers, salesgirls, receptionists,

domestic servants, factory workers, and laborers. The percentage distribution of females employed in the principal occupations compared to the male can be seen from Table 6.

Table 6 shows that the most significant change appeared to be the decline in the proportion of the female labor force employed in agriculture, forestry, and fishery sectors which showed a decline of 7.2 percent, i.e. from 50.0 percent in 1975 to 42.8 percent in 1979. On the other hand, the proportion of the female labor force employed in almost all non-agricultural sectors during the same period registered an increase. The increases are more pronounced in categories of workers registered as professional and technical, administrative and managerial, clerical work and services, production process, laborers and communications. The decline in the proportion of those in agricultural and related occupations and the corresponding increase in non-agricultural fields between 1975 and 1979 indicates the changing economic structure and the increasing urbanization and industrialization that was taking place.

Despite increasing participation of women in many sectors in recent years, they are still under-represented in the skilled, high income-earning categories but over-represented in the unskilled, low income-earning group. This is, of course, a legacy of the earlier structural conditions of Malaysian society where women were considered to be responsible for the production of labor, the rearing of children, and the maintenance of the home. Their work was regarded as "secondary labor."

The traditional belief has been well-preserved that women should be at home undertaking domestic chores while men played the "breadwinners" role. This explains the small number of women occupying managerial, professional, and technical positions. (See Table 6)

In 1975, women comprised about 0.1 percent of the labor force employed in administration and management on the Malaysian peninsula. In the professional and technical services sector, in 1975 women constituted 5.6 percent of the labor force in peninsular Malaysia. In 1979, their participation rose to 6.6 percent. These relatively high percentages can be explained by the inclusion of teachers, nurses and librarians in the categorization. They reflect aspects of women's domestic duties—home management, moral and nurturing roles, and

Table 6
Percentage Distribution of Employed Persons by
Principal Occupation and Sex in 1975 and 1979

	Male		Female	
	1975	1979	1975	1979
Sector:				
Agriculture	38.2	32.5	50.3	43.8
Industry	29.3	34.9	19.1	22.6
Services	32.5	32.6	30.6	33.6
Total	100.0	100.0	100.0	100.0
Occupation:				
Professional and Technical Workers	5.5	5.6	5.6	6.6
Administrative and Managerial Workers	1.9	2.0	0.1	0.1
Clerical Workers	6.9	7.3	7.2	9.8
Sales Workers	11.6	11.5	8.0	8.3
Service Workers	6.8	7.6	10.7	11.6
Agricultural, Fishing, Hunting and Forestry	37.6	30.9	50.0	42.8
Production, Laborers, and Communication Workers	29.6	35.0	18.1	20.7
Total	100.0	100.0	100.0	100.0

education. The number of women employed in the medical, legal, and accountancy professions remains insignificant because they are traditionally considered "male" occupations. In March 1983, women lawyers formed only 16.1 percent of the total number of lawyers in private practice.[9] Where engineering is concerned, from 1970 to 1980, the number of women engineers increased only from one to thirty-eight. In medicine, local universities produced only 140 women doctors from 1975 to 1980.

Industrial employment by gender is associated with differential incomes. In 1980, the average monthly wage to female workers was between $9.00 and $209.00 less than those paid to male workers. This was a marginal improvement from 1974 when the wage differential was between $17.00 and $243.00. In the case of daily rates, women received between 74 and 79 percent only of the rates paid to their male counterparts.[10]

A few reasons can be offered to explain the great increase in the proportion of women wage-workers in the labor force. First and foremost, the increase should be viewed as part of the inexorable process of releasing labor formerly occupied in home/farm production to wage work – a process following the separation of the peasant from his land (means of subsistence). This trend is strengthened by the government's policies:

(a) Agricultural policies based largely on existing unequal distribution of land, thus accelerating the dispossession of peasant-owned small plots whilst aiding land acquisition by landowners and others from outside the village, for example, government officers controlling subsidiaries and middlemen.

(b) State industrial policies which provide investors with generous tax incentives for setting up labor-intensive industries and locating enterprises in rural areas.[11]

(c) 'Pro-employer' labor policies which firmly guard against the formation of unions in certain industrial zones.[12]

Secondly, in spite of the exploitation of the rural labor force, the generally improved educational standards of women have enabled more of them to take on an outside job.

Thirdly, in consequence of the greater dependence of the cash economy on wages for survival and the low level of wages commanded by male workers, many more married women are now forced to work outside the home to supplement the household income.[13]

A recent trend of the female employment is that many women from rural and urban areas are engaged in production work. In 1931, women formed less than 10 percent of the labor force engaged in manufacturing in Malaya. In 1983, the proportion rose to 50 percent. My study also showed that more than 80 percent of women were employed in electronics companies.

Most of the electronics companies employed 50 percent
Malays, 30 percent Chinese, and 20 percent Indians in order to
comply with the government's New Economic Policy.[14]

Table 7

Population Engaged in Manufacturing

(Selected Industries) in Malaysia: 1970-1980

| Industry | 1970[1] | | | | 1980 | | | |
| | Males | | Females | | Males | | Females | |
	Total	%	Total	%	Total	%	Total	%
Manufacturing	178,881	71	73,058	29	357,350	60	238,920	40
Food Manufacturing	34,401	69	10,701	31	46,546	67	23,009	33
Textiles	5,402	43	7,308	57	13,975	38	23,031	62
Manufacturing of wearing apparel and footwear (excluding rubber footwear)[2]	11,607	38	19,055	62	15,213	23	49,937	77
Electrical Machinery apparatus and appliances	5,080	85	895	15	19,581	27	53,604	73
Professional and scientific equipment					934	40	1,374	60

Source: Census Reports 1970 and 1980

1.Peninsular Malaysia only
2.For the 1980 census, this category excludes plastic footwear as well.

Table 7 showed female labor force participation in selected
industries in 1970 and 1980. Their participation in these industries has increased in absolute numbers and in terms of the
percentage employed. Such a high level of participation actually
reflects certain characteristics of the Malaysian industrial structure. The characteristics are as follows:

Firstly, most manufacturing industries are labor-intensive
and export-oriented enterprises. Women are employed in tex-
tiles, garment, electronics, and food-processing industries, or
those industries which require certain characteristics that are
classified as "feminine."

Women workers are considered to have naturally nimble
fingers; they are docile and compliant; they do not get involved

in trade union activity and are reluctant to go on strike. They are good workers, tolerant of routine, repetitive and monotonous tasks which men dislike.

Secondly, women's employment in such industries represents the exploitation of cheap labor, and the women are paid near subsistence wages only. They work mainly as operatives or semiskilled workers and are given virtually no training. My study showed that chances of promotion are almost nonexistent and the supervisors are invariably male.[13] The multinational corporations have conjured up the myth that women do not need to earn as much as men. They are not breadwinners; they are just "secondary workers" providing extras, not essentials. Their wages do not have to support a family.[15]

Thirdly, most of the industrial investment in Malaysia is dominated by foreign capital which is attracted to the region by the availability of cheap labor and industrial incentives such as "pioneer status." "Pioneer status" qualifies the multinationals for tax relief for up to ten years, minimal customs fees for import and export of materials, and free transfer of capital and profits. Labor laws have been tightened to ensure that the labor force is politically controlled which actually offers a very favorable opportunity for profit maximization to the company. These foreign corporations are consequently able to escape U.S. and European trade union demands for certain health and safety standards as well as higher wages and benefits. In practice, Malaysian labor legislation, both by omission and weak enforcement, has enabled the multinational corporations to manipulate the local population as a labor reserve to be hired and fired according to their "whims and fancies."

Furthermore, women factory workers work under unfavorable conditions that are both hazardous to their health as well as nerve-wrecking. For instance, the U.S. National Institute on Occupational Safety and Health (NIOSH) has placed the electronics industry near the top of the list of high health-risk industries. The workers develop eye problems after only one year of employment and are regularly exposed to toxic chemicals. In garment and textile factories, back pain and brown lungs are amongst the most common industrial hazards.[16]

Most factories operate on several shifts, requiring workers to rotate day and night shifts every week or two. These irregular schedules wreck havoc with sleep patterns and foster nervous ailments and stomach disorders. Lunch breaks are short and visits to the bathroom are treated as a privilege.[17]

Sexual harassment is another hazard of factory work, especially for women who are out late at night working in the so-called "graveyard shift."

Finally, although the government intends to create an industrial labor force in both urban and rural areas, women factory workers as a group remain both passive and ignorant of their own rights. My observation indicated that they are not class conscious and, since they lack collective means to channel their grievances, they express their anger and dissatisfaction by other means.[18]

Conclusion

The conclusion emerging from this discussion is that "capitalism" was the vital factor that changed Malaysian women's economic role in this century. Before the advent of capitalism and industrialization, the women's role was confined to performing only daily household chores and bearing children. Women then became more a part of the productive contributors to the household economy. This, unlike in the traditional moral economy, means that women work to earn outside income that, later, became an obvious and quantifiable part of the household.

The increasing job and educational opportunities for women also mean that more women are taking on new roles outside their homes. But, as most studies show, even though women now have equal rights in employment, they are still concentrated in the lower ranking occupations with low pay.

Studies also show that there still exists a social stigma towards women's participation in industry. For example, society, till this day, still frowns upon female workers coming back from work escorted by their male counterparts. This attitude is attributed to the traditional view that women have no personal or sexual freedom. In the olden days, women were only confined to their homes; but in the modern era, they became independent and free to mix with the opposite sex, which led to a change in their moral values. This change in moral values was what earned women the social stigma. Prevailing traditions and values determined what is appropriate work both for men and women. Sex role prejudices concerning patterns of behavior supposedly common amongst women are still prevalent.

Although both men and women construct society, deep inside, the male dominance persists. As a result, men always decide what is most appropriate for women. Women's vocations are perceived in terms of running households. Thus, women's vocational training is trimmed to suit home management. This is because of the previous colonial policy and practice, and a socialization process of which women were also a part. Under the British, the system of education emphasized women's nurturing and domestic roles. Subjects offered to girls included domestic science where the basic craft of sewing and needlework was taught. Similarly, in boys' schools, basic carpentry subjects like woodwork and metal work were emphasized.

This attitude of always looking at women as domestic chore performers might well have been in existence in Malayan society for ages; but the institutionalization of such a view by the colonial administrators enhanced this belief further. Even in the socialization process, this attitude persisted. It is not a wonder even till today to see girls being given dolls, tea sets and toy sewing kits to play with, while the boys are given toy cars and construction sets as play-things. Thus the colonial attitude plus the socialization process fostered the notion that women do not have the natural affinity with machines that men have. As a consequence, women were not (and still are not) encouraged to develop competence and familiarity with machinery. Also, since the present national education policy also partly followed the previous colonial system of education (in spirit), it is therefore partially to blame for the inculcation of this distinctive "female model temperament" attitude. Negative attitudes towards factory workers in particular arises from the process of unequal trade and production relations. The term cheap labor often carries with it undertones of contempt for the workers. There is an implication that cheap labor also suggests lack of self-respect amongst these workers.

Factory work offered women some autonomy because

earning power and freedom from parental control subsequently made these women relatively independent, with a changed lifestyle, coupled with westernized dress. Nevertheless, some women were disapproved of outright by their families so that they faced severe difficulties in reassimilation once they were no longer employed on the assembly lines. These women are thought to possess a loose morality and are often scorned by men as unsuitable marriage partners. Of course, this male attitude is also imbibed by their womenfolk.

The issue of women factory workers' character and morality remains a burning moral issue in this country. The debate is still raging, with several organizations and public interest groups giving their views and findings on the matter.

Such is the alarming intensity of the problem that at one stage, political leaders (particularly the women), in national platforms and forums, were prompted to press for changes in the working conditions, accommodation and entertainment facilities for women factory workers.

The cries for changes and reforms aside, there are also women who, influenced by their menfolks' attitudes, denigrated the work done by the factory women as not a worthwhile enough effort, if they did so at the expense of their own social and moral virtues. And if this public scorn by their own sex was not enough, women factory workers were also expected to conform to certain male demands or orthodoxy. Women must retain their traditional images despite their involvement in the modernization process. Failure to conform to these values created another fresh problem for the workers, i.e. social isolation.

It is clearly evident that women's entry into previously male-occupied vocations does not merely involve participation in work roles but also entails an exposure to specific socio-cultural patterns predominant especially in the manufacturing sector. These socio-cultural patterns, as discussed earlier, may cause specific implications injurious to the women's status and character. And in the long run, it is feared that continuous exposure to these socio-cultural patterns may inadvertently implant distinctive cultural values and behavioral patterns detrimental to the society in general and to women in particular.

References

Amarjit Kaur, "An Historical Study of Female Labor Force Participation in Malaysia," paper presented at the colloquium on Women and Industrialization held at University of Malaya, Kuala Lumpur, 1985.

Chapkis, W. and Enloe, C. eds., *Of Common Cloth: Women in the Global Textile Industry*, Amsterdam: The Transnational Institute, 1983.

Clark, A., *Working Life of Women in the Seventeenth Century*, London, Routledge and Kegan Paul, 1919.

Daud, Fatimah, *Socio-Economic Problems of Women Workers: A Case of Electronics Workers in a Multinational Japanese Firm*, Ph.D. Thesis, University of Malaya, 1984.

_____, *'Minah Karan', The Truth about Malaysian Factory Girls*, Kuala Lumpur, Berita Publishing, 1985.

Department of Statistics, *1947, 1957, 1970, 1980 Population Census Reports*, Kuala Lumpur, Government Printer, 1911 (microfilm), 1971, 1981.

_____, *Report on the Labor Force Survey, 1979*, Kuala Lumpur, Government Printer, 1980.

Federation of Women Lawyers, "Women and Employment in Malaysia," paper presented at the Seminar on Women and Law, Kuala Lumpur, 1983.

Fifth Malaysia Plan 1986 - 1990, Kuala Lumpur, National Government Printing Department, 1986.

Grossman, R., "Changing Role of Southeast Asian Women: The Global Assembly Line and the Social Manipulation of Women on the Job," *Southeast Asia Chronical*, January-February, 1979.

Hing Ai Yun, Nik Safiah Karim, Rokiah Talib, eds., *Women in Malaysia*, Kuala Lumpur, Pelanduk Publication, 1984.

Malaysia Industrial Development Authority, *Investment Incentive Act*, Kuala Lumpur, 1968.

_____, *Industrial Digest*, Second Quarter, 1973.

_____, *Investment in Malaysia - Policies and Procedures*, Kuala Lumpur, 1981.

Ministry of Labor and Manpower, *Occupational Wage Surveys, 1974*, Kuala Lumpur, 1980.

Mitchell, J., "Women, the Longest Revolution," *New Left Review*, November-December, 1976.

Pinchbeck, I., *Women Workers and Industrial Revolution, 1750 - 1850*, London, Frank Cass & Co. Ltd., 1969.

Shorter, E., "Women's Work: What Difference did Capitalism Make?", *Theory and Society*, 1976.

Schreiner, O., *Women and Labor*, London, Allen and Unwin, 1911.

Yuen-Ching, Linda, *Multinational Firms and Manufacturing for Countries: The Case of the Electronics Industry in Malaysia and Singapore*, Ph.D. Thesis, University of Michigan, 1978.

Notes

1. Amarjit Kaur, "An Historical Study of Female Labor Force Participation in Malaysia," paper presented at the colloquium on Women and Industrialization held at University of Malaya, Kuala Lumpur, 1985. p. 3.
2. *Ibid*, p. 4.
3. *Ibid*, p. 6.
4. *Ibid*, p. 7.
5. Hing Ai Yun, Nik Safiah Karim, Rokiah Talib (eds), *Women in Malaysia*, Pelanduk Publications, 1984, p. 5.
6. *Population Census Report, 1980*, Department of Statistics, Kuala Lumpur, 1981, p. 112.
7. *Fifth Malaysia Plan, 1986 - 1990*, National Printing Department, Kuala Lumpur, 1986, p. 39.
8. *Population Census 1980, op.cit.*, p. 126.
9. Federation of Women Lawyers, "Women and Employment in Malaysia," 1983, p. 7
10. *Occupational Wage Surveys, 1974*, Ministry of Labor and Manpower, Kuala Lumpur, 1980, p. 35.
11. Hing Ai Yun, Nik Safiah Karim, Rokiah Talib (eds), *op. cit.* p. 9.
12. My study showed that the electronics workers in the Free Trade Zone Areas are not allowed by the government to form a trade union.
13. Hing Ai Yun, Nik Safiah Karim, Rokiah Talib, *op.cit.*, p. 9.
14. See Fatimah Daud, *Socio-Economic Problems of Women Workers*, Ph.D., thesis, University of Malaya, 1983, p. 314.
15. Amarjit Kaur, *op.cit.*, p. 19.
16. *Ibid*, p. 20.
17. *Ibid*, p. 21.
18. For details see Fatimah Daud, *'Minah Karan' The Truth About Malaysian Factory Girls*, Berita Publishing, Kuala Lumpur, 1985, p. 4.

The Development Of Malay Entrepreneurship Since 1957
A Sociological Overview

Mohd. Fauzi Haji Yaacob

Introduction

The decades following Malaysia's independence saw increasing participation of Malays in the business system of the nation. This increase is reflected both in terms of the number of business firms owned and managed by them and also in terms of their share equity in the corporate sector. In 1954 for example, only 7,878 units or 10% out of a total of 79,673 business units registered in the then Federation of Malaya, were owned and managed by the Malays (Goh Joon Hai, 1962: 84). But in 1970, the number of Malay businesses increased to 21,763 or 14.2% of the total, and it further increased to 78,961 or 24.9% of the total in 1980 (*Fourth Malaysia Plan, 1981*). Their share equity in the corporate sector also increased. There was no figure for the pre-independence period. But in 1970, their share was 2.4%, rose to 9.4% in 1975, and 12.4% in 1980 (*Third Malaysia Plan, 1976*: 99; *Fourth Malaysia Plan, 1981*: 62).

Despite this development, however, the phenomenon of under-representation of Malays in the rapidly expanding modern commercial and industrial sector still remains. The Malays, despite their numerical strength, still lagged behind the other major ethnic groups in the country, particularly in this field of economic endeavour. But what is important, however, is that changes had been and still are, taking place within them. The development in this direction can be viewed as one of the numerous changes affecting them since 1957, all of which resulted from the interplay of various social, economic and political forces. It is, therefore, the aim of this paper to detail some of the salient emerging patterns of increasing Malay participation in the business system, the growth of Malay entrepreneurship, and to outline some of the factors that affect the changes. The argument to be posited here is that the growth of Malay entrepreneurship in post-colonial Malaysia was closely related to the rapid urbanization of the community, the increasing educational opportunities, and the increasing government support. It is also argued that underlying these developments was Malay nationalism, the origin of which could be traced back to the very beginning of colonial administration.

The paper shall begin by sketching the changes from 1957 to 1980, followed by a discussion of the factors causing the changes.

Development Since 1957

In this section of the paper, we will trace the changes in the level of participation of the Malays in business and industry in post-independent Malaysia. As backdrop, we will, however, focus a little attention on the situation during the colonial period, to show that the Malays' relatively poorer economic status vis-a-vis the Indians and the Chinese and their under-representation in the industrial and commercial sector is actually a carry-over of the earlier period.

As early as 1830, Abdullah Munshi, a noted Malay writer of the period, intimated the problem in his autobiography (1964). Later, in 1927, Zaaba, in one of a series of articles wrote:

> "Their country is rich and received abundant blessings from God, but the Malay people did not recieve profit or benefit from the wealth, such as, agriculture, business, carpentry, shoemaking, tailoring, sundry shop, rubber trading, coffee

shops...... it was not the Malay people who were doing these
businesses."
(Zabba 1927; Quoted from Ungku Aziz, 1975: 48)

However, it is from Emerson that we get some statistical
insights into the problem. Writing in 1937, Emerson gave
some figures concerning some aspects of businesses of the
period. For example, working on the 1931 census, he noted
that there were 475 (not including 574 immigrant Malays)
Malay proprietors and managers of businesses in the then
Federated Malay States of Perak, Pahang, Negeri Sembilan
and Selangor, as compared to 16,894 Chinese, 4,428 Indians,
and 246 Europeans (1937: 183). He further noted that,

> ...the larger concerns are generally in European hands al-
> though the Chinese, and to a lesser extent the Indians, offer
> vigorous and adroit competition, and the Chinese and Indians
> dominate the smaller enterprises ...as well as most of the petty
> traders, although in both categories there are occasional
> Malays. (1937: 185)

Emerson also gave information on Malay stake in other
industries in the then Federated Malay States. In the rubber
industry, for example, there were 1,803 Malays and 910 Malay
immigrants listed as rubber estate owners and managers in
1931, as compared to 1,514 Chinese, 58 Indians and 1,121
Europeans. But the relatively large number of Malays listed as
owners dwindled into insignificance when the relatively tiny
size of the usual Malay estate was compared with the vastness
of the European and at least certain of the Chinese and Indian
estates. Emerson showed the insignificance of the Malay share
in these estates and the relative importance of the holdings of
other races by providing the following table (Emerson, 1937:
184):

	Europeans	Malays	Chinese	Indians
100 - 1000 acres	357	23	287	118
1000 acres or over	296	-	12	-

The same was true for tin mining. According to Emerson,

"The Malays have for practical purposes no share whatsoever. The ownership of the mines is almost exclusively European or Chinese ..." (1937: 1815). This is very interesting considering the fact that in the early 19th century, mining was very much in the hands of the Malays (Wong Lin Ken, 1965: 17). According to Winstedt, even in 1886 there were 350 private Malay mines in Kinta alone (1947: 131).

The situation remained unchanged even up to the eve of independence. In 1954 3 years before independence, there were 79,673 units of businesses registered in the then Federation of Malay. Out of these, only 7,878 or approximately 10% were Malay-owned. The Chinese owned 58,005 or 73% and the Indians owned 12,696 or 17% (Goh Joon Hai, 1962:84). Out of 58,005 Chinese-owned enterprises, about 70% were sole proprietorships. Limited liability companies accounted for less than 2%; the rest were partnerships (Goh Joon Hai, 1962: 90). It can be assumed that similar patterns characterized Malay enterprises. It is also interesting to note at this point that the domination of the non-Malays in trade and industry took place not only in the states where they formed the majority, as in Selangor or Perak, but also in the states where they constituted a minority, like Kelantan or Trengganu. The percentage of Chinese population in Kelantan in 1954 was 5.7%, which was the lowest in the then Federation of Malaya, but they owned slightly less than half the businesses in the state. There were 2,972 units of businesses in the state then, out of which 1,441 were Chinese-owned. Similarly in Trengganu, where the percentage of Chinese population in 1954 was 6.6%, the second lowest in the Federation. But there again the Chinese owned almost half the businesses in the state, owning 996 units out of a total of 1,995 (Goh Joon Hai, 1962: 87).

As far as it affects the position of the Malays in the business system of the nation, the scenario of the 60s did not see a radical departure from that of the previous decades. There were slight changes, but the overall picture remained almost the same. For example, December 1961, there were 84,930 sole proprietorships in the then Federation of Malaya. Out of these, 11,648 or 12% were owned and managed by the Malays. Out of 16,103 partnerships, only 4.5% were Malay. The ratio of Malay firms to non-Malay firms was 1:7 (Ungku Aziz, 1962: 10, footnotes).

The fact of under-representation is also reflected in other statistics of the period. For example, in 1968, the Statistics Department carried out a survey on retail trading in urban centers of 10,000 population and above. The result of the survey revealed that there were 59,737 such units, out of which only 3,993 or approximately 7% were Malay-owned (Statistics Department, 1968).

Further indications regarding the nature of Malay participation in business and industry up to 1970 can be seen from Table 1 below:

Table 1
Number of Malay Businesses by Industrial Category 1970

Category	Malay	Total	Percent
Oil Palm Estates	2	360	Insign.
Rubber Estates	46	2,059	2.0
Rubber Dealers	629	2,833[1]	22.0
Mining	28	1,506	2.0
Manufacturing	143	3,192	4.5
Contractor > $100,000	45	895[2]	5.0
< $100,000	2,098	2,679[3]	78.0
Selected Services	3,494	17,156[4]	20.4
Wholesale	184	6,874	2.67
Retail	3,993	25,660	15.6
Total	10,662	63,214	16.9

Source: Charlesworth, 1974: 63.

1, 3 and 4 - No survey in 1970, 1971 figure used; 2 -25% of 1971 total.

As the table shows, the Malay control of many of the business categories was rather insignificant. The only exception was in the area of contractors licensed to undertake work of less than $100,000. In this area, the Malays constituted 78.0% of the total. The other area where Malay participation was of some significance was in rubber dealership where they formed 22.0%

of the total.

A similar picture emerges when we look at the ownership of share capital in corporate sector. In 1969, Malay individuals owned only 1.0% or 1.5% if we include that share which was held in trust for them (*Second Malaysia Plan, 1971*: 40). Their share capital in manufacturing industry was about 2.2% out of the estimated $1,087 millions and 2.4% in mining industry out of estimated $336 millions (Abd. Rahim Said, 1974: 158). These figures appeared more insignificant when compared to those owned by Chinese and foreigners. In 1969, the Chinese owned 23%, the foreigners 62% share capital in the corporate sector.

However, the 70s appeared to present a different picture. There had been some changes in terms of both the number of business units owned and operated and in terms of their share equity in corporate sector. More significantly, there were also some qualitative changes relating to the types and scale of business operations that they ventured into and also in the socio-economic background of those who made up the emerging Malay business class.

The changes in numbers of business units are borne by the following statistics. In 1970, the number of business units owned by Malays in peninsular Malaysia was 21,763 or 14.2% of the total. The number of units rose to 78,961 or 24.9% of the total in 1980 (*Fourth Malaysia Plan, 1981*: 66).

A look at some of the categories of business and industry will provide further insights concerning the development mentioned earlier, as exemplified by the transport trade and contracting business. In 1970, 249 Malays held permit A. This figure represented 10.0% of the total. In 1975, there were 2,234, representing 54% of the licenses issued (*Third Malaysia Plan, 1981*: 230). There were 1,191 Malays in contracting business and who were registered with the Public Works Department in 1970. The number increased to 4,331 in 1975 and 7,834 in 1980. More significantly, their number in bigger contracting job categories had also increased rapidly. In 1970, there were only 9 (6.3%) class A contractors among the Malays, but there were 48 (21.2%) in 1980. Among the bigger categories of class A, B, Bx and C, the number of Malay contractors was 37 (6.2%) in 1970, 142 in 1975 and 321 (24.1%) in 1980 (*Third Malaysia Plan, 1976; Fourth Malaysia Plan, 1981*: 67).

There was also a corresponding increase in the ownership of share capital in the corporate sector, as reflected by Table 2 below. As shown by the Table, in 1970, the Malays and Malay interests owned 2.4% of the total share, 9.2% in 1975 and 12.4% in 1980 (TMP, 1981: 99; FMP, 1985: 62).

A more detailed picture of the Malay share as it existed in the various commercial and industrial sectors and the changes from 1970 to 1975 is presented in Table 3 below.

Table 2
Malaysian Ownership and Control of the Corporate Sector
1970-80 ($ Million)

	1970	%	1975	%	1980	%	Annual Growth Rate 1972-80 %
a) Bumiputera Individuals [1]	84.4	1.6	549.8	3.6	1880.1	5.3	23.5
b) Bumiputera Trust Agencies [2]	41.2	0.8	844.2	5.6	2170.4	6.7	39.0
2) Other Malaysians [3]	1826.5	34.3	5653.2	37.5	14442.9	44.6	18.8
3) Foreigners	3377.1	63.3	8037.2	53.3	13927.0	42.9	13.3
Total	6564.1	100.0	15084.4	100.0	26323.0	100.0	16.7

Source: Adapted from Third Malaysia Plan, 1981: 99, and Fourth Malaysia Plan, 1985: 62 and Mid-term Review of FMP, 1984: 112.

Notes: 1. Includes institutions channeling funds of individual Bumiputeras such as Lembaga Urusan dan Tabung Haji, Amanah Saham Mara, and cooperatives.
2. Shares held through institutions classified as Bumiputera trust agencies such as PERNAS, MARA, UDA, SEDCs, Bank Bumibutera, BPMB, FIMA, and PNB. Previously this item was classified as Bumiputera interests.
3. Includes shares held by nominee and other companies.

The quantitative changes that took place during the 1970s elaborated in the preceding pages find support in a number of micro studies. In a study of 400 Malay businessmen in peninsular Malaysia, Charlesworth found that 45% of them started their business operations during or after 1970 (1974:31). A 1976 report by Malaysian Center for Development Studies of

Table 3
Ownership and Participation in Industrial
and Commercial Sectors 1970; 75

	1970	1975
Industry		
Mining	0.8%	2.1%
Manufacturing	0.9%	3.6%
Construction	3.8%	4.5%
Trade		
Wholesaling	0.7%	1.7%
Retailing	3.0%	4.2%
Transport		
Taxi	47.7%	65.5%
Bus	18.0%	18.6%
Haulage	14.5%	39.0%

Source: Fourth Malaysia Plan, 1981, 64.

the Prime Minister's Department, now renamed Socio-Economic Research Unit or SERU, revealed that 32% of Malay businesses in Kelantan were started after 1970 (1976: 26). Based on a study of 186 businessmen of Kota Bharu, Mohd Fauzi found that 39.8% started their business enterprises in and after 1970 (1981:86). In another study on Kelantan businessmen, Amir Sharifuddin found a higher percentage of 78.0% of businesses that were started in and after 1970 (1984: 161). In Selangor, 72.6% of Malay entrepreneurs studied by Abd. Aziz Mahmood started their business operations after 1970 (1977: 145).

However, it should be borne in mind that this increase in number of business firms and their share equity in corporate sector was not solely the result of more Malay individuals and institutions channelling funds, individual Malays starting firms of their own or investing their money into business. Also important in the development in this direction was the government factor. Since 1970 the government had begun a policy of direct involvement in private sector activities. This point we shall take up in greater detail later. At this juncture, suffice it to mention that the government, through its numerous agencies, had set up companies that involved themselves in various types of business activities. These companies had been regarded as Malay or Bumiputera owned. Their direct involvement in trade and industry had boosted tremendously the Malay share in it. For example, of 2.4% of the share capital defined as Malay-or Bumiputera-owned in 1970, about 33.0% were contributions by these agencies (TMP, 1976: 99), about 60.1% in 1975 and about 65.3% in 1980 (FMP, 1981: 62).

Similarly, but to a lesser extent, the increase in the number of firms defined as Malay-owned could be attributed to government factor. There was no nation-wide statistic to show the distribution of Malay firms according to its equity source. But a sample of 106 firms that had been officially, in 1975, categorized as Malay-owned or controlled and were involved in distributive trade may provide some indications. This is presented here as Table 4. As shown by the Table, close to 30.0% of the sample were firms that were started by government agencies and only 25.0% of them were wholly owned by Malay individuals. Such a distribution may not reflect the true picture on the ground, especially concerning the share of Malay individuals. But the pertinent point here is the extent of the government's involvement in private sector activity, which could be termed as rather significant.

This had led to observations that in doing so the government appeared to be "more entrepreneurial than the group it is trying to develop" (Abd. Rahim Said, 1974: 203).

Notwithstanding what had just been mentioned, and apart from the quantitative changes described earlier, the 1970s also saw some significant qualitative changes. These qualitative changes took place in three major areas: in the type of goods and services offered by newly set up business enterprises; in the scale of operation of these enterprises; and in the socio-economic origin of the individuals who started these enterprises.

Up to the end of the 1960s, the majority of Malay business concerns were in the retail trade, offering for exchange a rather limited range of grocery or other consumer items; in coffee or eating shop business; in service sector like tailoring, laundering

Table 4
106 Malay Companies in Distributive Trade
According to their Equity Source, 1975

	Number	%
Statutory bodies, subsidiaries of State Economic Development Corporations and Pernas	31	29.2
Cooperatives and subsidiaries of Banks	7	6.6
Wholly-owned by Malays	27	25.5
51% Malay-owned	41	38.7
Total	106	100.0

Source: Bumiputera Participation Division, Ministry of Trade and Industry, Kuala Lumpur.

or hairdressing. In the manufacturing sector Malay concerns were largely in the production of batik, brassware and other handicrafts. Market for these goods and services were usually confined locally. Malay business enterprises of the pre-NEP era also shared another characteristic: that they were largely sole-proprietorships. Of 8,464 Malay firms registered in the country at the end of 1957, only 267 or 3.1% were partnerships of some sort. The rest were sole-proprietorships. In 1960, sole-proprietorships accounted for 95.0% of Malay firms, and in 1964, 91.2% (Zaman Hamzah, 1967: 15). These firms were small-scale in terms of initial capital and annual turnover and rarely employed more than two or three assistants.

Businesses on the scale and that dealt with the type of goods and services described above had for centuries been part and parcel of the traditional socio-economic patterns for the Malays. Perhaps, for convenience, these could be described as bazaar or traditional type. Businesses of this nature were to be found in most of the Malay villages throughout the country and in many of the major towns, especially where the Malays formed the majority of the population, like Kota Bharu and Kuala Trengganu on the East Coast of peninsular Malaysia or Alor Setar and Kangar in the North. Even in the bigger towns like Kuala Lumpur, Ipoh or Penang, most the Malay businesses of the period were of the bazaar category.

With a fair degree of accuracy, it could be asserted that much of the increase in the number of Malay business concerns described earlier took place in the so-called traditional or bazaar sector. The number increased because there were more Malays, after 1970, who started retail shops selling ordinary consumer goods like sugar, milk, kerosene and the like; or opened up foodstalls and small restaurants; producing and retailing batik, silver and brassware and other products of cottage industry; or providing services like hairdressing or laundering. But at the same time, there was sufficient evidence to suggest that part of the increase was attributable to some Malays who ventured into areas that had not been attempted seriously by other Malays previously. Such ventures included insurance and reinsurance business, property and housing development, consultancy services, security trading, import and export trade, advertising, film making, logging, travel agency and the like. It also included producing consumer goods; banking and hotelling. Even if the newly set-up firms were involved in retail trading, the goods and services offered for exchange were in demand as part of modern living. These included cars, motorcycles, motor spare parts, petrol and its related products, electrical goods, building materials, and the like.

As a rule, these business concerns were operated on a bigger scale, both in terms of initial and operating capital and also in terms of the number of people employed to run them. Markets for these goods and services were no longer confined to a limited parameter. Rather, they were aimed at regional, national or international markets. Running such enterprises therefore demanded a high level of management skill.

As a matter of record, businesses of this scale and dealing with this sort of goods and services had for a long time been part and parcel of the business and commercial system of the nation. But strictly in the context of Malay participation, these areas can be considered as new. Venturing into these new areas, to our mind, had been a high point of the post-1970 development. Their share in these new areas, just as their share in the total system, was still very low. For example, in 1983 of the 47 stockbroking companies in the country, six were Malay-owned (Ranjit Gill, 1985: 102). Distributive

Table 5
Malays in Distributive Trade, 1973-75

| Year | 1973 | | 1974 | | 1975 | |
Goods distributed	No.	%	No.	%	No.	%
Cement	3	14.3	16	43.2	24	48.9
Steel	29	29.9	53	41.1	59	43.4
Asbestos, Terrazo and paraguat	-	-	3	37.5	3	37.5
Paint	-	-	22	10.4	34	14.9
Roofing Sheet	-	-	2	28.6	5	35.7
Steel casting corrugated steel and other steel products	-	-	4	14.3	6	17.1
Sugar	-	-	114	14.0	186	19.0
Flour	-	-	44	8.0	51	8.5
Milk	-	-	33	11.3	59	18.0
Bottled drink	-	-	17	2.7	68	10.6
Cigarette	4	3.2	14	10.6	24	17.0
Motorcycle	9	15.0	30	36.0	35	40.0
Car/Lorry	-	-	20	16.0	68	39.0
Petroleum	-	-	129	11.8	141	13.4

Source: Bumiputera Participation Unit, Ministry of Trade and Industry, Kuala Lumpur.

trade provided another example which is presented in Table 5.

Though still low in degree of participation, of importance is the fact that a beginning had been made. This pioneering venture was initiated by a group of Malay entrepreneurs whom we can call the new breed. This new breed of Malay entrepreneurs stood apart from the rest of Malay businessmen of their time and differed significantly from the older generation of Malay businessmen in a number of ways. Firstly, they differed in terms of the type of businesses that they started and in the scale of operation of these businesses. Most of the ventures in the newer fields and on the scale described earlier, were undertaken by businessmen of this group. These ventures were no longer sole-proprietorships or simple partnerships. Rather they were private limited companies. In the 1980s, a significant number had even turned into public companies. Secondly, but more importantly, they differed from other Malay traders, past and present, in terms of educational background. Perhaps with some exceptions, this new breed of Malay businessmen were all educated, with a significant number of them holding diplomas, degrees, and other professional qualifications. In the past, the Malays who had educational qualifications were drawn into government service. Government service, and other white collar jobs had been traditionally favored over careers in other fields. Occupations with fixed salary, regular hours and personal security were considered to carry greater prestige than commercial ones, even when the latter may confer greater wealth (Tham Seong Chee, 1971; Judith Nagata, 1972). We shall return to this point in the latter part of the paper. At this point suffice it to say that the presence of this group in business and industry gave a new dimension to Malay entrepreneurship.

Another development worthy of note is the growth of joint ventures between Malay and non-Malay entrepreneurs, especially the Chinese. Without doubt, there were still not many of these enterprises, even when compared to the pre-1970s period. Based on a sample of 106, as indicated in Table 4, there were 41 concerns that were active in distributive trade in 1975. Certainly, there was an over-representation here. But of pertinence is that ventures were beginning to be looked upon in a new perspective by the Malays generally. Previously, such partnerships were derogatively termed Ali-Baba. Ali was the Malay partner who loaned his name for obtaining government privileges while Baba was the Chinese who managed the business giving the Malay a percentage of the income for the use of his name. Even well into the 1970s, Ali-Baba partnerships were prevalent. For example, in 1978, it was revealed by the Menteri Besar of Kelantan that 99.0% of Malay logging firms in the state were being run on this basis (*New Straits Times*, 19/4/78). It was thought that such a practice was detrimental to the development of Malay entrepreneurship in the long run, and that changes were called for. So, of late, these partnerships changed somewhat, with Ali equally active in the day to day management of the enterprise. He was no longer a sleeping partner whose primary waking function was to get more government assistance. A number of the businesses started by the new breed of Malay entrepreneurs were joint ventures of this kind.

As this development was occurring, other changes took place almost simultaneously. One of these was rapid urbanization. Prior to the colonialisation of the country, the Malays were predominantly rural dwellers, living in villages which "varied from hamlets of some five houses to large settlements of a hundred houses or more" (Gullick, 1958: 27). The larger ones, invariably the residence of a chief, were the capital of the district, and usually contained about 1000 people. The majority, however, were much smaller (Lim Heng Kow, 1978: 30). These were agriculture based and self-sufficient, without substantial cultivation for commercial gain.

This was the situation the British found when they started intervening in the Malay States in the 1870s. When they and other immigrant groups started to develop Kuala Lumpur, Seremban, Ipoh, and Penang among others, and thereby transforming the economy, the Malays never became a party to it. The growth of these two centers of intense economic activities were the results of British and Chinese enterprises. These new growth centers were not Malay settlements that developed into urban centers. "They were a foreign creation in a landscape originally barren of urban settlements" (Lim Heng Kow, 1978: XXV). The Malays remained in their villages, with their subsistence agriculture. They continued to form the bulk of rural agriculture population, so that by 1931 only 6.6% of them were to be found in urban centers and by 1947, 8.2% (Hamzah Sendut, 1965:).

The percentage of Malays to total urban population was also small. In 1931, they constituted 19.0% of the urban population and remained at that level up to 1947 (Hamzah Sendut, 1965:). The ethnic composition of Kuala Lumpur and George Town for the intercensal period 1911-1947 provide us a more detailed picture which is shown as Table 6 and Table 7.

By the time of political independence in 1957, only 13.6% of the Malays were living in towns and cities, forming 21.3% of the total urban population (Hamzah Sendut, 1965:). The point to be stressed is that though there were Malays in urban centers during the colonial period, they did not participate in the commercial activities that formed the mainstay of urban economy. The aristocratic class had been absorbed into the colonial government machinery. They and later some of their children became junior officers in the then new administrative set up. The ordinary citizens, on the other hand, preferred to work as clerks, peons, drivers and laborers in the various government departments and in the private sector. Some were policemen and soldiers. There were some who went into trading, but these were largely petty and small-scale, perhaps with a few exceptions. Large scale trading was very much in the hands of the Europeans and Chinese merchants.

But after independence, as a greater proportion of the Malaysian population became urbanized, so too the Malay population. In 1970, 14.8% of them were in the urban areas in peninsular Malaysia. By 1980, their proportion rose to 21.3% forming 32.8% of urban population (FMP, 1981: 78). As more of them became urban dwellers, they became involved in the modern economy. Hence, their level of participation in the industrial and commercial sectors increased.

While this development was taking place, the Malays were also experiencing some changes in the field of education. After 1957, and especially following the implementation of national education policy in 1961, educational opportunities were made available to the Malays, even to those who lived in the remotest area. During the colonial period, liberal secular education of the type that prepared its recipients for occupations in the modern sector, as a rule, was available only in the major towns. In the rural areas, there were only the vernacular schools, which prepared the pupils for four years of schooling in the basics. The children were taught simple arithmetic for the first three years, and in the fourth year, Malayan weights and measures. They were also taught some geography of the world in general and Southeast Asia in particular, and some exercises in composition (Chan Hon Chan, 1967: 251). It was considered that this curriculum would be,

> "sufficient for the ordinary requirements of Malay boys who will be bullock-wagon drivers, padi growers, fishermen, etc... or to keep accounts if they become small shopkeepers ..." (Quoted by Chan Hon Chan, 1967: 251 from The System of Education in the Federated Malay States, KL 1902: 9)

Table 6
Bandar Kuala Lumpur - Ethnic Composition 1891-1947

Year		Malays	Chinese	Indians	Others	Total
1891	%	12.4	73.2	12.4	2.0	99.8
	No.	2,333	13,927	2,367	393	19,020
1911	%	9.0	66.6	19.4	4.8	99.8
	No.	4,226	31,152	9,068	2,272	46,718
1931	%	9.6	60.9	22.7	6.6	99.8
	No.	10,769	67,929	25,342	7,378	111,418
1947	%	12.4	63.4	17.9	6.0	99.7
	No.	21,989	111,693	31,607	10,672	175,961

Source: McGee, 1971: 155.

Table 7
Georgetown - Ethnic Composition 1911-1947

Year	Malays	Chinese	Indians
1911	15.63	63.00	17.46
1921	13.86	67.09	15.88
1931	12.81	67.79	16.14
1947	11.15	72.4	13.87

Source: Timothy Lam Thim Fook, 1967.

And as quoted by Wheeler, the Annual Report of the Federated Malay States Government for 1920 stated that the aim of education for the Malays was,

> ...not to turn out a few well-educated youths, nor a number of less well-educated boys; rather it is to improve the bulk of the people and to make the son of the fishermen or the peasant a more intelligent fisherman or peasant than his father had been, and a man whose education will enable him to understand how his own lot in life fits in with the scheme of life around him. (Wheeler, 1928: 155)

To train a few well-educated Malay youths, the British government started the Malay Residential School, later renamed Malay College, at Kuala Kangsar in 1905 (Chan Hon Chan, 1967: 247). Those who were sent to this school were mainly the children of the traditional ruling class, though commoners were admitted as well. Upon completion of their education, they were drafted as junior officers in the colonial administrative machinery.

As educational opportunities were made available to more people in the years following independence, more Malays became its recipients. In the field of higher education, it can be asserted that the 70s marked a new beginning as far as Malays were concerned. The enrollment of Malay students in institutions of higher learning in the country increased greatly during the period. The changes in racial composition of the student population at the Universiti Malaya from the mid-60s to 1980 can illustrate this point. In 1966, the university's enrollment consisted of 70.0% non-Malays and 30.0% Malay students (Universiti Malaya, 1967). In 1970, Malay students formed 39.0% of population of the university (Universiti Malaya, 1972: 109). In 1980, they constituted 49.8% of the University's enrollment (Universiti Malay, n.d.: 156). By the same year, Malay students formed the majority group in other universities of the country, namely Universiti Kebangsaan Malaysia, Universiti Teknologi Malaysia, Universiti Pertanian Malaysia, and Universiti Sains Malaysia. Institute Teknologi Mara (ITM), which developed out of Dewan Latihan Rida of the late 50s, had always accepted only Malay and other bumiputera students. The combined Malay student enrollment of universities and ITM was 25,444 in 1980, as compared to 7,392 in 1971 (FMP, 1981: 65). Therefore, more Malay youths had access to education that enabled them to secure jobs in the modern sector in urban areas. From the midst of this group of educated Malays grew what we earlier called the new breed of Malay entrepreneurs. Previously, Malays with education preferred government jobs which were held in high esteem. Because of the pervasiveness of this attitude, not many of them, particularly the diploma or degree holders, ventured into the business world, even up to late 1960s. When they did, they set up private practice in the area of their expertise, such as legal, medical or accountancy. Even then, there were not very many of them. Those with, for example, B.A. qualifications were more attracted to jobs like ADO (Assistant District Officer) than to business.

The business world, up till then, save for an insignificant exception, attracted only the less educated Malays. Most of these were the Malays who aspired to join the ranks of white collar workers but lacked necessary paper qualifications. The result of several micro studies provide support for the claim. Studies by Mohd Fauzi, Charlesworth and SERU, among others, revealed that more than 50% of their samples consisted of individuals who had had 6 or less years of formal education. A period of schooling up to 6 years can be equated with primary level in the present national education system. Of those who passed the primary level, many did not complete their secondary level education. With some insignificant exceptions, most of them became small businessmen, involved with retail trading which requires small capital outlay (1981: 1974; 1976). Some of them fit what Judith Nagata termed "last resort" category, which refers to the fact that "these individuals did not originally or willingly aspire to a business career, and indeed evaluate such occupations negatively." (Nagata, 1972: 1141). The Kota Bharu study revealed that a number of operators of family businesses were, more or less, forced into entrepreneurship. More often than not, they were the sons who did not quite make the grade while they were at school. Their siblings who performed better at school sought salaried employment elsewhere (Mohd. Fauzi, 1981).

With the advent of the 1970s, this attitude gave way slowly. We have more and more of the educationally qualified Malays, the holders of diplomas and degrees and other professional qualifications, drawn into areas that had little or nothing to do with their professional training. There had been cases of lawyers or doctors going into property development, real estate agency, mining or the like.

When this group entered the business world, they went into sectors shunned by the earlier Malays. They set up firms that were involved in housing and property development, manufacturing, film-making, book production, distributive trade, and the like. These concerns demand large capital outlay, running into hundreds of thousands, employ a large number of personnel and other staff, and the area of activity, sometimes extends beyond state boundaries.

What motivated them was the belief that commerce and industry could also bring wealth and status. Therefore, even if they possessed the necessary academic qualifications to enter fixed, salaried, regular hours-government jobs, they chose to go into business. As a matter of fact, a good number of them had been in government service, but chose to go into business which now began to be viewed as confering wealth and status. Being educated they felt that they were able to fulfill their role as entrepreneurs more effectively. Because of the increasing state control in the running of present day businesses, the businessmen had to deal more and more with the government officials. Because there was no significant social difference between traders and the government officials, they could relate to each other better. The businessmen did not feel inferior to the officials, a feeling that existed with the small traders who usually had inferior educational background. Similarly, these Malay businessmen were better able to relate to other parties as well, for example the banks or other financial institutions which were instrumental to them and their businesses. Their similar social background, particularly in terms of education, enabled them to speak the same language, and therefore facilitated the running of their business affairs. "Old school" ties too, facilitated many of their business deals. Contacts with former school colleagues went a long way in determining whether their businesses were going to do well.

To date, a good number of the entrepreneurs from this category have become successful. They controlled, or at least owned shares in, firms whose activities were wide ranging or diversified. Some of them have been deeply involved in the corporate culture, dabbling in mergers, share-swaps, and take-overs. Through such measures they had managed to turn their companies into conglomerates. Names like (Tan Sri) Ibrahim Mohamed, (Datuk) Syed Kechik, (Datuk) Azman Hashim, (Datuk) A. Rahim Abd. Rahman and Daim Zainuddin (now a state Minister) were some of the corporate captains produced by the decade of the 1970s.

There were also from amongst this group those who though

they did not possess high scholastic achievements had nevertheless achieved similar successes as entrepreneurs. Through sheer grit and hard work, connections and some luck, they too had emerged as corporate champions, involved in huge projects. Names such as Abu Bakar Lajim, Mat Sarikun Abd. Hamid, and Mohd Noor Yusof were cases in point.

The presence of this group in business and industry gave a new dimension to Malay entrepreneurship. They were part of the educated Malays who worked towards the realization of personal dreams. But in doing so, they also proved that the hitherto widely held view that Malays cannot be successful in business ought to be viewed in a different perspective. That there was no substantial number of Malays in this sector in the past was, amongst other factors, because they were shielded from exposure to non-traditional economic activities of the urban centers.

Apart from rapid urbanization and the impact of education, Malay entrepreneurship in recent years also received government support, a factor conspicuously absent during the colonial period. As observed by Emerson,

> "In the political sphere it has been felt necessary to maintain a facade of Malay rule, or at least, of Malay participation in government, but there was no such necessity in the economic sphere". (1937: 185)

Instead the Malays were allowed to carry on their life in their accustomed ways, playing neither creative nor servile roles in the economy which had supplanted theirs as the dominant and dynamic force in the country.

It was only as late as 1950 that some effort was made by the colonial government to improve the lot of the Malays, when the Rural Industrial Development Authority, more commonly known as RIDA, was set up. But Rida's objective was to stimulate development in the rural areas, and its original activities included:

(i)   the provision of physical improvement to rural areas;

(ii) changing the structure of rural economy through provision of rural credit, marketing and technical assistance; and

(iii) fostering in the rural people a spirit of self-reliance and initiative (Gayle Ness, 1967: 123).

Rida was not set up with the specific purposes of fostering Malay business class, but rather with a more general purpose of improving the rural situation. So it is hardly surprising that there were no significant changes recorded for the period. What was remembered of Rida, were its fiascos. As observed by Hanna,

"the common judgement is that Rida lacked either a competent administration or a coherent programme; it subsidized a widely-assorted lot of individual projects after only the most perfunctory investigation, lending money without security, failing to collect payments, providing little guidance and often neglecting even to keep notations of its outlays". (1968: 5)

Hanna further noted that,

"Malay beneficiaries of Rida's largess were enabled to set up little transport companies, construction firms, rubber processing centers, fruit canneries, fisheries, rice mills, village shops, tanneries, and the like. Many, probably most of them, promptly failed; and if they did not fail, they were taken over by Chinese, the original Malay owner becoming a 'sleeping partner' whose primary waking function was to get more government credit". (1968: 5)

Rida's failure gave birth to Majlis Amanah Rakyat or the Council for Trust for the Indigenous People, better known by its Malay acronym, Mara. Mara was established as a corporate organization in July 1965 with the stated purpose, "to find realistic and practicable methods to stimulate, assist, and facilitate Bumiputera participation in commerce and industry." Mara was in fact the result of Kongress Ekonomi Buniputera which was held earlier the same year. This Kongress "was attended by a significant number of local Malay business leaders, criticizing the government's economic policies for the Malays" (Abd. Rahim Said, 1974: 140). One of their targets was Rida. The delegates passed a resolution, that since Rida was not performing its functions effectively, it should be dissolved. As a result, "Rida was killed off, at the same time, being reborn phoenix-like, a new agency Mara" (Abd. Rahim Said, 1974: 140). Another resolution passed by the Kongress was the setting up of Bank Buniputera Malaysia Berhad. Its objective, as envisaged by the participants, was to extend to Bumiputera traders credit and other facilities so that they can participate more extensively in trade and industry.

The setting up of these institutions spurred the Malays tremendously, because of the adequate opportunities created. Mara also trained Malays and other Bumiputeras to be equipped and willing to seize opportunities offered. These developments marked the beginning of the intensification of the policy of giving top priority to the welfare of the Malays and other Bumiputeras, and was described by Hanna in 1968 as "the latest development in Kuala Lumpur" (Hanna, 1968: 1).

The effort was further intensified after the launching of Second Malaysia Plan (SMP) in 1971. The plan, which outlined the government's development programs for the 1971-1975 period, introduced an approach it called the New Economic Policy (NEP). The NEP had as its objectives the restructuring of society and eradication of poverty, with increased national integration as its ultimate goal. Operating on the premise that most of Malaysia's problems had been essentially economic in origin, NEP believed its ultimate goal would be achieved through a radical re-allocation of basic economic resources and opportunities between the ethnic groups. The May 13 (1969) Incident had been used as the basis for the premise.

As far as it concerned the restructuring objective, the particular emphasis of NEP was on incorporating the Malays and other Bumiputera groups into the commercial and business sector and inducting them into the complexities of this mode of life. The plan had established a target whereby "within two decades, at least 30% of the total commercial and industrial activities of all categories and scale of operation should have participation by Malays and other indigenous people in terms of ownership and management" (SMP, 1971: 158).

In order to achieve the objective, the NEP formulated and, since then, implemented a number of programmes which included training, credit assistance, advisory and technical services and administrative support. As part of the overall plan and with the idea of further accelerating the growth in the direction,

NEP also provided for direct government participation in private sector activities. These measures were taken based on the belief that these were the problems that faced Malay entry into business and industry.

The implementation of these programmes was carried out by several government or government-backed agencies, which included MARA and Bank Bumiputera (BBMB) which had been mentioned earlier. Other agencies included Malaysian Industrial Development Finance Berhad (MIDF), Malaysian Industrial Development Authority (MIDA), Bank Pembangunan Malaysia Berhad (BPMB), National Productivity Center (NPC), Credit Guarantee Corporation (CGC), Perbadanan National Berhad (PERNAS), Urban Development Authority (UDA), and the Economic Development Corporations of all the states of Malaysia (SEDC's).

Some of these agencies, for example MARA, BBMB and SEDC's of the various states were already in operation at the time of the launching of NEP. But most of the rest were created after 1971 with the expressed objective of helping the NEP to achieve what it set out to do. UDA, for example, was established in 1972; so was FIMA. While some of these agencies were assigned specialized tasks, the others had diffused functions. NPC, for example, was involved only with the task of providing training and technical assistance and CGC with credit assistance. MARA and UDA, on the other hand, were involved with fulfilling several functions, like providing credit assistance, training, consultancy, creation of space for trading activities and also direct business ventures through their subsidiaries.

As a result of the activities of these agencies, the Malay share in the business and industrial sector showed an all-round improvement. This shows that successful entrepreneurship needs some measure of government support, which the Malays did not get, or was denied to them, during the colonial government. One of the problem areas that faced Malay businessmen of the past was credit assistance. There were not many financial institutions that were prepared to assist Malay ventures. For example, of the total loans and advances given by commercial banks and finance companies to finance business ventures even as late as 1971, only 4.0% or $149.3 million were given out to Malays. But as a result of efforts by bodies like MARA, UDA, and commercial banks administered within the framework of CGC, they managed to secure loans and advances amounting to 12.0% in 1975 and 20.6% in 1980 of the total given out (FMP, 1981: 65). As a comparison, banks and finance companies gave loans and advances amounting to $2,851.4 million in 1971 and $18,440 million in 1980 to other Malaysians (FMP: 1981: 65). Through the process of helping the Malays within the context of an expanding economy, other Malaysians also benefit from the expanding range of facilities and services.

Under the impact of these measures, the Malays, in just one decade, had managed to increase their stake in the commercial and industrial sector of the nation. In quantitative terms, the enlargement of their share took the form of more business establishments owned and operated by them and in the bigger equity share in the corporate sector. In qualitative terms, it was reflected in the transition from bazaar to stores, from cottage industry to factory. Largely due to the support of NEP, Malay businesses were beginning to appear in the major urban centers. Malay businessmen entered society and started to play an increasing role in many spheres of Malay life, particularly politics. Previously, UMNO leadership, locally and to a lesser extent nationally, was comprised of school teachers who formed the bulk of Malay intelligentsia in the earlier Malay social formations. But with the advent of the 1980s the businessmen challenged them. As evidenced by the May 1985 election results at divisional level, some businessmen had successfully challenged the school teachers for these posts. Perhaps, it may be worth noting that the period that saw the businessmen's increasing role in UMNO politics also witnessed the rise of another phenomenon, that of "money politics". Simply put, it was the use of money to buy political positions. It had been widely reported that many people aspiring to be leaders were prepared to spend from $400,000 to $600,000 for a divisional post (*New Straits Times*, 3/2/86).

Thus far, we have considered the development of Malay entrepreneurship in the light of the rapid urbanization of the community; their greater participation in education, particularly higher education; and the increasing government support given to them. It is also the contention of this paper that underlying all these developments was Malay nationalism, the origin of which could be traced back to the very beginning of colonial administration and the great influx of immigration that followed colonial economic development (Roff, 1967). Malay nationalism could be viewed as economic, political, and cultural; all these elements were inter-related (Abd. Aziz Mahmood, 1977: 59). Its economic dimension stemmed from the fact that colonial economic development, which relied on Chinese and Indian labor, had isolated the Malay Society from the processes of economic change. After several decades, the Malays were the most economically backward segment of the plural society just created. This situation, as observed by Golay *et. al.*, had sown amongst Malays a feeling of insecurity (1969). Many Malay social thinkers of the colonial era expressed this feeling as evidenced in the writings of Zaaba and Syed Shikh al-Hadi in the 1920s and 1930s and Ibrahim Yaakob and Ishak Haji Mohamed in the 1940s and 1950s.

The expression of this sentiment continued well into the 1960s. As a matter of fact, throughout the decade political tensions increased over the economic position of Malays. As mentioned earlier, this question was heatedly debated at the Kongress Ekonomi Bumiputera of June 1965, where the government was strongly criticized for its lack of adequate assistance in helping Malays enter the commercial world.

These continued expressions of basic economic insecurity and discontentments led to formulation and implementation of policies that favored Malays in many spheres of life, including education, employment, and business permits and licenses. The culmination of such a policy was the NEP of 1970, which was in effect an extension of many previous policies, "linked together to form a coherent whole" (Gale, 1985: 2).

Following implementation of these policies, the Malay position in many aspects of their life changed. They were beginning to become more urbanized, participating increasingly in higher education and in the business and industrial system of the nation. But the achievement of these results brought problems. The policy of giving preference to Malays, as can be recalled, was aimed at rectifying the various racial imbalances that existed at the time of independence. These imbalances were seen as impediments to national integration. It was thought that if Malaysia were to emerge a strong and united nation, the indigenous population had to be raised to the level already achieved by Malaysians of other ethnic origins. And this was to be done through measures that gave preference to them. But this policy was criticized as "further communalizing an already communal situation" (Chandra Muzaffar, 1978: 8). It had been pointed out that, apart from overt expression of resentment, the policy encouraged the growth of racially-based enterprises and institutions. For example, it was pointed out, the Chinese, through MCA, had formed the Multi-Purpose Holding Berhad (MBHB) in 1975. The MPHB was described by Gale as a response by the Chinese to the establishment of various government-owned "Bumiputera" companies in the 1970s (1985: 11). MPHB had its forerunner in the Koperatif Serbaguna Malaysia (KSM) which was formed in 1968. The Indians, through MIC, reacted by forming Kerjasama Nesa in 1974 (Gale, 1985: 36). The changing recruitment pattern in the universities also prompted similar reactions. The setting up of Kolej Tunku Abd. Rahman and the unsuccessful attempt to set up Merdeka University by the MCA were cases in point. There was some indication that MIC was also interested in setting up an Indian college in the tradition of MCA supported ventures (Chandra Muzaffar, 1978: 8).

The other criticism levelled at the policies that favor Malays is that in practice these had proven to be a bonanza for well-placed, well-connected Malays who operated with special licenses, in protected markets, with guaranteed credit, selling goods and services, often to the state, at fixed prices with guaranteed profits. It had been argued that the creation of a business class based on such foundations was untenable in the long run (Young et.al, 1980; Ozey Mahmet, 1986).

However, recognizing the merits of such arguments, can it also be argued that the enlargement of the Malay share was to have taken place in the context of an expanding economy and that the implications for national integration would have been worse if the question of racial imbalance were left unresolved?

Conclusion

From the foregoing discussion, it can be concluded that Malay entrepreneurship after 1970s developed at a rate unparalleled by any other period of its past history. This development can be said to have its origin in a number of factors, the most important being urbanization, education, and government support. Underlying these developments was Malay nationalism.

However, despite the development, achievement in the desired direction was not spectacular. A small class of nouveau riche, whose life style set them apart from other Malays, was created. But the phenomenon of under-representation persisted. The government, as expressed by the Deputy Prime Minister in Johor Bahru recently, was not happy with the results attained so far (*New Straits Times*, 21/12/85). Indeed, Malay entrepreneurship was still at its formative stage and had a long way to go.

References

Abd. Aziz Mahmood (1977), *Malay Entrepreneurship: Problems in Development - A Comparative Empirical Analysis*, Unpublished Ph.D. Thesis, University of Southern California, USA.

Abd. Rahim Said (1974), *Developing Indigenous Entrepreneurship in West Malaysia*, Unpublished M.Sc. Thesis, Cornell University, USA.

Abdullah Munshi (1964), *Hikayat Abdullah*, Pustaka Antara, Kuala Lumpur.

Chandra Muzaffar (1978), "The New Economic Policy and the Quest for National Unity," Paper presented at *Fifth Malaysia Economic Convention*, Organized by Malaysian Economic Association, 17th - 25th May, Penang.

Chan Hon Chan (1967), *The Development of British Malaya*, Oxford University Press, Kuala Lumpur.

Charlesworth, H.K. (1974), *Increasing the Number of Bumiputera Entrepreneurs*, A report submitted to Director ITM, Shah Alsam, Selangor.

Cooper, E. (1951), "Urbanization in Malaya," *Population Studies*, Vol.V, No.,2.

Emerson, R. (1966), *Malaysia*, University of Malaya Press, Kuala Lumpur.

Gale, Bruce (1985), *Politics and Business, A Study of Multi-Purpose Holdings Berhad*, Eastern University Press (M) Sdn. Bhd., Singapore.

Gill, Ranjit (1985), *The Making of Malaysia Inc.*, Pelandok Publications, Kuala Lumpur.

Goh Joon Hai (1962), "Some Aspects of Chinese Business World in Malaysia," *Ekonomi*, Vol. III, No. 1, Kuala Lumpur.

Golay F.H., et. al. (1969), *Under-development and Economic Nationalism in Southeast Asia*, Cornell University Press, Ithaca.

Gullick, J.M. (1958), *Indigenous Political Systems of Western Malaya*, The Anthlone Press, London.

Hamzah Sendut (1965), "Some Aspects of Urban Change in Malaya, 1931;1957," *Kajian Ekonomi Malaysia*, Vol. II, No. 1, Kuala Lumpur.

Hanna, W.A., (1968), "The Day of the Bumiputera," *Southeast Asian Series,* Vol. VI, No. 6 and 7.

Lam Thin Fook, T. (1967), *Population Data of George Town*, Kuala Lumpur.

Lim Heng Kow (1978), *The Evolution of the Urban System in Malaya*, Penerbit Universiti Malaya, Kuala Lumpur.

Malaysian Govt. (1971), *Second Malaysia Plan, 1971-1975*, Government Printer, Kuala Lumpur.

---------- (1976), *Third Malaysia Plan, 1976-1980*, Government Printer, Kuala Lumpur.

---------- (1981), *Fourth Malaysia Plan, 1981-1985*, Government Printer, Kuala Lumpur.

---------- (1984), *Mid term Review of Fourth Malaysia Plan, 1981-1985*, Government Printer, Kuala Lumpur.

McGee, (1971), *The Urbanization Process in the Third World: Exploration in Search of a Theory*, London.

Mehmet, Ozay (1986), *Pagar Makan Padi*, Nadi Insam, Kuala Lumpur.

Mohd Fauzi Haji Yaacob, (1981), *Peniaga dan Perniagaan Melayu*, Dewan Bahasa dan Pustaka, Kuala Lumpur.

---------- (1984), "Keusahawanan Melayu Semenanjung Malaysia, 1960-1980" in Khoo Kay Kim, et. al. (eds.), *Malaysia Masa Kini*, Persatuan Sejarah Malaysia, Kuala Lumpur.

Nagata, J. (1972), "Muslim Entrepreneurs and the Second Malaysia Plan Some Socio-Caltural Considerations," *Asian Research Bulletin*, Vol. II, No. 4.

Ness, G.D. (1967), *Bureaucracy and Rural Development in Malaysia*, University of California Press, Berkeley, USA,

New Straits Times, 21/12/85; 19/4/78; 3/2/86.

Popenoe, O. (1970), *Malay Entrepreneurship: An Analysis of the Social Backgrounds, Careers and Attitudes of Leading Malay Businessmen in West Malaysia*, Ph.D. Thesis, London School of Economics and Political Science, London.

Puthucherry, J.J. (1979), *Ownership and Control in the Malayan Economy*, University of Malaya Cooperative Bookshop Ltd., Kuala Lumpur.

Roff, W.R. (1967), *The Origins of Malay Nationalism*, Pustaka Ilmu, Kuala Lumpur.

SERU (1976), *Laporan Akhir Kajian Penyertaan Bumiputera Dalam Bidang Perusahaan dan Perniagaan Di Kelantan*, Kota Bharu.

Statistics Department (1972), *Panduan Pertubuhan Jual Runcit dan Jual Borong Yang Dimiliki Oleh Orang Melayu Di Kawasan Bandar di Malaysia Barat*, Vol. III, Kuala Lumpur.

Tham Seong Chee (1971), *Corak-corak Pekerjaan Dalam Masyarakat Melayu*, Ph.D. Thesis, National University of Singapore.

Ungku Aziz (1962), "Fact and Fallacies about Malay Economy - In Retrospect, with New Footnotes", *Ekonomi*, Vol. III, No. 1, Kuala Lumpur.

---------- (1975), *Jejak-jak di Pantai Zaman*, Penerbit Universiti Malay, Kuala Lumpur.

Universiti Malay (1967), *Laporan Tahunan ke-18*, Kuala Lumpur.

---------- (1972), *Laporan Tahunan ke-22, 1970-71*, Kuala Lumpur.

---------- (N.D.), *Laporan Tahunan ke-22, 1980-81*, Kuala Lumpur.

Wheeler, L.R. (1928), *The Modern Malay*, Allen and Unwin, London.

Winstedt, R.O. (1947), *The Malays: A Cultural History*, Routledge and Kegan Paul, London.

Wong Lin Ken (1965), *The Malayan Tin Industry to 1914*, The University of

Arizona Press, Tucson.

Young, Kevin et. al (1980), *Malaysia, Growth and Equity in a Multi-racial Society*, Johns Hopkins University Press, Baltimore.

Zaman Hamzayh (1967), *Kemunduran Orang Melayu di Dalam Perniagaan*, Unpublished B.A. Graduation Exercise, Malay Studies Department, Universiti Malaya.

7

The Rubber Smallholding Sector: Ethnic Perspectives And Policy Implications

K.T. Joseph

"Rubber is the one commodity whose price fluctuations have a far reaching impact on Malaysia with its millions of smallholders and their dependents."

Malaysia is the largest producer of natural rubber accounting for about 40% of the worlds' total. In 1985 Malaysia produced 1.51 million tons of rubber (valued at Ringgit $2921 million) of which 940,000 tons (63%) came from the smallholder sector, which accounts for about 75% of the total area under rubber in Malaysia. The dualistic nature of the rubber industry in the form of a large scale estate sector and a large number of smallholdings, differentiated legally by an upper size limit (up to 100 acres), arose in the early days of the 20th century.[1]

The birth of the rubber industry was caused "by a series of fortuitous circumstances" in the 1900s (Drabble) which eventually led to high rubber demand and prices. By 1914 there were a million acres under rubber and by 1930 nearly 3.1 million acres had been developed. Although rubber had become primarily an estate industry, there arose in various parts of the country a spontaneous process of Malay pioneering in the development of small holdings. In the 1930s nearly two-thirds of the total acreage under rubber were estates which produced three fifths of total peninsular production. The history of rubber has been characterized by great fluctuations in world rubber market prices. The serious recession of 1918-1921 resulted in the Stevenson Plan which had an adverse effect on smallholders whose expansion was curtailed.[2] There was therefore little expansion between the early thirties and the late fifties due to the Rubber Restriction Scheme (the Great Depression in the Thirties), the Second World War, the Japanese Occupation from Dec. 1941 to 1945, and the Communist insurrection from 1948 to 1960.

The distribution of rubber according to smallholdings (A rubber smallholding can vary from less than 1 acre to 99.99 acres in size.) and estates for the period 1960 to 1985 is given in Table 1 and illustrated in Figure 1.

Table 1
Proportion Of Rubber Land According To Smallholdings And Estates

Year	1960	1965	1970	1975	1980	1985
Smallholdings	50.3%	57%	62.5%	67%	73%	75%
Estates	49.7%	43%	37.5%	33%	23%	25%

For purposes of comparison with the earlier periods of the rubber industry, and in view of the fact that about 98% of the rubber comes from peninsular Malaysia, this paper will exclude East Malaysia (Sabah and Sarawak).

In 1960, estates accounted for 1.9 million acres and smallholdings coverage was estimated as 1.8 million acres. Rubber was the largest single crop by acreage (68%) and was the largest source of employment. In 1960, the Federation of Malaya produced 706,000 tons of rubber of which 413,200 (58.5%) came from the estate sector and 292,800 tons (41.5%) came from smallholdings. There were 2,300 estates and 282,300 smallholdings growing rubber.[3]

By 1982 there were only 1,624 estates but the number of smallholdings had increased substantially. Total rubber produced was 1.46 million tons of which 554,000 tons came

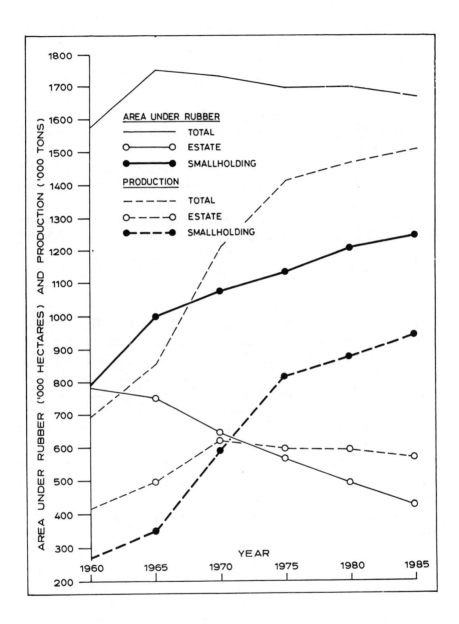

Figure 1. Rubber Cultivation and Production in Pen. Malaysia

from the estate sector comprising 473,000 hectares and 902,300 tons came from smallholdings covering 1.228 million hectares. The total number of hectares under rubber in peninsular Malaysia for 1982 was 1.7 million.

The planted area of rubber estates in peninsular Malaysia declined from 1.96 million acres in 1950 to 1.94 million acres in 1960 to 1.5 million acres in 1970 and to 1.22 in 1980. The corresponding areas for smallholdings were 1.73, 2.11, 2.67 and 2.77 million acres respectively.

The downward trend of the estate sector in the fifties and early sixties has been ascribed to fragmentation[4] of estates into smallholdings.

Planted acreage under estates declined over the years from 647,200 hectare in 1970 to 507,100 hectares in 1980 and its production decreased by 40% due to the continued conversion of rubber estates to oil palm and due to some subdivision of estates (see Figure 1). The overall acreage under rubber of 2.1 million hectares was sustained by the smallholder sector through new land development. As at the end of 1981, RISDA replanted and opened up a total of 783,283 hectares of rubber land involving some 412,250 smallholders. Further encouraging smallholders with less than two hectares of rubber land to replant, RISDA (Rubber Industry Smallholders' Development Authority) began the Replanting Incentive Scheme (Sepentas) which provides among other incentives, interest free credit of $100 per month for six years to supplement smallholders' incomes before the rubber trees mature. RISDA also set up eight nursery centers covering 355 hectares to produce high quality seedlings to smallholders.

Similarly, the Federal Land Development Authority (FELDA) is developing new rubber land. Felda developed about 373,700 hectares mainly in the states of Johor (22%), Negri Sembilan (17%), Pahang (46%) and the Federal Land Consolidation and Rehabilitation Authority (FELCRA) 50,700 hectares. In the case of rubber, almost the total acreage under the crop would have been planted and replanted with high yielding varieties by the end of the 70s with the full impact on production being realized by the early eighties. Output growth would be mainly the result of new plantings. There is the need for opportunities for excess rural labor to find employment in new land development (slow) and in non-agricultural sectors (off farm labor). Total employment creation in agriculture is estimated at only 445,000 persons over the 20 year period 1970-1990. A major part of the task of absorbing the creations in the labor force as well as those currently under-employed will fall upon the non-agricultural sectors of the economy. The relatively faster rates of growth of non-agriculture in GDP from 30.8% in 1970 to 22.2% in 1980. Significant structural changes in the composition of output also occurred within the sectors, especially in agriculture. Notable features in

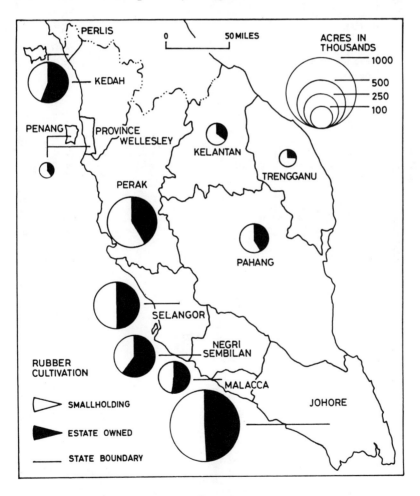

Fig. 2: Land Under Rubber In Pen. Malaysia - 1962

Table 2 *
Peninsular Malaysia: Incidence Of Poverty By Rural Strata 1970, 1975 And 1980

	1970				1975				1980			
	Total house-holds (000)	Total poor house-holds (000)	Incidence of poverty (%)	Percentage among poor (%)	Total house-holds (000)	Total poor house-holds (000)	Incidence of poverty (%)	Percentage among poor (%)	Total house-holds (000)	Total poor house-holds (000)	Incidence of poverty (%)	Percentage among poor (%)
Rural:												
Agriculture	852.9	582.4	68.3	73.6	915.1	576.5	63.0	69.0	963.2	443.7	46.1	66.6
Rubber smallholders	350.0	226.4	64.7	28.6	396.3	233.8	59.0	28.0	425.9	175.9	41.3	26.6
Oil Palm smallholders	6.6	2.0	30.3	0.3	9.9	0.9	9.1	0.1	24.6	1.9	7.7	0.3
Coconut smallholders	32.0	16.9	52.8	2.1	34.4	17.5	50.9	2.1	34.2	13.3	38.9	2.0
Padi farmers	140.0	123.4	88.1	15.6	148.5	114.3	77.0	13.7	151.0	83.2	55.1	12.5
Other agriculture	137.5	126.2	91.8	16.0	157.4	124.1	78.8	14.9	172.2	110.5	64.1	16.6
Fishermen	38.4	28.1	73.2	3.5	41.6	26.2	63.0	3.1	42.8	19.4	45.3	2.9
Estate workers	148.4	59.4	40.0	7.5	127.0	59.7	47.0	7.1	112.5	39.5	35.1	5.9
Other industries	350.5	123.5	35.2	15.6	433.3	153.4	35.4	18.4	546.4	124.8	22.8	18.7
Subtotal	1203.4	705.9	58.7	89.2	1348.4	729.9	54.1	87.4	1509.6	568.5	37.7	85.3
Urban: Subtotal									774.4	97.6	12.6	14.7
Total	1606.0	791.8	49.3	100.0	1901.4	835.1	43.9	100.0	2284.0	666.1	29.2	100.0

Note: 1. The calculations took into consideration the effects of programmes implemented during 1971-80 as well as changes in other factors, such as prices and costs.

2. Data from studies conducted by Economic Planning Unit and Socio-Economic Research Unit in the Prime Minister's Department, Ministry of Agriculture, Department of Statistics and other agencies were used in the computations.

* quoted from 4th Malaysia Plan - Government of Malaysia

the growth of the sector during the period were the rapid expansion of palm oil output which contributed about 40% of the increase in the sector's output, and the decline in the dominant role of rubber in output expansion. Rubber production expanded by 2.3% per annum while the acreage under rubber cultivation decreased by 0.2% per annum during the decade. This period witnessed a marked decline in estate acreage of about 14,100 hectares, due to continuing conversion into oil palm and other crops. Despite the decline in the acreage, output from the estate sector remained almost at the same level due largely to increases in yield at an average rate of 2.6% per annum during the period. Smallholders' production expanded by 4.4% per annum during the period as a result of the government efforts at large-scale new planting and replanting schemes. A total of 76,180 hectares and 115,870 hectares were newly planted during 1971-75 and 1976-80 respectively, in addition to replanting of 172,500 hectares during 1971-75 and 106,500 hectares during 1976-80. These efforts, coupled with improvement in yield, resulted in the smallholder sector contributing 60% of national rubber output in the 1980 output from the estate smallholder sectors. The share of rubber in total agriculture output declined from 34.3% in 1970 to 24.9% in 1980.

Marked shifts in the structure of the estate sector over the last decade arising from the conversion of rubber acreage with oil palm has reduced estate employment. These reductions have affected Indian workers on rubber estates most severely.

Rubber Smallholders

As shown in Table 2, the incidence of poverty among the rubber smallholders in peninsular Malaysia declined from 64.7% in 1970 to 41.3% in 1980, due to productivity improvements in the sector and the prevalence of high rubber prices in the second half of the decade. In 1980, the estimated yield per hectare was 1,105 kg compared with 750 kg and 1,0969 kg in 1970 and 1975, respectively. This was largely due to replanting efforts undertaken prior to 1970, which also influenced productivity among the rubber smallholders during 1971-80. About 77,900 holdings covering 172,500 hectares which were

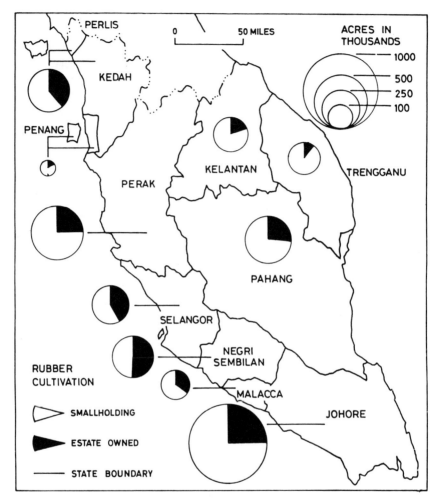

Fig. 3: Land Under Rubber In Pen. Malaysia - 1982

replanted during 1971-75 began to mature during 1976-80. However, during 1976-80, only 57,200 holdings covering 106,500 hectares were replanted. This decline in the total number of smallholdings replanted was due partly to the high price of rubber after 1975 making it difficult for small-holders to replant. Access to better processing facilities improved throughout 1971-80 with the provision of about 1,903 small-holders development centers implemented by Rubber Industry Smallholders' Development Authority (RISDA). In addition, purchases of smallholder rubber by the Malaysian Rubber Development Corporation (MARCDEC) also expanded from 35,400 tons in 1976 to 55,000 tons in 1980, an increase of 55%. The combined effect of these measures coupled with good rubber prices was to raise the average monthly income of rubber smallholders from about $228 in 1973 to about $450 in 1979.

Figs. 2 and 3 show land under rubber cultivation in peninsular Malaysia at 1962 and 1982. In 1962 the proportion of estates to smallholdings was greater in Kedah, Negri Sembilan, and Malacca. In Johor and Selangor, the sectors of smallholders and estates were about equal. Perak, Penang, Pahang, Kelantan, and Terengganu were dominated by smallholdings. By 1982 (Fig.3) apart from Negri Sembilan, smallholdings were dominant in all the other states in peninsular Malaysia.

Table 3
Registered Rubber Smallholdings By Size Of Holding And Race

	Total	0-5 acres	5-15 acres	15-30	30
Malays					
Total number of smallholders	335,637	246,505	84,722	3,581	829
Total area under rubber	1,450,021	694,743	648,044	73,463	33,771
Chinese					
Total number of smallholders	154,426	57,843	81,102	10,207	5,274
Total area under rubber	1,255,481	243,893	654,233	181,941	175,414
Others (Mainly Indians)					
Total Number of smallholders	7,982	4,215	2,784	558	425
Total area under rubber	65,020	13,847	23,867	9,775	17,531
Total Number of Registered Smallholders	498,048				
Total Land Under Rubber by Smallholdings (acres)	2,770,000				

Source: RISDA as of 31 Dec. 1984.
These exclude Felda and Felcra schemes.

Table 4
Registration Of Rubber Smallholdings By State And Race

	Malays			Chinese			Others			Total		
	No.	Acre	Avg.	No.	Acre	Avg.	No.	Acre	Avg.	No.	Acre	Avg
Johor	72,071	309,616	4.3	62,522	489,812	7.8	713	8,028	11.3	135,306	807,457	6.0
Kedah	34,783	156,044	4.5	7,480	90,182	12.1	1,712	12,329	7.2	43,975	258,555	5.9
Kelantan	52,849	190,168	3.6	1,818	16,367	9.0	49	422	8.6	54,716	206,957	3.8
Melaka	15,333	49,866	3.3	8,956	73,138	8.2	346	3,547	10.3	24,635	126,552	5.1
N. Sembilan	22,293	76,331	3.4	12,689	101,607	8.0	482	5,103	10.6	35,464	183,041	5.2
Pahang	34,536	178,374	5.2	16,620	135,663	8.2	656	5,332	8.1	51,812	319,370	6.2
Perak	46,449	222,367	4.8	25,747	176,021	6.8	2,390	18,133	7.6	74,586	416,521	5.6
P. Pinang	2,461	11,324	4.6	3,729	44,711	12.0	87	1,353	15.6	6,277	57,388	9.1
Perlis	1,412	5,558	3.9	591	5,659	9.6	65	721	11.1	2,068	11,938	5.8
Selangor	16,672	66,034	4.0	11,754	93,134	7.9	1,423	9,236	6.5	29,849	168,404	5.6
Terengganu	36,778	184,340	5.0	2,520	29,188	11.6	59	815	13.8	39,357	214,344	5.4
TOTAL	335,637	1,450,023	4.3	154,426	1,255,484	8.1	7,982	65,021	8.1	498,045	2,770,528	5.6

There are presently about 498,000 smallholdings in peninsular Malaysia covering an area of 2.777 million acres (see Table 3). Each of the main ethnic groups found in peninsular Malaysia is represented amongst smallholders: 67.4% of the smallholders were Malays; 31% Chinese; and 1.6% Indians. 62% of the smallholders had holdings of less than 5 acres. 34% had holdings of between 5 and 15 acres, 2.9% had holdings of between 15 and 30 acres, and 1.3% had holdings larger than 30 acres. The smallest sized holdings (0-5 acre) were dominated by the Malays (80%). For the category (5-15 acres), 50% were Malays, 25% Malays were in the third category (15-30 acres), and 12.7% Malays for the holdings that were greater than 30 acres. The Chinese have larger size holdings; 81% were in the greater than 30 acres group and 71% in the 15-30 acres category. 6.5% Indians were in the greater than 30 acres group and about 4% in the 15-30 acres group.

The ethnic representation for total acreage under rubber for each of the size group categories are as follows:

Table 5
Percentage Of Rubber Land According To Race

	Malays	Chinese	Indians
Johor	38.3	60.7	1.0
Kedah	60.3	34.9	4.8
Kelantan	91.9	7.9	0.2
Melaka	39.4	57.8	2.8
N Sembilan	41.7	55.5	2.8
Pahang	55.8	42.5	1.7
Perak	53.4	42.3	4.3
P Pinang	19.7	77.9	2.4
Perlis	46.6	47.4	6.0
Selangor	39.2	55.3	5.5
Trengganu	86.0	13.6	0.4
Total	52.3	45.3	2.3

Table 6
Production Of Smallholding By State 1982

	Production	Acreage	lbs/ac.
Johor	262,648	780,749	672.8
Kedah & Perlis	121,495	265,001	916.9
Kelantan	28,724	199,245	288.3
Melaka	51,979	126,679	820.6
Negeri Sembilan	103,231	179,839	1,148.0
Pahang	89,258	303,488	588.2
Pulau Pinang	29,425	56,606	1,039.6
Perak	153,613	402,649	763.0
Selangor	44,868	164,265	546.3
Terengganu	17,020	205,468	165.7

Rubber: Statistic Handbook 1982.

The Chinese owned 77% of the total land area of holdings greater than 30 acres and 67% of land in the 15-30 acres grouping. The Malays held 73% of land in the 0-5 acres category, 7.7% of land area of holdings greater than 30 acres were in Indian hands and 4% in the 15-30 acres category. The average Malay size holding was 4.32 acres compared with 8.13 acres for both the Chinese and Indian. In the smallest category of holdings namely 0-5 acres, average for the Malays was 2.8 compared with 4.2 for the Chinese, and 3.3 for the Indian.

From a preliminary socio-economic study of smallholders carried out by RISDA in 1977, of all smallholdings between (0.1 - 2.4 acres), 93% were Malays and 18% were Malays who owned from 0.1 to 2.4 acres. These represent the absolute poor, about 43% of all holdings which were smaller than 5 acres in size – the acreage of a high yielding holding needed for a family to rise above the poverty line, provided that rubber prices were adequate. The threefold factors of low yields, inadequate sized holdings and low prices determine the level and extent of poverty in this important sector.

From Table 4, note the extremely high percentage of rubber land owned by Malays in Terengganu and Kelantan comprising about 374,000 acres and representing 30 percent of all land owned by Malay rubber smallholders in peninsular

Malaysia. The low yields recorded in both these states as deduced from the production figures for 1982, 5 to 6 fold differences, would suggest the extreme poverty conditions operative there. See also Table 6 which clearly illustrates the unfavorable conditions (climatic) for rubber. The average holding for the Malays is 3.6 for Kelantan and 5.0 for Terengganu. Chinese holdings are much larger in these areas as well as in the states of peninsular Malaysia. It should also be noted that Chinese smallholding areas were dominant in Penang, Johor, Malacca, Negri Sembilan and Selangor, all areas of high rubber performance.

Table 7 shows 10 year rubber yields from estates in the states of peninsular Malaysia. The significant fact is the consistently low yields obtained in Terengganu which substantiates the belief that the rubber smallholders of Terengganu must represent the poorest rubber smallholders in peninsular Malaysia.

Table 8 summarizes the amount of replanting grants which have been made to the various ethnic groups in relation to the states of peninsular Malaysia from 1953 to 1984. The response to the replanting program undertaken by RISDA, however, was more from the larger holdings despite the increase in the replanting grant from $2,223 to $2,964 per hectare for holdings of 4.1 hectares and below due to the reluctance of smallholders to replant for fear of losing their incomes. As a result, the rate of replanting by RISDA declined from 34,500 hectares per annum replanted during 1976-75 to 21,500 hectares per annum replanted during 1976-80. In view of this, the replanting grant was further increased recently from $2,964 to $5,434 per hectare for holdings of 4.1 hectares and below and from $2,223 to $3,705 per hectare for holdings of more than 4.1 hectares. (Government of Malaysia, *Fourth Malaysia Plan*, p. 166.)

It should be noted that the Chinese received 52.3% and the Malays 45.4% of this replanting program. The government's policy of supporting the program of replanting was carried out effectively and in favor of the larger holdings which were owned by the Chinese. There is a need to give priority to the smallest holdings. There is also an urgent need to reconsider the legal upper limits of a smallholding as presently defined, which is a hundred acres, as most of the smallholdings are less than 10 acres and that the minimum size holding with a high yielding

Table 7

Estate Rubber Yields In The States Of Peninsular Malaysia, kg/ha

	1969	1970	1971	1972	1973	1975	1976	1977	1978	1979	Average [1]
Johore	1050	1099	1209	1300	1343	1211	1406	1404	1398	1397	1282 abc
Kedah & Perlis	1206	1227	1352	1379	1430	1349	1506	1481	1580	1581	1409 d
Malacca	1390	1378	1435	1474	1461	1279	1481	1444	1469	1478	1429 d
Negeri Sembilan	1279	1321	1419	1418	1447	1378	1515	1448	1421	1465	1411 d
Pahang	920	928	1003	1066	1203	1110	1313	1282	1323	1242	1139 abc
Pulau Pinang	1174	1191	1300	1350	1401	1273	1455	1437	1504	1551	1364 bcd
Perak	1139	1177	1243	1278	1354	1300	1538	1499	1520	1508	1358 bcd
Selangor	1193	1233	1412	1321	1401	1254	1457	1406	1372	1405	1345 bcd
Trengganu	669	738	789	918	881	875	1151	986	857	717	858 a
Average [2] $x^2 = 69.31$	1115 a	1159 ab	1247 abcd	1281 abcde	1328 bcde	1272 abc	1460 e	1430 de	1439 de	1439 cde	1317

[1] Difference between states' yields significant at more than 0.001 by Friedman Test ($x^2 = 83.17$). Yields with same letter not significantly different at 0.05.

[2] Difference between yearly yields significant at more than 0.001 by Friedman Test. Yields with same letter not significantly different at 0.05.

[3] Spearman's Rank Correlation between pooled state's yields of 1969 to 1973 and those of 1975 to 1979 gives coefficient of 0.7667, significant at 0.01. The average yearly yields correlate with time giving coefficient of 0.8100, significant at 0.01.

Table 8

Land Areas Under Rubber Receiving Planting Grants According To Race From 1953-1984

State	Malays			Chinese			Others			Total	
	No.	Acre	%	No.	Acre	%	No.	Acre	%	No.	Acre
Johor	67,165	223,384	33.3	68,450	439,145	65.5	862	8,160	1.2	136,477	670,689
Kedah/Perlis	35,180	123,502	59.1	7,656	76,383	36.5	1,527	9,244	4.4	44,363	209,129
Kelantan	45,116	123,815	91.3	1,389	11,371	8.4	76	434	0.3	46,581	135,620
Melaka	19,506	49,963	39.0	11,557	75,027	58.6	403	3,071	2.4	31,466	128,061
N. Seremban	21,709	64,413	38.7	13,089	98,001	58.8	522	4,124	2.5	35,320	166,538
Perak	41,121	138,506	44.1	25,926	163,656	52.1	1,765	12,139	3.8	68,812	314,300
Pahang	22,486	85,037	48.1	12,443	89,050	50.3	396	2,762	1.6	35,325	176,849
Pulau Pinang	2,485	9,072	18.8	3,760	38,270	79.6	81	756	1.6	6,326	48,099
Selangor	15,125	53,583	34.3	14,304	95,792	61.3	1,095	6,785	4.4	30,524	156,160
Trengganu	27,867	86,245	84.5	2,447	15,672	15.3	39	208	0.2	30,353	102,125
Total	297,760	957,520	45.4	161,021	1,102,368	52.3	6,766	47,684	2.3	465,547	2,107,572

Source: Laporan Tahunan 1984 RISDA.

clone (RRIM 600) at least 15 acres would be needed to provide earning above the poverty line (poverty at $300/month).

Future Prospects and Policy Implications

Rubber smallholders form a major component of the poverty group in Malaysia. In absolute terms the largest number in poverty are rubber smallholders in the less than 5 acre group. Malay smallholders occupied a total area under rubber of 1.45 million acres while Chinese smallholders (31%) occupied 1.26 million acres (45.5%) and represent a major component of smallholdings in peninsular Malaysia. Malaysian rubber smallholders were a disappointed lot in 1985. Not only did the rosy projections for the commodity not come true, but

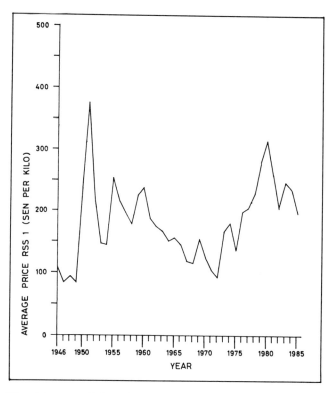

Fig. 4 Average Prices for Rubber in Peninsular Malaysia

rubber prices sank to the lowest level in 10 years with near-term price prospects unlikely to improve (see figure 4). Many Malaysian rubber smallholders still survive under poverty conditions. In 1985 NASH (National Association of Smallholders) suggested the government fix a guaranteed minimum price for rubber at 210 sen/kg to protect the interests of smallholders who account for 65% of the country's total rubber output.

The preamble of the *Third Malaysia Plan 1976-1980* objectives and policies has this to say about rubber smallholders. The accelerated replanting of smallholdings with high yielding stock will remain the principal means for reducing poverty among rubber smallholders. The government in addition will continue to deal with the basic problem of inadequate-sized holding.

The welfare of rubber smallholders is markedly influenced by rubber prices and productivity. The cultivation of inter-crops on replanted holdings during the gestation period increases the earning capacity of smallholders making them more responsive to replanting programs. Improvement in marketing and processing of smallholder rubber is essential. More effort is needed to process rubber into more value added products. The bulk of Malaysian rubber exports still remains in the unprocessed form due to slow absorption into semi processed or manufactured goods.

Natural rubber will continue to play an important part in the economy of Malaysia. The Malaysian Rubber Research and Development Board (MRRDB) in a global study of rubber use in major applications including tires, suggests natural rubber's potential share of the market is about 40% (*Malaysian Rubber Review*, Vol. 1, No. 1, July 1976). This is due not to any superior type of synthetic isoprene rubber but to the gap between world demand and natural rubber supply. Natural rubber is preferred in the manufacture of products that require high strength and low generation of heat such as airplane tires, giant truck tires, and technical products needing high resistance to fatigue. To increase its share of the market, Malaysia must increase its production. This increase will have to be borne by smallholders of the rural work force (despite the drift of the young to urban areas), old and unproductive rubber trees, and traditional methods of production which continue to affect the performance of the rubber smallholding sector. It is essential that the present proportion of estate rubber is at least maintained (or preferably increased) and further loss of existing rubber estates through conversion to oil palm discouraged except where ecological conditions favor such a switch. Rubber is more labor intensive than oil palm which makes it more advantageous from the point of view of providing employment. From a national strategic point of view it is essential to consider a suitable long term commodity mix in export crop production. Legislation is needed to prevent rubber estates from switching further to oil palm in rolling terrain where slopes of 6-12 and above are common. A land use policy based on matching landform to appropriate farming systems, and not purely on free market forces needs to be adhered to. More effective nutrient cycling and lower levels of nutrient removal from latex as against palm oil also favors rubber over oil palm in addition to the more effective protective canopy that a rubber forest develops for both soil and water conservation on the sedentary soils of Malaysia. Rubber forests as a source of timber and fuel wood for the future is another spin off from such a policy.

The disadvantage of the domination of rubber smallholdings over estates is that during boom times of high rubber prices, the extra money is likely to be frittered away and not reinvested in the holdings and thus in the rubber industry, whereas, during low price periods, unstable conditions are created.

It is essential to have a significantly large estate sector which can more effectively ride over the lean periods as rubber prices fluctuate (see Fig. 4). A change in government policy is required to encourage estate development of rubber by the private sector.

This paper has demonstrated that holdings formed by smallholders of Chinese and Indian origin are larger than holdings owned by Malays and that more government aid has been given to Chinese owned rubber holdings than to those owned by Malays. In a survey carried out by RISDA in 1977, it was shown that of the smallholders whose size of holding was less than 1 hectare i.e. between 0.1 to 2.4 acres, 93% were Malays. There are about 100,000 Malay smallholders in this category of land ownership. They represent the poorest of the poverty groups in Malaysia. The problem of low income, and under-employment in the rubber smallholder sector is compounded by the fact that Malays are much more adversely affected than the other races in Malaysia. Although the government has improved many smallholders through accelerated replanting, a large number of Malay smallholdings remain unplanted. The lack of credit facilities appears to be the most serious inhibiting factor. The scattered distribution of smallholdings and inaccessibility has precluded benefits from group processing and central marketing facilities. Under the present marketing system about 90% of smallholders' rubber is still marketed through a chain of agencies ranging from local dealers and middle dealers to remillers, and exporters. The production and sale of wet sheets results in very low returns to the small operators. About two thirds of the dealers numbering over two thousand were Chinese.[5] Malay smallholdings also dominate areas of relative unsuitability to rubber e.g. Terengganu and coastal Kelantan (monsoonal effects). In Johor large numbers of Malay smallholdings are on peat where yields are low. Government attention needs to focused on the smaller Malay smallholdings. These areas have been registered and are identifiable. Where possible there is the need to consolidate these small parcels into larger working units. The rate of replanting of high yielding material needs to be stepped up with intercropping. Advanced planting material and agronomic advances can reduce the immaturity period and yield stimulation practices have been shown to increase yields substantially. Increased planting densities (larger number of trees per acre) is recommended. The diffusion rate at which these innovations are implemented will depend on the organizations that deal with this important group.

The need for decision making at ground level, transfer of resources, matched by effective delivery of services in the field, would suggest a decentralization and re-distribution of scientific and technical personnel from large top heavy federal departments to the mukim, district and state level. The need to restructure agricultural organizations (rather than create new ones) is essential, if the vast sums of money which the government is planning to use to uplift smallholders are to be effective. RISDA needs to increase its effectiveness by increasing its ground staff in areas where the holdings are isolated and scattered and through better implementation and coordination of policies.

Expansion of the programs especially for assisting the smaller smallholdings is essential if the incomes of the large number of poor are to be increased. In the long run, programs for increasing incomes of the traditional rubber smallholders will become of great importance in eradicating poverty in Malaysia.

Notes

1. See John Drabble, *Rubber in Malaya 1876-1922, the Genesis of the Industry*. Oxford Univ. Press. Kuala Lumpur, 1973.
2. Lim Chong Yah, *Economic Development of Modern Malaya*. Oxford Univ. Press, Kuala Lumpur, 1967.
3. C.R. Wharton, *Rubber Supply Conditions: Some Policy Implications in the Political Economy of Independent Malaya*. A.N.U. Press, Canberra, 1963.
4. See Ungku Aziz, *Subdivision of Estates in Malaya 1951-1950*. Kuala Lumpur, University of Malaya, Sept. 1962.
5. Lim Sow Ching, *Analysis of Smallholder's Rubber Marketing in West Malaysia*. Nat. Rubber Conf., 1968.

Chinese Economic Activities In Malaya
A Historical Perspective

Khoo Kay Kim

A cursory survey of the principal Chinese dialect spoken in each major town in peninsular Malaysia will reveal that Hokkien is most widely spoken in all the port towns, for example, Penang, Teluk, Intan, Klang, Pekan, Kuala Trengganu, and Kota Bharu.[1] It has been traditionally the *lingua franca* among Singapore Chinese too and continues to be popular despite official promotion of mandarin in recent years.

This, in effect, means that the earliest Chinese to settle in peninsular Malaysia were Hokkien. They were also traders. It is known that:

> From the ninth century, Fukien (Hokkien) has been one of the major provinces actively involved in sea trade. The Fukienese people were also the first important segment of the Chinese population to establish themselves in trade overseas and to set up permanent settlements there. Their communities were widespread, ranging from Japan to Nanyang (Southern Ocean, or present-day Southeast Asia), and were also found in many other parts of China, particularly in Taiwan.[2]

Until the beginning of the nineteenth century, it was trade primarily which induced the Chinese to come to the Malay peninsula. The Chinese participated actively in the trade of

Melaka in the fifteenth century. The following is a general description of that trade in terms of Chinese imports into Melaka.

> A very large assortment of the more varied merchandise was brought by the Chinese junks to Malacca. It included musk, rhubarb, camphor, pearls, a small amount of gold and silver, large amounts of raw and woven silk, expensive fabrics such as damask, satin and brocade, and cotton materials, the trade in which was conducted from China by Chinese wholesale merchants. Then there were goods... such as alum, salpetre, sulphur, copper, iron, large quantities of copper utensils, cast iron kettles, and the familiar products of Chinese handicraft-lacquered boxes, elaborate cabinets, fans and fancy hair ornaments, and many worthless trinkets such as copper bracelets, for example. Each cargo also included an enormous quantity of porcelain and pottery - plates, dishes, cups and bowls.[3]

But presumably the Chinese were inactive during the period when the Portuguese controlled Melaka. A Dutch source indicated that by 1641 the trade of Melaka was to a large extent monopolized by Indian merchants.[4]

A census of Melaka taken by the Dutch Governor, Balthasar Bort, in 1678 nevertheless showed that there were no less than 852 Chinese in Melaka territory outside the fortress; but within the fortress there were only 40 of them. The Dutch population itself numbered 4,884 persons. However, Baretto de Resende's Account of Malacca, written in 1646 but referring to the period c. 1638, and Francois Valentijn's *Account of Malacca*, published in 1726, make practically no mention of the Chinese.[5]

There is sufficient evidence to indicate that throughout the greater part of the 18th century, at any rate, the Chinese preferred the east coast of the peninsula to the west. A French ship *St. Jean Baptiste* was in Trengganu in late July 1769 and four accounts of the visit are extant. While they provide no statistics as regards the number of Chinese resident in Trengganu, these accounts are nonetheless enlightening. One referred to the existence of three bazaars in Trengganu, "one for the Malays, another for the Siamese and the largest for the Chinese: their street is a pleasant one, their houses better built than the others and in front they have their shops where you can find Chinese and European goods."[6] Another remarked that "Since there are numerous Chinese a street is allocated to them; it is the only passable one, it is well laid out, the houses are very clean and the shops fairly well stocked."[7] A third account confirmed that the Chinese were largely traders; the writer said:

> There are numbers of Chinese people settled here who are all small tradespeople and have five or six vessels which they dispatch to various places. The King (Sultan) has a share in this and does all the sea trade on his own account with Europeans....[8]

A Chinese source published in 1938 contained an account of the travels of Hsieh Ching Kao who visited Kelantan in the late 18th century and witnessed the existence of a Chinese population there. He recorded:

> The Hokkiens live in the town and the Cantonese in the rural areas. Those in the rural areas engage in gold mining, while those in town do business or plant pepper.
>
> Visiting vessels are taxed according to their size, big ones pay 500 to 600 silver coins each, and small ones 200 to 300 coins each. Visitors are taxed a silver coin each; after a year they must pay another silver coin. Such taxation is called 'hasil'. Taxation on goods is called 'machi' (masysul?). Those who have been engaged in gold mining and wish to return to China must first come to town and present a tahil of gold to the Sultan. Those who are too old to earn a living any more, may pay only half a tahil. A poor man may be exempted from paying on the recommendation of the *Kapitain*. The *Kapitain* is a Chinese chief. Those who live in the town are exempt from paying this tax.
>
> If a foreign ship fails to report her presence, the *chin chew* has to pay *hukom*. The *chin chew* is the man who owns the merchandise. The ship owner is called *pan chew*. A navigator is called a *ko chang*, and; the person who mans the rudder a *tai kong*. The crew take their orders from the *chin chew*.[9]

The Chinese settlements on the east coast of the Malay peninsula were still there during the first three decades of the nineteenth century. No precise figure is available for the size of the Chinese population in Kelantan but there was a contemporary reference to "the numerous body of Chinese, which reside in the interior." In the case of Kuala Trengganu, the number of Chinese was said to "amount to some hundreds, dwelling principally in strong brick built houses, which have every appearance of being erected many years ago."[10] But the largest Chinese population at that time was, apparently, to be found in Pahang. The population of the state was then computed at about 40,000 comprising chiefly Malays and Chinese. It was estimated that the Chinese numbered probably about 12,000 and, as in the case of Trengganu and Kelantan, they were employed in mining and agriculture.[11] Beyond that, however, little is known of the Chinese in Pahang.

By the mid-nineteenth century the situation had changed drastically. Civil wars in Kelantan and Trengganu in the 1830s and in Pahang in the 1850s and early 1860s disrupted economic activities on the east coast. Most of the Chinese left. On the other hand, the year 1786 marked an important turning point in Chinese migration to the west coast of the peninsula. Hardly two months after Penang had been opened as a port that year, Francis Light wrote to Calcutta saying that:

> Our inhabitants increase very fast - Chooliahs (Tamils), Chinese, and Christians; they are already disputing about the ground, everyone building as fast as he can.[12]

About a year later, most the shops in the bazaar, which was then quite extensive, were owned by Chinese. In early 1794, Francis Light, addressing the governor-general of Bengal, wrote:

> The Chinese constitute the most valuable part of our inhabitants, they are men, women and children, about 3,000, they possess the different trades of carpenters, masons, and smiths, are traders, shopkeepers and planters, they employ small vessels and prows and send adventures to the surrounding countries. They are the only people of the east from whom a revenue may be raised without expense and extraordinary efforts of the government.[13]

The arrival of the Chinese in Penang marked the beginning of a continually growing settled Chinese population in the Malay peninsula. Although the trading community was predominant, by the close of the eighteenth century the Chinese in Penang were already cultivating the ground. They grew pepper and gambier; they were also the only regular cultivators of indigo which, however, was not of any importance until after 1822.[14] It was sugar planting which eventually proved most valuable to Penang.

The cultivation of sugar was first commenced by Chinese from Swatow who settled in the central and southern portion of Province Wellesley which was ceded to the British in 1800. In China itself, throughout the nineteenth centruy, the Teochiu region of south China was known for its production of sugar for export.[15]

In Province Wellesley, the pioneer Chinese sugar estates were opened between 1810 and 1820. There was further expansion in the following decade, indicated by an increase of the Chinese population from 325 in 1820 to 2,259 in 1833. However, when European planters also began engaging in sugar cultivation, the expansion of the Chinese-owned sugar estates slowed down. By 1858 they comprised only about 1,000 acres.[16] The next phase of expansion occurred in the 1870s which saw the Chinese pushing their way into northern Perak.

Meanwhile, there was almost a simultaneous movement of the Teochiu into the southern part of the Peninsula. But many did not come to Johor direct from China. The Chinese had been involved in the planting of pepper and gambier in Riau since the mid-eighteenth century. Some of these and possibly a small number too from Siam had moved into Singapore to grow gambier and pepper even before 1819, the year the British took formal possession of the island.[17]

The first three decades after the opening of Singapore in 1819 witnessed a rapid expansion in agriculture in which gambier and pepper accounted for about three-quarters of the total acreage. By the mid-nineteenth century, the cultivation of gambier in Singapore had begun to decline as a result of soil exhaustion. The Chinese turned to Johor with every encouragement given by the Temenggung, *De facto* ruler of peninsular Johor. Initially, the gambier and pepper plantations on the mainland were concentrated along the rivers flowing into the Johor Strait. These provided the most convenient means of entry for settlers moving from Singapore. This movement into Johor was probably augmented by a further migration from the exhausted plantations of Riau. By the early 1860s there were about 1,200 gambier and pepper plantations in Johor, employing a labour force of about 15,000.[18]

It was here among the Chinese planters that the well-known *Kangchu* system developed. The plantations were divided into small villages along each river, these were known as *kangkar* (literally foot of the river). Each *kangkar* was governed by a headman known as *kangchu* (head of the river) who held the land from the Malay ruler, receiving as a grant a *surat sungai* (literally river letter).[19] Gambier and pepper continued to be a major export until the first decade of the twentieth century and it was the primary factor influencing Teochiu migration to the state so that, until today, the Teochiu dialect is widely spoken in southern Johor as it is widely spoken in Province Wellesley owing to the presence of large numbers of Teochiu sugar planters in the nineteenth century.

It may appear a matter of coincidence that it was also during the same period that an increasingly larger Chinese mining population moved into the territories of Larut, Klang, Lukut, and Sungai Ujong. But even a cursory glance at the changing political scenario after 1824 will reveal that the withdrawal of the Dutch from the Straits of Melaka after the signing of the Anglo-Dutch Treaty (1824) encouraged the Malay ruling elite to expand their mining activities. These had been greatly curtailed previously, owing to the proclivity of the Dutch (in Melaka) to try to obtain a monopolistic control over the export of tin from the Malay states.[20]

There had been Chinese mining tin in Perak and Selangor even before the turn of the nineteenth century but for reasons which are not clear, they did not stay. Contemporary British observers noted that in 1815, there were Chinese miners in Lukut. By 1824, their number; (about 200) was sufficiently large for a *Kapitan China* to be appointed.[21] Lukut's development, thereafter, was rapid despite ethnic conflict in 1834. In the early 1860s it was practically the most modern town in the peninsula.[22]

Sungai Ujong had an even larger Chinese population by 1828. The estimated figure was 1,000. But here too ethnic conflict occurred which led to the departure of the Chinese. By 1832, however, they started to return.[23] Lower Perak also had a sizeable Chinese population by the early part of the nineteenth century. Tan Ah Hun, Teochiu, was appointed Kapitan China. His son, Tan Seng Poh, born in Lower Perak, was to become a wealthy and influential merchant in Singapore by the third quarter of the nineteenth century. The Chinese in Lower Perak were both traders and miners.[24]

But it was in the 1840s that discoveries of rich and extensive ore deposits first occurred. The success of the Lukut mines has been mentioned but it was in the Klang Valley that tin mining achieved its greatest success in the state of Selangor. The mines were opened by Malay chieftains with capital borrowed from Straits merchants. The mining workers initially were brought to Ampang from Lukut. By 1859 tin was first exported from the depot, Kuala Lumpur, a village which was soon to develop into a prosperous township. The majority of the mining population in the Klang valley comprised Fui Chiu Hakka. Further north in the territory of Kanching, the mines were worked by Kah Ying Chiu Hakka.[25]

An even larger spurt of mining activity occurred in the territory of Larut in Perak. The discovery of tin in Klian Pauh led to the growth of a large Chinese population there by the 1840s. The first group of Chinese to work the mines there were Chen Sang Hakka. Subsequently, tin was also discovered in an adjacent area known as Kamunting. In the mid-eighteen sixties, the total population of the two villages was estimated at slightly over 6,000.[26]

Within the next few years, disturbances broke out in all the major mining territories. The areas worst affected were the Klang valley and Larut, the Fui Chiu miners left after they had been severely beaten in 1865; Kamunting was next occupied by a group of Cantonese (San Neng). Their clash with the Chen Sang Hakka eventually involved Chinese from Penang and Province Wellesley as the Larut Chinese were of Penang origin.

The cessation of mining and commercial activities leading to heavy losses incurred by Straits merchants was one reason which influenced the British government to intervene in the affairs of the Malay states in 1874.[27] The British, however, needed about six years to consolidate their position in the mining states. Once political stability had been effected, the development of mining activities occurred at a rapid rate especially in the 1880s when steps were taken to mprove the system of transport and communication.

By 1885 railway services had begun in Larut linking the mining district with its nearest port, Port Weld. In the following year, Kuala Lumpur was linked to Bukit Kuda in Klang. As the railway extended to the north and south, new mining villages appeared. This was particularly evident in Selangor where Rawang, Sungai Choh, Serendah, Ulu Yam, Rasa, and Kuala Kubu became busy commercial centres. The Chinese mining population in that area, in 1900, numbered over 20,000.[28] Similar developments took place in Perak where Ipoh and Kampar soon rivalled Taiping in importance owing to the discovery of richer mines in the Kinta valley.

The growth of new townships owing to mining activities was a phenomenon of the last two decades of the 19th century. It was in Perak that this process of urbanization occurred most rapidly and the majority of these towns, for example, Chemor, Pusing, Papan, and Tronoh, apart from Ipoh and Kampar, are located in the Kinta valley. To these may be added Sungai Siput further to the north and Tapah as well as Bidor, situated south of Kampar. All these towns had a high concentration of Chinese residents. Therefore, although a large proportion of the Chinese were mining workers, those involved in providing diverse services were equally numerous. By the turn of the present century, the majority of the Chinese in Malaya were located in Penang, Singapore, the town of Melaka, and the numerous townships which had emerged on the western part of the peninsula.

Often described in those days, as ubiquitous, it was also said of the Chinese by J.D. Vaughan that they "are everything," meaning that:

> ...they are actors, acrobats, artists, musicians, chemists and druggists, clerks, cashiers, engineers, architects, surveyors, missionaries, priests, doctors, schoolmasters, lodging house keepers, butchers, porksellers, cultivators of pepper and gambier, cake-sellers, cart and hackney carriage owners, cloth

> hawkers, distillers of spirits, eating house keepers, fish-mongres, fruitsellers, ferrymen, grass-sellers, hawkers, merchants and agents, oil-sellers, opium shopkeepers, pawnbrokers, pig dealers, and poulterers. They are rice dealers, ship chandlers, shopkeepers, general dealers, spirit shop keepers, servants, timber dealers, tobaconists; vegetable settlers, planters, market-gardeners, laborers, bakers, millers, barbers, blacksmiths, boatmen, book-binders....[29]

Vaughan's list is too comprehensive to be cited in full here; suffice it to say that the Chinese were extremely versatile but it was primarily in the area of trade, tin mining, and commercial agriculture that they were dominant up to the time of British intervention in the Malay states. In later years, British capital took control of, first, agriculture and then tin mining.[30]

Chinese trading activities, however, continued to devlop. Speaking of the Chinese involvement in local trade, Tan Teck Soon, [31] in a lecture delivered at the Chinese Christian Association in Singapore (August 1902) remarked that "almost the whole trade of the Colony [is] in their hands," adding, "The Chinese are not only producers but also importers, exporters, and distributors, beside being, as the principal purveyors, the intermediate link between the distant Malay villages and the chief centres of trade in the Colony."[32]

His description of what he termed the "pushing trade" is illuminating. Chinese traders in those days often travelled in the jungles of the Malay peninsula for months. Though cut off from the society of their own people, they perseveringly and tenaciously pushed their wares among the Malays. These hawkers were mainly Hokkien, the newly arrived rather than the Straits-born. The latter, though enjoying the advantage of being culturally more harmonious with the Malays, did not take to this line of business, though, as entrepreneurs, they invested heavily in the Malay states. The Straits-born did not like the lonesome and toilsome life of a hawker with its slender chance of making a rapid fortune.

As regards the *modus operandi* of the hawkers, Tan Teck Soon said:

> The Hokkiens...take to hawking regularly, study the tastes and requirements of the natives, and soon make themselves indis-

pensable to the latter. Such Hokkiens begin by borrowing or scraping together a small capital to pay the costs of an outfit, consisting, say, of rice, salt, saltfish, tobacco, kerosine, matches, sugar, biscuits, cotton goods, umbrellas, and other petty wares enough to fill a cart. They then proceed to a distant village. There they start operations by building a hut, planting a small vegetable garden to supply their own wants and opening a 'kedeh' [kedai] or shop. The next step is to pay court to the village officials, and to give credit to the more prominent villagers. The natives soon flock to the shop, and barter jungle produce for the shopman's wares. The shopman swindles them right and left but with such dexterity and kindliness that the Malays stand the cheating. The shopman gets all he can out of them, until he finds, in a few years' time that the gains admits of his moving off. He then sells off the goodwill and business to another hawker, loads in carts the accumulated produce from bartering, and starts for the nearest seaport. There he sells his 'trade' pays his debts, and either returns to China or takes a holiday. The profit of these hawkers comes, on the average, to about $200-$300 each from, say, three years shopkeeping. This hardly comes up to the like earnings of a day coolie, or of a house servant in town. But hawkers have the additional advantage of gaining hard-won experience to profit by after-life.[33]

Chinese success in economic ventures may be attributed, to a large extent, to their ability to organize systematically and effectively. A number of organizations existed which were important socially and, even more so, economically. Perhaps most important of all was the secret society, also sometimes referred to as lodge (somewhat in a Masonic sense). The British administration, initially unable to cope with the Chinese *imperium in imperio,* tended to view Chinese secret societies as essentially turbulent in nature. But such societies were not without constructive functions as explained, in 1939, by the Acting Secretary for Chinese Affairs:

> In the early days, the various lodges of the Triad Society which until 1890 were not illegal fulfilled some of the functions normally covered by trade associations. They were large mutual benefit and protection societies covering between them practically the whole of the Chinese population. The spheres of influence of the various lodges were mainly territorial, but, in so far as it is customary for Chinese establishments carrying on a particular trade to group themselves

together in one area, the tendency was for those engaged in
particular trades to join particular lodges, though a particular
lodge might embrace several trades in its own territorial
sphere.[34]

All secret societies were equipped to function as para military
organizations for each had a group of fighting men who could
be used as enforcers in collecting debts, ensuring obedience
among members, or in the control of labor.

Another organization which was not entirely separated
from the secret society was the *pang* organization.[35] This was
based on the territorial-dialect origin of the Chinese. Within
large secret socieities such as the Ghi Hin, there often existed
Cantonese, Hokkien, Teochiu, etc. branches. In the earlier survey of the beginnings of large scale Chinese economic activities
in the Malay states, it has been shown that each territorial-
dialect group tended to engage in a particular occupation, such
as the Teochiu gambier and pepper planers, the Hokkien
traders, and the Hakka mining workers (divided into Fui Chiu,
Kah Ying Chiu or Chen Sang). Territorial-dialect associations,
apart from secret socieities, were therefore among the earliest
Chinese associations to be formed whenever the Chinese
population in a particular area had reached a sizable proportion. Common language, customs, and, in many instances, blood
ties, provided a sense of unity difficult to achieve with other
groups of persons who were socio-culturally as well as linguisti-
cally different.

In the case of tin mining, while the secret society and *pang*
elements were undoubtedly important in organizing production, the whole system was, in fact, more complex. In general,
when a mine was opened there was a *taukeh labur* and a *taukeh
lombong*. The first was the advancer of capital and the second
the headman of the mine. Although the advancer ran all the
risks, the miner himself was seldom rich. All he possessed was
his mine. His water-wheel for pumping purposes, sheds for the
labourers, and other trifling mining plants as well as everything
else depended for value on what he produced. However, so
long as tin was produced in small quantities, even to half the
value of the advance, the *taukeh labur* was not likely, according
to customary practice, to cease advancing. It was only in the

event of serious reverses, such as the cessation of credits from the advancer's own source of capital, or if there was an absolute loss of confidence after repeated futile endeavors in working the land, that the advancer would cease to advance. As long, however, as he continued advancing to the same headman and working party, even if they should move to other mining land the debt was still in force. The miner, on the other hand, could not abandon his advancer or take advances from others without his advancer's consent. In the event that the miner himself became rich, he could not close his account with his advancer, but he could, in turn, advance to other mines. On the other hand, there was nothing to prevent the advancer from being the mine owner or owner of the mining grant. This often happened when the advancer prospered. The system, it may be emphasized, was supported by law.[36]

Martin Lister, the Superindent of Negeri Sembilan in 1889, gave the following details with regard to the *labur* system:

> It is the supplying or advancing in cash and kind, and is used in connection with other industries besides mining. In advancing for tin it may reasonably be expected that the advances bear a very enhanced rate over cash purchases. Supposing the local market rates of opium to be $23, the *labor* or mines advancing rate would be $28. rice at local market rates being $4.00 a pcul (133 1/3 bls.) the *labor* rate would be $5.00. This is a proportion that may fairly be awarded in a mining case between advancer and miner in court. The advancer naturally prefers giving in kind, such as all food and drink, clothing, etc. etc. His profit is larger on goods, and his risk is less, as he never knows exactly whether his cash advances may not be disposed of outside the mine and not brought to bear on the production of tin, the recipient gradually enriching himself. All tin is the property of the advancer, subject to certain conditions. The advancer, when he commences trade with the miner, arranges that he should receive the tin at, say, $5.00 a *bhara* below market rates. It has been the custom, and is quite recognized between advancer and miner that the weighing scale for goods issued gives an extra percentage of profit to the advancer and the scale for receiving tin equally so. The system, however, is really to be deplored. It is not cheating but is a Chinese custom which every mining coolie is well aware of, but it has always appeared to me that it would be far better for the advancer to charge rather more on his advances and receive the tin at a lower rate.[37]

There was, of course, always the possibility that an advancer might run short of capital. He could then apply to another person for assistance. This was known as *bantu* (assistance). In the earlier years of the 19th century, Malay chieftains who brought in Chinese to work the mines were, in fact, *taukeh labur* and they often obtained *bantu* from the Straits merchants. After approximately the 1840s the Straits merchants themselves became *taukeh labur*.[38] *Bantu* was given at a different rate (usually a fifth of the total advanced) for *labur*. The *taukeh bantu*, however, had the first charge on the tin produced, to the extent of the assistance given. Again as Martin Lister explained:

> Thus supposing $5,000 to have been invested by the mines advancer and $1,000 by the trader, if only 20 bharas of tin were produced, the trader can claim tin to the full extent of the $1,000, the balance going to the mines advancer.

Prices, in the case of the *bantu* system, would be based on what was known as shop rates or *harga pekan* (shop prices), and differed from that of the *labur* system.

It is pertinent to refer also to the system governing relationship between the *taukeh lombong* and his laborers or coolies. There were various forms employed but the two principle ones were known as *kongsi* and *hoon*. Under the *kongsi* system the *taukeh lombong* was very much a middleman. He received the advances and supplied the laboreres. He usually held the cooking of boiled opium on which he made a profit. If he was the mine owner and not merely headman, he received his royalty on the tin produced. If the advancer was mine owner, the *taukeh lombong* received nothing; his own interest was a small profit on opium and advances.

Under the *hoon* (share) system, the laborers in the mines were all shareholders. The headman or *taukeh lombong* had two or three shares against the laborers' one. This form of working required that the land should be previously tested in order that the laborer might agree to work on a share. The test had to be made by first employing the *kongsi* system. The *hoon* system was by far the most satisfactory as the man worked harder and gave fewer difficulties. As far as the advancer was concerned, even if he was the mine owner, the same laws applied.

Europeans who did not fully understand the workings of Chinese organizations could not initially compete with the Chinese in the tin mining industry,[36] but a few who adopted the Chinese system succeeded. One example was that of John Muir who in 1883 opened up mines in Rawang. According to a report in the *Straits Times*:

> The Rawang mines are being worked on the 'tribute' (*labur*) system, that is to say that the Chinese miners work for their own account on the concession, subject to certain conditions. All payments made to them either in cash or goods are in the form of avances merely, and bear interests and margins of profit, against which the Chinese return the tin they produced from their excavation at a margin below current rates, subject to a tax of 10% for the use of pumping machinery which is provided by Mr. Muir. The Chinese thus have every incentive to increase the output, and this arrangement is in every respect suited to the conditions of the tin mining industry of the country.[37]

In the urban areas, however, one other form of Chinese association soon emerged. This was the guild. Trade guilds had existed in China since very ancient times and included master craftsmen, journeymen, and apprentices. In Malaya they were especially common among the old-established trades such as tailors, shoemakers, goldsmiths, and carpenters. Rates of wages, hours of work, holidays and terms of apprenticeship were decided by the guilds. In addition, they frequently fulfilled the role of friendly societies, providing funeral benefits for the members, and accommodation for the unemployed. Among the earliest guilds may be mentioned:[38]

Kwong Ngi (Cantonese Domestic Servants), Singapore	1890
Loh Pak Hong Kongsi (Carpenters), Singapore	1890
Ban Gim Kongsi (Drapers' Guild), Penang	1890
Ta Kam Hong (Cantonese Goldsmiths), Penang	1891
Lun Seng Thong (Hakka Stone-cutters' Guild), Penang	1895
Van Fa Hong (Hakka Goldsmiths), Melaka	1890

For reasons not clear the establishment of guilds in the

Malay states was a later development. Few of them were formed before the 1920s. It is important to note that these early guilds comprised both master and men. In fact, the officers of such guilds were usually the employers. Disputes were settled within the guild. In later years, with the spread to China of Western ideas the guilds gradually became more akin to trade unions which began to appear in Malaya, at first clandestinely, after World War I.[39]

Yet another important vehicle of Chinese commercial organization was the chamber of commerce which made its appearance after the turn of the present century. The first to be established was the Penang Chinese chamber of commerce in 1903. The object of its promoters was not only the protection of common trade interests, but also the collection and classification of mercantile information and the establishment of a court of arbitration to adjust commercial differences. However, the constitution of each chamber tended to vary in different parts of Malaya. In Singapore, it was controlled very largely by Chinese business interests represented by Hokkien and Teochiu firms. Significantly, it was a body which was dominated primarily by the views of the China-born; the Straits-born had practically no representation. This was in contrast to the Penang situation where the chamber was controlled by what was known as the Chinese Twon Hall Group, a conservative body composed of Straits-born Chinese. In both Selangor and Perak, the influence of the mining community was, understandably, very strong. But, in later years, other trade guilds began to make their impact in both the Selangor and Perak chambers.[40]

No discussion of Chinese economic activities in the early years of British administration would be complete without a reference to the farming system[41] which may be compared to the privatization scheme now very much in favour with the Malaysian government. Revenue farming, although profitable to the colonial government, was, from time to time, criticized and the *Straits Times* (already very influential in the 19th century), on 27 June 1890, commented lengthily on the subject. It was of the opinion that "the idea of revenue farming commends itself on the score of expediency, considering the Asiatic preponderance among our mixed multitude, and it has long taken practical shape in China." It then proceeded to trace the origins of the system in the archipelago:

> The Dutch, from the early days of their dominion in the Ar-
> chipelago, have found excise farming to be the best way of
> raising revenue from the consumption of luxuries. The British
> took the system over from the Dutch, and 'farmers' have been
> the revenue mainstay of the colony since the foundation of
> Penang. In the infancy of the Settlements, the excise farms
> were wider in area and took in pork and betelnut leaves, be-
> sides gambling, which later proved an important source of in-
> come here from 1820 to 1829. In 1828-29, opium yielded
> $32,640, spirits $15,600, and gambling $33,864. These figures
> show how largely the gambling farm, abolished in 1830, bulked
> in the revenue of the Settlement and the importance of the
> issue under review arises from the fact that 67% of the
> colonial revenue comes out of excise licenses.

A year earlier the same paper had occasion to comment on
the importance of the railway "in opening up new countries and
furthering that settlement of the people on the land which
alone can develop the resources of the state," and, in doing so,
pointed out that:

> The railway in Selangor is farmed out to a syndicate of
> Chinese traders under a lease which runs out in March 1890.
> The revenue farming system so often objected to has, in this
> instance, been crowned with success. The renters bound them-
> selves to pay the Government $25,000 a month. Large as this
> amount may appear, the traffic returns, since the new manage-
> ment took charge in March last, show that they work the line
> at a high profit.[42]

Apart from the single instance in Selangor where the state
railway was farmed out in the early years of its existence, the
revenue farm in practice covered, separately, items such as
opium, pawnbroking, gambling, and spirits or, as in the case of
Pahang, for the period 1902-1904, it was referred to simply as
the Pahang General Farms. The contract, however, comprised
"the chandu, opium, spirits, gambling, pawnbroking, and tobacco
farms for the whole state, excepting for the farms for the district
of Bentong, which ... are treated separately...."[43]
Apparently direct revenue collection by the government

then would mean not only expensive European management but no European agents under government would have much of a chance of successfully contending against "the knavery of our Asiatic population."[44] This was because "the native underlings through whom they must operate would not resist temptation, and serious revenue leakage would result." Therefore, in areas where the Chinese formed the major portion of the population, it was more expedient to farm out revenue collection. It was argued that:

> Under Chinese excise farmers, who know all the dark ways of their countrymen, and employ people of their own clan and nationality as agents, these difficulties are reduced to a minimum. Certainly the Government could not collect, after deduction of the cost of a department, a sum nearly so largely as they now get from the farms; and the question at issue seems to be whether it would be worthwhile to sacrifice a portion of the revenue in order to have the satisfaction of collecting it in a fashion more in accord with European ideas.[45]

The system of revenue farms hence enriched the Chinese merchants as well as gave them great economic power. Some of the leading personalities of the late 19th century, many of them important tin miners, were revenue farmers. One of the more successful farmers in the 1880s was Khoo Thean Teik of Penang well known as the leader of the secret society known as Toa Pek Kong. It is known that, between 1880-1882, he obtained the following farms in Perak:[46]

The Krian and Kurau General Farm
The Krian and Kurau Attap Farm
The South Larut General Farm
The Perak River Farm of Opium Duties
The Perak River Farm of Tobacco Duties

Yap Ah Loy, Kapitan China of Kuala Lumpur, a town which he almost single-handedly rebuilt after the Klang War (1867-1873), held the Kuala Lumpur Spirit Farms from 1882-1884,[47] and possibly during the preceding years too. Chung Keng Kwee, one of the protagonists of the Larut Wars before British intervention in 1874, held the Larut Gambling,

Pawnbroking, Spirit and Tobacco Farm from 1880-1882, and probably many years more; he also held the Perak General Farm from 1898-1900 which was subsequently extended for another two years. Chung Keng Kwee, however, passed away in December 1901.[48] Loke Yew, acknowledged as the richest man in Malaya in the early years of the 20th century, was another important revenue farmer. Although his interests were largely concentrated in Selangor, his commercial ventures extended to other states, notably Pahang where, in 1900, he held the Pahang Tobacco Farm which gave him the right to collect $10 per picul of native tobacco imported into the state.[49] He was also offered the Perak General Farm in 1903 and the Selangor General Farm, including the Coast Chandu Farm, for the period 1905-1907. Indeed, it was said of him in 1902 that "He has worked farms for many years to the entire satisfaction of the government."[50]

The revenue farm system combined with what was known as the *truck system* gave the Chinese merchants and mine owners the opportunity to make substantial profit from their mining ventures. The truck system was explained very clearly by J.B. Massey Lech, an administrative officer, in 1904:

> I came to Perak at the end of 1879. The mines were then nearly all in Larut and were almost without exception worked on the truck system, nine-tenths of the tin produced going to the coolies and one-tenth to the *tokway*, who supplied the coolies with their food and stores at mining prices - i.e. about double the market rates. The settlements were annual - at the Chinese New Year, when the books were made up, the coolies credited with nine-tenths of the amount of tin sold and debited with the amount of stores consumed, and received the balance, if any. If the coolies were in debt to the mine - and they very often were - they went on and worked for another year, and still another if they did not get out of debt. The punishment for absconding was flogging.[51]

The farming system was, however, from 1909 onwards rapidly abolished. Since 1906 questions about government policy with respect to opium and gambling in Malaya were raised yearly in the British Parliament. Also agitation against gambling and opium-smoking in China inspired the Chinese in Malaya to call for their suppression as well. It was, moreover, pointed out by certain European mining interests that the farming system enabled the Chinese to mine at an apparent loss and yet acquired substantial profit much to the disadvantage of Western enterprise. Opium nonetheless was recognised as an important source of revenue even though, among mining labourers, opium smoking had radically declined by the turn of the century. Although opium farms were abolished, opium became a government monopoly and continued to fetch substantial revenue.[52]

The abolition of the revenue farms which coincided with the introduction of more advanced technology in the mining enterprise enabled Western capital steadily to overtake Chinese capital in the production of tin. As early as 1904, the largest ouput of tin in the Kinta valley was from mines owned by the French company The Societe de Etains de Kinta:[53]

Leading Mines in Perak	Output in Piculs
The Societe de Etains de Kinta	29,000
Tronoh (a Limited Company)	21,600
Tambun (Leong Fee)	17,000
Gopeng Hydraulic (F.D. Osborne)	8,500
Kampar (Foo Choo Choon)	6,000

The state assistant warden of mining pointed out that the methods of mining had become so much more skilled and economical that European capital was more largely invested and European supervision deemed more necessary and he remarked that:

> ...the old-fashioned prejudices of the Chinese against machinery have been overcome, and they now realise that earth containing tin ore can be put into a machine and that, by the adoption of certain principles, the ore can be absolutely separated from the dirt without constant handling.[54]

Then came the dredge in 1912 the first of which was built in Gopeng, Perak. This was a European capitalized venture. It marked a revolution in the history of the tin industry. Production from Chinese mines gradually decreased in comparison to European mines as the following chart indicates:[55]

Percentage of Tin Produced by European and Chinese Mines 1920-1938

	European %	Chinese %		European %	Chinese %
1920	36	64	1930	63	37
1921	39	61	1931	65	35
1922	38	62	1932	66	34
1923	44	56	1933	66	34
1924	45	55	1934	66	34
1925	44	56	1935	66	34
1926	44	56	1936	67	33
1927	41	59	1937	68	32
1928	49	51	1938	67	33
1929	61	31			

The gap between the two was, however, arrested since 1931 owing largely to the tin control scheme.[56]

As indicated above, important as tin was as a cause of large-scale Chinese immigration in the mid-nineteenth century, commercial agriculture was no less important even if the story of Chinese sugar, pepper, gambier, and tapioca planters is less dramatic. However, within about fifteen years of British intervention, European capital had begun to promote agriculture in the tin mining states. Coffee was the favourite crop then and for the next two decades it became a major export of the Malay peninsula. But when rubber arrived towards the close of the 19th century, the Chinese were among the first to cultivate it. Tan Chay Yan, a Melaka tapioca and coffee planter, in 1895 or 1896, planted forty acres at Bukit Lintang near Malaka town. In Selangor, Low Boon Tit, in 1898, planted fifty-four acres with rubber on his Semenyih Estate (Ulu Langat) and, in 1899, Chong Ong Sian was in the process of opening a large plantation at Kota Bahru in Kinta, Perak.[57]

The British adminstration in the F.M.S. indirectly encouraged the Chinese to plant rubber by introducing a special clause stipulating that a permanent crop such as rubber or coconut must be planted into all new grants of land made to

Chinese (after 1900) for tapioca or gambier or pepper cultivation. The rising price of rubber at the beginning of the 20th century helped considerably to encourage widespread planting of rubber among catch-crops of tapioca or gambier on Chinese-owned estates.[58]

By the early 20th century, there were a number of Chinese merchants who planted large sections of their estates with rubber. In Perak there was Chung Ah Yong, eldest son (adopted) of the influential Kapitan Chung Keng Kwee; he owned the Hearwood Rubber Estate in Sungei Siput which covered an area of about 3,000 acres. Heah Swee Lee, a member of the Perak State Council, owned the Hin Heng Estate, about 5,000 acres, in the Krian district. It was originally planted with sugar but changed to rubber. Lim Kek Chuan of Penang with A.R. Adams and George Stothard were directors of the Brieh Rubber Co. Ltd. in Bagan Serai.[59]

In Selangor, the Chua brothers (Cheng Tuan and Cheng Bok) of Cycle and Carriage fame, owned the Gonggang (Kuala Lumpur), Bernang (Ulu Langat), and Rumbia (Melaka) estates, all of which were planted with rubber. Chua Cheng Tuan was himself an estate manager.[60] But the leading Chinese plantation owner in Selangor was, as in the case of tin mining, Loke Yew. He owned the Hawthorden and Lincoln estates near Kuala Lumpur as well as the Kalumpang Estate which was part of the 20,000 acres of land which he possesed in the Tanjong Malim district. He began planting rubber on the Kalumpang Estate in 1902. The Changkat Asa Estate (Ulu Bernam) was also part of his 20,000 acres of land. This was originally planted with pepper but later switched to rubber.[61]

There were also Chinese estates in other states: the Khean Ann Estate in Province Wellesley planted with rubber, coconut and tapioca owned by Ban Eng & Co.; the Eng-Moh-Hui-Thye-Kee Estate in Semeling (Kedah), about 3,400 acres, partly planted with rubber, which was owned by Cheah Tek Thye of Penang and numerous estates in Melaka.[62] Chinese planters in Melaka who had, for many years previously, engaged in tapioca planting found it convenient to turn to rubber when tapioca planting was no longer profitable. Among some of the leading estate owners of the early 20th century may be mentioned Chan Kang Swi, Tan Jiak Lim, Tan Jiak Hoe, Lee Keng Hee, Kan

Keng Lim, Tan Hoon Choon, Tan Hoon Guan, and Ee Kong Guan, all of whom, were Straits-born.[63] Planting, however, was not their sole preoccupation. Many of them, such as Chan Kang Swi, Tan Jiak Lim, Lee Keng Hee, and Tan Choon Guan belonged to distinguished families which were involved in numerous branches of commerce in Melak and, more important still, Singapore. One of the major activities of these Melaka families was shipping.[64]

Apart from the larger estates, there were numerous small-holdings (generally less than 500 acres) owned by Chinese. The census of 1921 showed that the Cantonese on estates (in most instances rubber) were almost twice as numerous as any other territorial-dialect group; they numbered 22,828. Most of them were found in Negeri Sembilan, Johor and Perak. The Hakka estate population numbered 12,838. They predominated in Selangor, Negeri Sembilan and Johor.[65] The Hainanese were the third largest group of Chinese in the estates (approximately 11,000). Before World War I, many of them were estate labourers but their number decreased by the time of the 1921 census; according to the report:

> The most probable explanation of the large decrease in the Hailams on estates is their independence and eagerness to plant up land on their own account. In Johore especially, thousands of acres of land have been taken up in the last few years by Hailams (Hailanese), a large proportion of whom were formerly estate coolies. [66]

The Hainanese estate population was largest in Negeri Sembilan and Johor.

An important development during the period 1911-1921 was that in the Federated Malay States, agriculture had replaced mining as the principal occupation among the Chinese.

In 1911, 416 Chinese males in 1,000 were engaged in mining and 178 in agriculture, but in 1921, while the former figure has dropped to 169, the latter has risen to 295. Apart from the low price of tin, the cause lies in the increased use of labour-saving machinery on mines.[67]

In the Unfederated States most of the Chinese were estate labourers. In the Straits Settlements a larger proporation of the Chinese were engaged in commerce or transport (mostly rickshaw pullers or *sampan* men) than in agriculture.[68]

The 1931 census showed that the situation in the Straits Settlements remained relatively unchanged. The same applied to the Unfederated States except that in absolute numbers the estate population in Kelantan and Trengganu decreased slightly (in each case from a little over 2,000 to less than 2,000), whereas in the case of Kedah there was a drastic reduction (from 14,593 to 6,642), and in Johor a substantial increase (from 28,922 to 51,425).[69] Significantly, in the Federated States, the mining population (46,444) once more exceeded the estate (rubber) population (29,808).[70] The census report provided no explanation.

It is pertinent to note in the 1921 census no precise figures were given for rubber. It can be assumed, however, a very large section of the estate population was engaged in rubber cultivation. In the 1931 census, rubber (separated from coconuts and oil palm) was specifically mentioned as one category of occupation. It may be added, also apart from being owners, managers and labourers, the Chinese also played an important role as processors and middlemen in the rubber industry.[71]

Although the Chinese performed numerous functions in Malaya's rubber industry, in 1938 more than half the cultivated area was in British hands as the following figures indicate:

**Distribution of Rubber Estates
Among Ethnic Groups in Malaya (Acre)[72]**

	European (mainly	Chinese	Indian	Others[73]
F.M.S.	853,841	118,076	47,104	13,405
S.S.	132,165	61,011	12,036	1,646
U.M.S.	544,414	143,554	28,655	76,062

The Chinese share was about one-sixth of the total. Also, it should be noted that the larger estates were owned by Europeans as shown below:

Ethnic Ownership of Estates 1938 [74]
(Number of Estates)

Ethnic Group	5000 acres and over	1000-4999 acres	500-999 acres	100-499 acres
European	47	467	237	245
Chinese	1	47	94	911
Indian	-	5	21	343
Others	5	13	10	63

That the Chinese were very involved in the development of the tin and rubber industries is, in general, widely known. Those who have a fair acquaintance with the Malaysian society are probably aware too that the larger proportion of the fruit and vegetable growers have always been Chinese. In the Federated Malay States alone, they numbered about 20,000 in 1921 and 32,000 in 1931. [75]

Through their informal apprentice system the Chinese have provided the large majority of skilled workers: carpenters, mechanics, electricians, etc. But it is not common knowledge that the Chinese were the first to establish shipping companies and that they monopolized the pineapple industry and practically controlled the Malaysian fishing industry. Their role in banking has also been significant. A brief history of each of the above-mentioned will help provide a better perspective of Chinese economic activities in Malaya. It may be appropriate to begin with shipping.

Chinese control of coastal shipping in the Malay Peninsula became increasingly important after Singapore had become an established port in the Malay archipelago. Chinese merchants soon began to play an important role in what was known as the *sampanpukat* or *perahu-pukat* trade. [76] The majority of them were then residents of Singapore or Riau. A *sampan-pukat* or simply *pukat* was a large row-boat provided with the means of setting up an occasional sail. Each *pukat* could usually carry a crew of twenty-nine. The *pukat* was seldom owned by the crew; it generally belonged to a merchant. The cargo was purchased on credit supplied by the merchant who owned the boat. The crew did not receive wages but each had a share of the profits in proportion to the amount of capital contributed to buy the original cargo. However, if the venture was unsuccessful, often it was the *nakodah* (commander) who absorbed the losses.

The *pukat* trade was generally confined to the Straits of Melaka but the trade with the east coast, although affected by the monsoon, was even more valuable for it was from Pahang, in particular, that Singapore obtained the valuable imports of gold-dust. This trade with the east coast was shared by Malay traders using boats of one to eight *coyan*[77] but it was mainly in the hands of the Chinese. The speculative trade in opium was one of the most profitable ventures undertaken by the Singapore merchants to this part of the Malay Peninsula. This was due to the presence of a Chinese mining population in Kelantan and Pahang in the mid-nineteenth century.

Besides being engaged in the *pukat* trade, the Chinese traders of Singapore also had the major share of the trade of that port with Penang and Malaka. Beginning from about 1830, the principal feature of this trade was that it was mainly carried by square-rigged or European-rigged vessels. In the trade with Penang, native shipping was relatively unimportant but it enjoyed a fair share of the trade with Melaka. In 1838 it was estimated that in this trade there were about seven to eight Chinese-owned square-rigged vessels. Two years later, the number of Chinese-owned European-styled ships in the trade had increased to eighteen.

The imports from Melaka and Penang to Singapore consisted largely of Straits produce. Tin was a very important item of import. A large part of the tin was re-export from the neighbouring Malay states although a substantial amount was produced by Melaka itself especially in the period 1840 to 1850. The principal exports from Singapore to Melaka and Penang were beers, wines, and spirits, and other commodities for domestic consumption, especially Chinese foods suited to the palates of Chinese settlers. But most important of all there was a large speculative trade in opium among the three settlements.

Another valuable aspect of the trade of Singapore controlled by the Chinese was the junk trade. It has been noted that:

> The entrepot trade of Singapore with China, which constituted one of its most important branches of commerce, con-

sisted largely of the transhipment of Chinese manufactures and produce to Europe and America. The trade between China and Singapore was carried in Chinese junks and square-rigged vessels. In 1835, when the total trade of Singapore with China was $1,344,236, almost one-half of the trade... was carried by Chinese junks but the share of the junks in this trade...tended to decline in later years.[78]

With trading activity expanding there soon emerged Chinese shipping companies in Singapore. Among the better known companies in the mid-nineteenth century were Wee Bock Seng & Co., Cheng-tee Wat-seng & Co., and Lee Cheng Yan & Co. In 1866, out of 178 vessels - schooners, bargues, brigs, junks and ships - registered in Singapore, fifty-eight belong to Europeans, Indians and Malays while the rest were owned by Chinese.[79]

In the early years of British administration, communication between the ports of Penang and Singapore with the townships in the tin mining areas continued to rely on Chinese ships plying along the eastern and western coasts of the peninsula. By then steamships had been introduced; these were owned by Chinese merchants the majority of whom were Melaka-born. The better known among them were Tan Choon Bock, Tan Beng Swe and Lee Cheng Yan.[80] Although the railway had made its appearance by the 1880s, the north-south route was completed only in the first decade of the 20th century.

In 1890 the first European steamship concern having its head office in Singapore was established. This was the Straits Steamship Co. Ltd. But of the seven directors, three of them were Chinese, Tan Keong Saik, Tan Jiak Kim and Lee Cheng Yan, all of them Straits-born. The Company began with five ships, two were contributed by T.C. Bogaardt, the principal founder of the company, and three by Kim Seng & Company, the firm founded by Tan Jaik Kim's grandfather.[81] The company soon had the major share of the passenger and goods trade between Singapore and the ports in the Malay states.[82]

The Chinese, however, continued to play an important role in the coastal trade as well as the trade of the Dutch islands and the China ports. One of the principal firms involved in this trade was Tan Kim Tian & Co. Ltd. which had been active since the 1860s. In 1910, the *Hongkong Free Press*, comparing the shipowners in Hongkong and Singapore, concluded that the Babas in the Straits had far outdistanced the Hongkong Chinese. It was said that in one weeks' arrivals in Singapore, out of 83 steamers (not including deep-water steamers that sailed to Europe, Australia, Japan, and India where the Chinese did not compete), 45 were consigned to Chinese firms or individuals.[83]

The paper also related how the Straits Steamship Co., refusing to sell a share in their concern, Koe Guan & Co., decided to have their own fleet, and by purchasing a number of steamers from the Union Line of New Zealand, became the largest steamship concern in Penang,[84] a position which earlier appears to have been held by the Guan Lee Hin Steamship Co. established in 1895 by Quah Beng kee and his brothers. This company, in 1897, opened a ferry steamship service covering Penang, Province Wellesley, Kedah and the minor ports of Perak while other regular services were kept up by a fleet of three larger steamers and seven modern steam launches. The company had its own coal depots at Prai, and employed ten European engineers as well as several hundred Chinese and Malays.[85]

About thirty years later, out of the nine coastal lines operating from Singapore, six of them were Chinese owned and operated. The other three were the Straits Steamship Co. Ltd (with Chinese participation); the Ho Hong Steamship (1932) Ltd. which was a subsidiary of the Straits Steamship Co.; and the Koninklijke Paketvaart Maatschappij (KPM), a Dutch company founded in 1888 to operate as an exclusive and national shipping line in the Indonesian archipelago.[86]

The six Chinese companies were, in general, comparatively small. The Kheng Seng Steamship Co. owned one vessel that brought rubber from Melaka to Singapore. Tan Siew Inn was owner of *Hong Ho*, a ship running to ports between Kemaman and Kuala trengganu. Thong Ek Steamship Co. although operating from Singapore, was established in Pontianak. Hoe Aik Steamship Co. owned seven small coasters trading with the Karimon Islands, the east coast of Sumatra, and Kota Tinggi in Johor. The fifth shipping company was owned by a Singapore merchant, Teo Hoo Lye, who operated under the chop *Soon Bee*. In the late 19th century, he was owner of the steamers *Aing Hong, Flevo, Batavier* and *Benuit*. His firm acted as consignee of ships belonging to other Chinese firms. In the thirties his company ran various services to Sarawak (Sibu), Muar, and South Sumatra. They were then managed by his son, Teo Teow Peng. Heap Eng Moh Steamship Co. was the sixth of the Chinese-owned lines. It survived until only the early thirties. Established in 1912 by Oei Tiong Ham, the 'Sugar King' of Java, this line was a minor subsidiary of his many activities. After his death, the line was, in 1931, reorganized; it became linked to the KPM and by 1932 was no longer regarded as a Chinese firm.[87]

That fishing is an important occupation of the Malays is well known for it has been said that "No seas in the universe contain more edible fish than the seas of the Malay archipelago. The best quality is found in the comparatively shallow waters bordering the granitic and sedimentary formation of the peninsula's shores."[88] However, once the Chinese began settling down in large numbers in Malaya, they proceeded to play a controlling role in the fishing industry.

Unfortunately, no history of the fishing industry in Malaya has ever been attempted and the study of R. Firth[89] notwithstanding, present knowledge of the industry as it existed before World War II is vague. Available information in secondary sources is fragmentary but it clearly indicates that, by the early part of the 20th century, the Chinese had succeeded in controlling the fishing industry in Malaya. Traditionally, the Malays had been expert fishermen but, apparently, by the turn of the present century they had been "excelled, even in their own waters, by the Chinese, who make up for less skill by untiring application. The fishmongers are almost invariably Chinese."[90] In general, however, it was on the west coast of the peninsula that the Chinese played a more important part in the fishing industry than the Malays. For example, in 1906, of the 400 odd fishermen in the Klang district, 90 percent of them were Chinese. In the Kuala Selangor district, the larger fishing stakes were mainly worked by the Malays but the fishing industry, it was stated, was chiefly in the hands of the Chinese.[91] Many of the Chinese were dealers rather than fishermen. The situation remained unchanged in the thirties. The Trengganu *Annual Report* of 1935 explained it succinctly:

There are fisheries throughout the length of the State's coastline. The fishing is done entirely by Malays though the financing and marketing side of the industry is, as elsewhere, mainly in the hands of the Chinese.[92]

But important as the Chinese were in the Malaysian fishing industry, their methods were inclined to be unprogressive. Commenting editorially on the subject in 1931, the *Straits Times* said:

Fishing is another Malayan industry which promises valuable returns if put on a more scientific basis.... One of the prime needs of a properly organized fishing industry is the prompt marketing of catches. In Malayan fishing a large measure of rationalisation would seem to be necessary. There is too long an interval between the hauling abroad of catches and their appearance at market stalls and as a consequence the fish, when it is not positively unsanitary, has depreciated both in financial and in food value. One of the remedies for this state of affairs is the more extended provision of power boats to serve as collecting agents for the smaller fishing vessels, supply cold storage facilities and rush the catches to the markets in a fresh condition. The provision of these and other reforms, however, requires capital which those at present running the industry are not in a position to supply.[93]

The Fisheries Department was aware of the shortcomings but attempts to modernize the industry did not immediately follow. It was not until 1936 that an experimental vessel equipped with a refrigeration plant was used with encouraging results. The vesel which cost a total of $36,900 including $6,258 for the refrigeration plant had a capacity of 10 tons of fish packed in bulk. The chief object of the experimental refrigeration vessel was to put *kembong* (mackerel) on the Singapore market in bulk after prolonged storage had been achieved. The fish were caught off Pangkor Island in the district of Dindings, Perak, and were collected as they were caught by the Chinese purse seine netters who operated their nets by hand.[94]

By 1936, about 80,000 tons of fish, valued at $8,000,000 were landed in Malaya each year. The number of people involved in the industry exceeded 25,600 divided, ethnically, as follows:[95]

Malays	13,745
Chinese	9,701
Japanese	1,752
Indians	352
Siamese	66
Portuguese (Melaka)	38

On the eve of World War II, the pattern of ethnic involvement in the Malayan fishing industry remained unchanged. On the east coast the fishermen were almost all Malays, whereas on the west coast and in the south, many of them were Chinese.[96] In the state of Kelantan, boats and gear were nearly all owned by Malay fishermen; where fishermen used boats or gear belonging to others, the owner of the equipment was given a share of the catch. Further south in Trengganu and Pahan, boats and nets were often owned by Chinese fish dealers; and in this case the owner obtained his interest and return of principal indirectly through his monopoly of the purchase of the fish. Elsewhere the owner of capital was even more commonly a Chinese, again usually a fish dealer, and the fishermen received a price for the fish caught which took into account the dealer's ownership.[97] The situation, it may be added, has not radically changed even today.

Chinese venture into the world of banking before World War II is fortunately not *terra incognita*, thanks to the effort of Tan Ee-Leong.[98] In the earlier days of the Straits Settlements, Chinese businessmen were greatly dependent on the Chettiar for loans and indeed they never ceased to borrow heavily from the Chettiar until quite recent times. Still by the first decade of the 20th century, the first step had been taken to establish a Chinese bank. The Cantonese were the pioneers. The bank, founded in Singapore in 1913, was known as the Kwong Yik Bank; the managing director and principal promoter was Wong Ah Fook who came to Singapore in 1851 and later became an important gambier planter in Johor.

The second bank, established in 1917, also in Singapore, was known as the Sze Hai Tong Banking & Insurance Co Ltd. This was founded by members of the Teochiu community. It proved to be more solid than the first one. Unlike the Kwong Aik Bank which encountered serious difficulties during the period of the First World War, the Teochiu Bank weathered the storm.

Surprisingly the Hokkien businessmen, who formed the majority of the wealthy in the Straits Settlements, ventured into banking later than the Cantonese and the Teochiu. In 1912 the Chinese Commercial Bank Ltd. was founded in Singapore with a paid up capital of $1,000,000. Among those involved were Lee Choon Guan and Dr. Lim Boon Keng, both local-born Chinese. Dr. Lim was a Queen's scholar (1887) and a graduate of Edinburgh University. The history of the bank is eventful but it served as a good training ground for persons such as Yap Pheng Geck and Tan Chin Tuan who later became renowned bankers.

Dr. Lim Boon Keny together with Lim Peng Siang and Seow Poh Leng (both of whom had also been involved in the founding of the Chinese Commercial Bank) went a step further in 1917 by opening the Ho Hong Bank Ltd. in Singapore and its branch office in Melaka as well as a sub-branch in Muar simultaneously. A few months later another sub-branch was opened in Batu Pahat. The bank started with an issued capital of $3,500,000 half paid up. A notable feature of the bank is that it established branches outside Malaya: in Palembang, Batavia (Jakarta), and Hong Kong. An important addition to the directorship in 1930 was Aw Boon Haw, born in Rangoon, who became prominently known in Malaya as the "Tiger Balm King." He was also a shareholder and placed large sums on deposit with the bank.

Dr. Lim Boon Keng who was to become the first Principal of the Amoy University when it opened in 1920 was also involved in the establishment of yet another bank. In 1919 the Oversea-Chinese Bank Ltd. opened for business in Singapore. This time the founders derived from various territorial-dialect groups. There was Lim Nee Soon, a Teochiu, local-born and a staunch member of the Kuomintang; S.Q. Wong, lawyer and son of Wong Ah Fook, founder of the kwong Yik Bank; and Dr. S.C. Yin, a Hokkien but married to the daughter of J.H. Bowyer of London.[99] Oei Tiong Ham and Oei Ik Tjoe, the leading sugar merchants of Semarang, between them took $1,000,000 shares in the new bank.

Like the Ho Hong Bank, the Oversea-Bank Ltd. also opened up branches overseas — at Rangoon, Amoy and Jambi

(Sumatra) — in addition to Penang, Kuala Lumpur and Melaka. The 1930 slump adversely affected the bank and, with a view to solving common problems, directors of the Oversea-Chinese Bank and the Ho Hong Bank began talks on the possiblility of an amalgamation. It was later suggested that the Chinese Commercial Bank should be invited to join in the scheme. The amalgamation in 1932 led to the birth of the Oversea-Chinese Banking Corporation, popularly known as OCBC, which is one of the leading banks in Singapore-Malaysia today.

In the meanwhile, the Chinese continued to establish more banks. The Lee Wah bank, again a Cantonese venture, appeared in 1920 also in Singapore but two of the promoters — Eu Tong Sen and Cheong Yoke Choy, — were from the mining towns of Kampar and Kuala Lumpur respectively. In the same year the Batu Pahat Bank Ltd. was incorporated in Singapore although it operated in Batu Pahat, and, like the others, its founders were Chinese based in Singapore.

However, by then, two Chinese banks had been incorporated in the Federated Malay States. The first was known as The Kwong Yik (Selangor) Banking Corporation Ltd. Significantly, the incorporation of this bank, in 1913, was effected a few months before a receiving order was issued against the Kwong Yik Bank in Singapore. It is believed that some ties existed between the two institutions. The founders of the Kwong Yik Bank in Selangor included several well-known miners such as Cheong Yoke Choy, Chan Wing, San Ah Wing, and, a little later, even Loke Yew.

The other mining town, Ipoh, was not left out. In 1920 the Bank of Malay Ltd. was established there. Among its directors were Chin Sem Lin, a public-spirited miner, and Leong Sin Nam who, in the 1930s was to play a leading role in raising funds to support China in its war campaign against Japan. Although the bank had a paid-up capital of $1,000,000, it could not surmount the crisis arising from the slump of 1930 and had to go into voluntary liquidation.

Although the oldest of the settlements in Malaya with a substantial Chinese population, Penang was the last to have its own Chinese bank before the outbreak of war in 1941. The Ban Hin Lee Bank Ltd. which was registered in 1935 had offices in both Penang and Singapore. Its founder was Yeap Chor Ee, widely known as "Barber" Ee for he had been a barber when he was young. Although registered in 1935, as early as 1918 there had been, in effect, a banking department in Yeap Chor Ee's company, Chop Ban Hin Lee. Yeap Chor Ee's interest in banking was not confined to the Ban Hin Lee Bank as he was also one of the largest shareholders of the Oversea-Chinese Banking Corporation.

One more Chinese bank emerged in the same year in Singapore. This was the United Chinese Bank Ltd. which had a paid-up capital of $1,000,000. The notable feature of this bank was that its chief financiers were a Chinese (Wee Kheng Chiang) from Sarawak and a Penang Chinese (Khoo Beng Cheang), both Hokkien. Almost all the principal officers of the bank had gained experience in the older Chinese banks. This was the last bank founded by the Chinese before the outbreak of war. In the early post-war years, the Chinese continued to establish more banks and among those involved were famous names such as Aw Boon Haw, Tan Lark Sye who played a leading role in founding the Nanyang University, Col. H.S. Lee who later became the first finance minister of independent Malaya, and Lau Pak Kuan who led a delegation, representing Chinese guilds, to London to espouse the cause of the Chinese in the final negotiations on the 1957 Constitution.

On the eve of World War II, Malaya's pineapple industry became one of the largest fruit-canning industries in the world and ranked third among the country's export industries.[100] It had a modest start in Singapore in the 1890s. The first factory was established by a European in Bain Court. The cans were soldered by hand and the factory's capacity was quite small; only a few thousand cases were produced in a year. The supplies of the fruit were very limited, obtained almost exclusively from Singapore and the surrounding islands.[101]

By 1900 the Chinese had entered into the industry which was showing encouraging signs so much so that it attracted the attention of the Americans who were then beginning to pack pineapples in Hawaii. They sent representatives to Singapore to make a study of the industry there because Singapore was then the largest exporter of canned pineapples. The industry in Hawaii soon developed rapidly and in due course completely overshadowed the industry in Singapore in terms of factory equipment and the elimination of waste as well as in size and output. By 1931 Hawaii was able to pack about 16 million cases against 12 million in 1930 whereas Malaya could not reach 2 million annually.

Before the rubber boom in 1910, many of the pioneer rubber estates in Singapore were under pineapple: the enterprising planters dug just enough holes for the rubber seeds and seedlings between the pines. The estates were then floated in London and Singapore as rubber estates. Most of the factories were then located at Lavender Street, Sungei Road, Grove Road, Serangoon Road, and Seletar.

By 1912, however, the industry had been introduced in Johor and, although without success initially, became firmly established beginning from 1922. The area planted with pineapples for export in Malaya in 1930 was estimated at 52,000 acres, of which all but 3,000 acres contained pineapples interplanted as a catch crop between young rubber. The total exports in the same year amounted to 57,959 tons or 1,618,919 cases valued at $7,859,026. The average value of exports over the period 1928-1930 had been £1 million a year.

Johor at that juncture, was responsible for over sixty percent of the total Malayan pack. In 1930 Malayan pineapples constituted about eighty-five percent of the total imports of tinned pineapples into the United Kingdom. There was in the United Kingdom no competition with higher priced canned pineapple from Hawaii or South Africa. Reasonable price of local products placed it within the means of almost all classes. Outside the United Kingdom, the largest consumer of Malayan pineapples then were Canada, New Zealand, and the continent of Europe.[102] Significantly, the industry was practically entirely in the hands of the Chinese merchants.

R. Boulter, British Trade Commissioner in Singapore in 1931, was, however, critical of the Malayan pineapple industry. Commenting on the subject in his report entitled *Economic Conditions in British Malaya*, he said:

> In view of the success which Chinese have gained in various enterprises, it may appear to be a waste of time to attempt to offer any suggestions; but the fact remains that, wonderful businessmen though the Chinese are, they have not yet learnt all the possibilities of fostering an industry by means of large scale advertisement.[103]

Moreover, they lacked the capital and had no resources to enable them to hold their products for a satisfactory price. They had to dispose of them quickly in order to meet calls for payment for fruit, tinplate, and wages.

Boulter was referring to what he considered the actual potential of the pineapple industry because the export of Malayan canned pineapples had, in fact, since 1918, steadily increased. But it was believed that there were distinct possibilities of further expansion and development. In 1931, the industry was to some extent brought into prominence by the advertising efforts of the Malayan Agency in London, by the Department of Agriculture in Kuala Lumpur, and by the speech of Sir Cecil Clementi, High Commissioner of the Federated Malay States, at the Malayan Agri-Horticultural Association Exhibition held in Kuala Lumpur.[104]

Despite Boulter's criticisms and possibly because of more concerted support given by the government, the export of Malayan canned pineapples continued to increase and, in 1936, reached a record figure of 76,403 tons valued at $8,686,085. These represented roughly 2,377,000 cases of 48 cans of 1 1/2 lb. capacity. About 71% of the Malayan pack in 1936 was exported to the United Kingdom; at the same time, there were considerable increases in the exports to Canada, New Zealand, America and India. In 1935, 91% of the pineapples exported to the United Kingdom were Malayan.[105]

In 1940 the prices of most agricultural commodities declined except pineapples. The explanation given was that "reorganization put the pineapple industry on a fairly firm foundation and the Control Board of Pineapple Packers set to work and kept a fair balance between production costs and selling prices by eliminating waste."[106]

The success of the pineapple industry notwithstanding, until the 1930s, the Chinese barely ventured into the industrial sector. In fact, during the period of the depression, one complaint directed at the wealthy Straits Chinese in particular was that they were too content being landlords and mortgagees. The Straits Chinese British Association was asked by a correspondent of the *Straits Times* (7 March 1934) to "wake up their rich members to start some kind of industrial enterprises and make them realize their position that being a landlord or mortgagee they are not doing any good to the children of their own community who are at present unemployed."

Possibly one Chinese was, at that time, involved in manufacturing in a big way. Tan Kah Kee, China-born, had started a rice mill in Geylang in the early twentieth century. His employment register then numbered about 800 people. By the late 1920s he was running pineapple factories in Singapore, Johor, and Selangor (Klang), a 11,300-acre rubber estate, rubber mills (throughout the country), a tannery, a brickworks, soap, biscuit, and other factories, and gave work to 15,000 people. At his Sumbawa Road (Singapore) factory, he had machinery valued at $8 million turning out rubber goods on a scale never seen on the island before, and supplying all the wrapper, labels and cardboard boxes needed for their marketing. His manufacturing concern had few rivals in the Far East. It was said of him that:

> A Henry Ford in as much as he adopted the principle of making for himself every article required in his business, Tan Kah Kee, at the time producing 20,000 pairs of rubber and leather shoes a day and wishing to double his capacity, had been likened also to Bata, the late Czecho-Slovakian shoe manufacturer. His footwear similarly commanded worlwide sales.[107]

But during the period of the world depression, Tan Kah Kee & Co. also encountered difficulties. In August 1931, the company was registered as a limited concern with a capital of $2,500,000. In the same year, an issue of eight debentures for securing various sums amounting in the aggregate to $3,033,000 was made. The new concern covered a wide field of manufacturing activity and exported largely overseas. However, it did not operate many of the businesses which the founder of the original firm created. The rice-mill had closed down a long time ago, and Tan Kah Kee's interests in the cultivation and export of Malayan pines had been reduced; most of the rubber mills were in other hands. Nevertheless, up to early 1934, the company employed about 6,000 people principally at the Sumbawa Road rubber goods factory, a few hundred at the soap and biscuit factories, and at the sales branches from one end of the peninsula to the other. Even in China nearly 30 sales branches had been established, stretching from as far north as Peking to as far south as Hainan.

Tan Kah Kee's rubber shoes, in particular, commanded world-wide sales so much so that, in early 1934, questions were actually asked in the House of Commons in England concerning competition of rubber footwear from Hong Kong and Singapore in Canada and Britain. Although Britain had imposed duties, in 1933, on imports of foreign shoes, such duties were not aimed against those manufactured in British territory. Indeed, the Act introduced was designed, inter alia, to help local manufacture within the British Empire. But British and Canadian manufacturers soon realized that such large shoe-making concerns as Tan Kah Kee's of Singapore, whose labour costs were much lower, could produce shoes almost as cheaply as certain other foreign manufacturers; they, therefore, agitated for some relief. But on the 19th of February 1934, it was announced in the press that:

> The affairs of Messrs. Tan Kah Kee Ltd., the well known local rubber goods manufacturers, have been placed in the hands of a receiver and manager. Mr. David Phillip, the local Chartered Accountant, has been appointed to the post.[108]

The debit on profit and loss account at 30 June 1933 was $3,098,913; the company's capital had been wiped out. A large proportion of the profit and loss deficit was due to overvaluation of assets at the date of incorporation but some of the difficulties encountered by the company were caused by business depression, Japanese competition in foreign markets, tariff walls and the tightness of capital. It was, however, not a total setback for Tan Kah Kee for some of his factories were taken over by his son-in-law, Lee Kong Chian, who, by then had emerged as one of the most successful businessmen in Malaya.

Also China-born, Lee Kong Chian had a university education and served as an assistant surveyor in the Singapore Municipality before joining Tan Kah Kee Rubber Co., in 1918, as head of its rubber department. Later he married Tan Kah Kee's daughter. In 1931 he started in business on his own account. Thus was born the now well-known Lee Rubber Co. which was followed by Lee Produce Co., Lee Sawmills, the Lee Pineapple Factory, Lee Biscuits, and Lee Printing. He acquired thousands of acres of land and turned them into rubber and pineapple plantations. By 1937 he was popularly known as "the rubber and pineapple king of Malaya."[109] He was also instrumental in bringing about the amalgamation of three banks in 1932 which witnessed the formation of the Oversea Chinese Banking Corporation.[110]

Until the outbreak of war in 1941, not only were the Chinese reluctant to venture into the industrial sector, they continued to function along traditional lines. Sole proprietorship was still preferred to public companies. The banks apart, there appears to have been at least one attempt made to form a public company. In 1919, a company under the name of Chenglock Soohock & Co. Ltd. was floated with a nominal capital of $1,000,000 to carry on business as general import and export merchants, commision agents, and managers of rubber estates as well as household property in Singapore and Melaka. Soon after, branches were also opened in America, the United Kingdom, and China. The capital was divided into 10,000 shares of $100 each of which 3,500 shares had been issued towards the end of the year. this was very much a Straits-Chinese venture. The Chairman of Directors was Tan Cheng Lock who, today, is better known for his political rather than his economic activities although by 1919 he was already one of the major rubber plantation owners in the Peninsula. Also involved in the company were Tan Soo Hock and Chan Kang Swi of Melaka and Lee Choon Guan and Dr. Lim Boon Keng of Singapore.[111] Unfortunately, at this juncture, it has not been possible to trace the subsequent development of the company.

Although generally acknowledged as shrewd businessmen, the Chinese before World War II clearly lacked the knowledge of modern economic organization except for a handful with English education. This placed them at a disadvantage when competing with European capital. But there is one other factor which perhaps deserves special attention. As early as 1912, a Chinese reader wrote to the *Malay Mail* at a time when China was attempting to float a C$10 million[112] loan. He said:

...I would like to advise Straits-born and other Chinese against the foolish way in which they have been pouring money into China mines, banks and revolutionary funds, etc.

For the millions of dollars invested in the last few years by the Straits and F.M.S. in China I have not yet heard of the receipt of a single cent in dividends. Quite apart from any ethical question of patriotism and gratitude to the country in which we have made our homes and fortunes, is it a wise policy to drain dry of capital our own business-sphere, capital which if re-invested here would not only give better returns and greater security, but, by increasing the general commercial activity of the country, would doubly benefit us all? Think of the profitable scope there now is in our own country for investment in such secure local undertakings as coconuts, rubber, house property, motor-buses, the new Selangor coal-fields, etc., or, with a greater risk, in tin mining, and pause before investing in discredited loans.[113]

But the appeal made no impression on the Chinese who continued to send money to China. Remittances to families and relatives had become common practice practically from the beginning of permanent Chinese settlement in Malaya. Figures available for the period 1936-1940 show that the total amount remitted per year ranged from C$320 to C$1,329 million.[114] In addition, there were also contributions to "relief funds" when natural calamities occurred in China or when the Chinese government, favoured by overseas Chinese, was in dire need of financial assistance. This was particularly evident after the Marco Polo Bridge Incident in 1937 which sparked off the Sino-Japanese War.[115]

By October 1937, three months after the outbreak of war, the Chinese in Malaya were able to raise C$19.5 million which accounted for 43% of the total Southeast Asian Chinese contribution. From November 1938 to December 1940, the sum amounted to C$30.8 million or 47.5% of the total Southeast Asian Chinese contribution. In terms of Straits dollar, the sum totalled slightly over $8 million.[116]

There was a third form of assistance given to China. The wealthy Chinese in Malaya often responded quickly to calls for the purchase of Chinese government bonds. Again the war years found the Malayan Chinese at their most generous. Between July 1937 and October 1938, the amount of government bonds purchased totalled C$12.8 million. In 1937, C$1 million was worth approximately $520,000 Straits dollars.[117] When all three categories are added together, for the year 1937 alone, Malaya's contribution to China amounted to no less than $200 million Straits dollars.

World War II caused serious dislocation to the country but did little to alter the basic roles of the Chinese in Malaya's economy despite Japan's anti-Chinese policy and the massive migration of the Chinese from the urban to the rural areas. Indeed, by the middle of 1943, the Japanese military administration was compelled to modify its policy towards the Chinese because it "realized that the Malayan economy would grind to a halt without the Chinese business cooperation."[118]

At the time the country achieved independence, this was the observation made as regards the position of the Chinese in the Malayan economy:

> The Chinse own and operate most of the non-British commercial enterprises throughout Malaya and are second in terms of volume of capital investment. They are the chief middlemen and shopkeepers and generally dominate the service industries. Although their historical importance in tin mining has been lessened under European competition, they still account for over 40 percent of the annual tin production. Similarly, the Chinese dominate the pineapple industry and own many of the small and medium rubber holdings which account for a large proportion of the annual output. The Chinese also are the principal vegetable gardeners, supplying the urban centers with fresh produce.[119]

Government statistics released in 1973 revealed that the Chinese owned 26 percent of both the agricultural and industrial sectors; foreign capital still controlled both the sectors.[120] But the principal feature of the Chinese position has been, as in the past, the varied and multifarious roles which they play in the country's economy. In this respect, there has been no change to this day.

Notes

1. Although the focus here is on peninsular Malaysia, continual reference to Singapore is unavoidable as the economy of the Malay States was inextricably linked to that of Singapore since the 1820s. Moreover, many of the leading entrepreneurs in Singapore were of Melaka origin. For the sake of convenience the pre-war term of 'Malaya' (the Malay States and the Straits Settlements not the Federation of Malaya) is retained here.

   On 5 September 1893, the *Straits Times*, commenting on the *Pinang Gazette's* publication of a series of extracts from W.P. Groeneveldt's *Notes on the The Malay Archipelago and Malacca* (Batavia, 1879), remarked that "the greatest account of Chinese enterprise in Malay has yet to be written." It was not until 50 years later that Victor Purcell wrote *The Chinese in Malaya* (London, 1948). But Purcell devoted only one chapter to "The Chinese in Malayan Industry" where he acknowledged that "The Chinese in Malayan industry would form the subject-matter for an extensive study, and there is indeed room for one..." (p.235). However, he found that "the information on which it should be based is not readily available" (p.235). Official documents rarely provided figures according to the race of the persons concerned. Purcell is right if the intention of the writer is to provide precise statistics in every instance. The alternative approach is to examine the numerous functions performed by the Chinese in Malay's economy which, in a very modest way, is the principal aim of this paper.

2. Ng Chin-Keong, *Trade and Society: The Amoy Network on the China Coast 1683-1735*, Singapore, 1983, p.1.

3. M.A.P. Meilink-Roelofsz, *Asian Trade and European Influence in the Indonesian Archipelago Betwen 1500 and about 1630*, The Hague, 1962, p.76.

4. Rev. W.G. Shellabear, *The Chinese in Malaysia*, pp.502-6, cited by Victor Purcell, *The Chinese in Malaya*, Kuala Lumpur, 1967, p.19n.

5. Victor Purcell, "Chinese Settlement in Malacca," in *Journal of the Malayan Branch Royal Asiatic Society (JMBRAS)*, XX, 1, 1947, p.124.

6. Dr. John Dunmore (tr.), "French Visitors to Trengganu in the 18th Century" in *Journal of the Malaysian Branch Royal Asiatic Society*, XLVI, 1, 1973, p.147.

7. *Ibid.*, p. 152.

8. *Ibid.*, p.148.

9. M.W.F. Tweedie, "An Early Chinese Account of Kelantan" *JMBRAS*, XXVI, 1, 1935, p. 218. See also Wang Gungwu, An Early Chinese Visitor to Kelantan" in *Malaya in History*, VI, 1, 1960.

10. See M. Medhurst, *Journal of a Tour Through the Settlements on the Eastern Side of the Peninsula of Malacca 1828*, Singapore, n.d., pp. 14,19.

11. T.J. Newbold, *Political and Statistical Account of the British Settlements in the Straits of Malacca*, London, 1839, Vol. II, p. 56.

12. Victor Purcell, *The Chinese in Malaya*, p. 39.

13. *Ibid.*, p. 40.

14. *Ibid.*, pp. 45,46.

15. James C. Jackson, *Planters and Speculators: Chinese and European Agricultural Enterprise in Malaya 1786-1921*, Kuala Lumpur, 1968, pp. 128-129.

16. *Ibid.*, p. 129.

17. See Carl A. Trocki, "The Origin of the Kangchu System, 1740-1860" in *Journal of the Malaysian Branch Royal Asiatic Society*, XLIX, 2, 1976; Lee Poh Ping, *Chinese Society in Nineteenth Century Singapore*, Kuala Lumpur, 1978, p. 28.

18. James C. Jackson, op.cit., pp. 14-15.

19. See Carl A. Trocki, op.cit.

20. For a detailed study of Dutch attempts to control the tin trade of Perak, see Barbara Watson Andaya, *Perak:The Abode of Grace, A Study of an Eighteenth Century Malay State*, Kuala Lumpur, 1979, passim.

21. Wong Lin Ken, *The Malayan Tin Industry to 1914 with special reference to the States of Perak, Selangor, Negri Sembilan and Pahang*, Tucson, 1965, p.18.

22. Khoo Kay Kim, *The Western Malay States 1850-1873, The Effects of Commercial Development on Malay Politics*, Kuala Lumpur, 1972, pp. 72-73.

23. Wong Lin Ken, *op.cit.*, p.18.

24. Song Ong Siang, *One Hundred Years' History of the Chinese in Singapore*, Singapore, 1923, pp. 21, 131-133; Khoo Kay Kim, op.cit., pp. 34-35.

25. Khoo Kay Kim, *op.cit.*, p.74.

26. *Ibid.*,p.134.

27. See Khoo Kay Kim, "The Origin of British Administration in Malaya" in *JMBRAS*, XXXIX, pt.1, 1966.

28. "Mr. Choo Kia Peng recalls Old Kuala Kubu Days", *Malay Mail*, 2 February 1939.

29. J.D. Vaughan, *The Manners and Customs of the Chinese of the Straits*, Kuala Lumpur, 1971, p.15.

30. For a study of the rise of Western mining enterprise, see Wong Lin Ken, *op.cit.*,pp.211-216.

31. He was described as "a brilliant and thoughtful writer, especially on subjects relating to China and the Chinese." He was educated at Raffles Institution, where he won the Guthrie Scholarship for Chinese boys in 1873. He then proceeded to Amoy to prosecute his Chinese studies. (See Song Ong Siang, op.cit.,p.94).

32. "Local Chinese Trade. Lecture On The Subject," *Straits Times, 13 August 1902.*

33. *Ibid.*

34. Colonial Office Records 273/654, File No.5055/pt.II, Shenton Thomas to Malcolm MacDonald, 13 July 1939; encl. *Monthly Review of Chinese Affairs*, 7 July 1939, Section V "The Development of Trade Unions in

Malaya."
35. According to Taku Suyama, "The Pang society may be regarded as an organization of men which incorporates all aspects of the neighbourhood spirit in the broad sense." See "Pang Societies and the Economy of Chinese Immigrants in Southeast Asia" in K.G. Tregonning (ed.), *Papers on Malayan History*, Singapore, 1962.
36. "Mining Laws and Customs of the Malay Peninsula", *Straits Times*, 5 November 1889. This lengthy article is an extract from a pamphlet published by the Government Printing Office. The author, Martin Lister, was Superintendent of Negeri Sembilan. He believed that European capital could be introduced into alluvial tin mining if the Chinse methods were adopted.
37. *Ibid.*
38. See Khoo Kay Kim, *The Western Malay States &c.*, pp.67-79
39. Wong Lin Ken, *op.cit.*, pp.148-149.
40. *Straits Times*, 20 October 1886.
41. Colonial Office Records 273/654, file No.5055/pt.II, Shenton Thomas to Malcolm MacDonald, 13 July 1939; encl. *Monthly Review of Chinse Affairs*, 7 July 1939, Sect. V "The Development of Trade Unions in Malaya."
42. See Arnold Wright & H.A. Cartwright (eds.), *Twentieth Century Impressions of British Malaya: Its History, People, Commerce, Industries and Resources*, London, 2908, p.744; Colonial Office Records 273/580, No. 92036, Cecil Clementi to Gunliffe-Lister, 6 October 1932; encl. *Monthly Review of Chinese Affairs*, 3 October 1939, Sect. VI "Chinese Chambers of Commerce in Malaya."
43. *Straits Times*, 18 March 1889.
44. *Malay Mail*, 24 January 1902.
45. *Straits Times*, 18 March 1889.
46. *Pinang Gazette*, 14 October 1879.
47. *Straits Times*, 20 April 1885.
48. Pinang Gazette, 14 October 1879; *Malay Mail*, 29 September 1902.
49. *Perak Pioneer*, 28 March 1900; *Singapore Free Press*, 19 November 1904.
50. *Malay Mail*, 29 September 1902.
51. Cited by R.N. Jackson, *Immigrant Labour and the Development of Malaya*, Kuala Lumpur, 1961, p.40.
52. Wong Lin Ken, op.cit., pp.224-225; Li Dun Jen, *British Malaya: An Economic Analysis*, Kuala Lumpur, 1982, pp.21-23.
53. *Perak Pioneer*, 6 July 1905.
54. *Ibid.*
55. Victor Purcell, *op.cit.*, p.237.
56. *Ibid.*
57. James C. Jackson, *op.cit.*, pp.218, 222, 224.
58. *Ibid.*, p.224.
59. Arnold Wright & H.A. Cartwright (eds.), *op.cit.*, pp.377, 413, 423.
60. *Malay Mail*, 15 August 1906.
61. Arnold Wright & H.A. Cartwright (eds.), *op.cit.*, pp.435, 438.

62. *Ibid.*, pp. 384, 489.
63. *Ibid.*, p. 502.
64. This will be discussed subsequently.
65. J.E. Nathan, *The Census of British Malaya*, 1921, London, 1922, pp.138-139.
66. *Ibid.*, p.139.
67. *Ibid.*, p.120.
68. *Ibid.*
69. *Ibid.*, p.298; C.A. Vlieland, *British Malaya, A Report on the 1931 Census and on Certain Problems of Vital Statistics,* London, 1932, p.319.
70. *Ibid.*, p.294.
71. Norton Ginsburg & Chester F. Roberts, Jr., *Malaya*, Seattle, 1958, p.257.
72. Li Dun Jen, *op.cit.*, p.86.
73. This category included Malays and Japanese.
74. Li Dun Jen, *op.cit.*, p.86.
75. J.E. Nathan, op.cit., p.294; C.A. Vlieland, *op.cit.*, p.294.
76. Wong Lin Ken, "The Trade of Singapore, 1819-69" in *JMBRAS*, XXXIII, Pt.4, 1960, pp.78-82.
77. One *coyan* = 40 piculs (approximately).
78. Wong Lin Ken, "The Trade of Singapore", p.106.
79. Song Ong Siang, op.cit., pp.118-119.
80. K.G. Tregonning, *Home Port Singapore: A History of Straits Steamship Company Limited 1890-1965*, Singapore, 1967, pp.6-10.
81. *Ibid.*, p.17.
82. Arnold Wright & H.A. Cartwright (eds), *op.cit.*, p. 174.
83. Song Ong Siang, *op.cit.*, p.349.
84. *Ibid.*, pp.349-350.
85. Arnold Wright & H.A. Cartwright (eds.), *op.cit.*, p.177.
86. K.G. Tregonning, *Home Port Singapore &c.*, p.12.
87. Song Ong Siang, op.cit., p.350; and *ibid.*, pp.138-139.
88. Arnold Wright & H.A. Cartwright (eds.), *op.cit.*, p.554.
89. Raymond Firth, *Malay Fishermen: The Peasant Economy*, London, 1946.
90. Arnold Wright & H.A. Cartwright (eds.), *op.cit.*, p.554.
91. *Ibid.*
92. *Straits Times*, 11 September 1936.
93. *Ibid.*, 7 August 1931.
94. *Pinang Gazette*, 2 July 1937.
95. *Ibid.*
96. See Moira Rowland, "The Malayan Fishing Industry" (M.A. Thesis, Australian National University, year?), p.3.
97. *Ibid.*, pp.19-20; see also Raymond Firth, op.cit., pp.59-62.
98. See "The Chinese Banks Incorporated in Singapore and the Federation of Malaya" in *JMBRAS*, XXVI, Pt.1, 1953. I have relied solely on this source for a historical sketch of the development of Chinese banks but have added biographical information with regard to certain well-known personalities.

99. They were the parents of Leslie Chateris Bowyer Yin, famous author of "The Saint" series.

100. Norton Ginsburg & Chester F. Roberts, Jr., *op.cit.*, p.264.

101. "50,000 A Year From Pines," *Straits Times*, 27 August 1931.

102. *Ibid.*

103. Editorial, *Straits Times*, 5 August 1931.

104. "$50,000 A Year From Pines", *op.cit.*

105. *Straits Times*, 31 July 1937.

106. *Malaya Tribune*, 1 July 1940.

107. "Remarkable Record of Tan Kah Kee's," *Straits Times,* 21 February 1934.

108. *Straits Times*, 7 February 1934.

109. *Pinang Gazette*, 26 January 1937.

110. Dick Wilson, *Solid As A Rock The First Forty Years of the Overseas-Chinese Banking Corporation*, Singapore 1972.

111. *Malaya Tribune*, 15 october 1919. Others involved in the company were: Lee Choon Guan, Koh San Hin, Tan Kheam Hock, Tan Kwee Wah, all of whom were well-known in Singapore, and Tan Soo Ghi of Melaka.

112. C$ = Chinese dollars *(yuan)*.

113. *Malay Mail,* 9 December 1912. He was naturally chided by another correspondent calling himself "A True Son of China" and was accused of being "most unpatriotic and selfish." (*Malay Mail*, 13 December 1912)

114. Stephen M.Y. Leong, "Sources, Agencies and Manifestations of Overseas Chinese Nationalism in Malaya, 1937-1941" (Ph.D. dissertation, University of California, 1976), p.325.

115. *Ibid.*, p.261

116. *Ibid.*, p.312

117. *Ibid.*, p.325

118. Yoji Akashi, "Japanese Military Administration in Malaya - Its Formation and Evolution in Reference to Sultans, the Islamic Religion, and the Muslim Malays - 1941-1945" in *Asian Studies*, Vol.VII, No. 1, 1969, p.103.

119. Norton Ginsburg & Chester F. Roberts, Jr., *op.cit.,* p.244.

120. See Lim Mah Hui, *Ownership and Control of the One Hundred Largest Corporations in Malaysia*, Singapore, 1983, p.19.

About the Editor

Manning Nash is an educator and an anthropologist. He was born in Philadelphia, Pennsylvania in 1924 and graduated from Temple University in 1949. Nash went on to the University of Chicago where he earned his masters degree and later, in 1955, his Ph.D. Nash served as an instructor at UCLA from 1955 to 1956, and as Assistant Professor at the University of Washington from 1956 until 1957 when he joined the faculty at the University of Chicago. In 1964 he became a professor of Anthropology. He married June C. Bousley in 1951. They have two children, Eric and Laura.

Doctor Nash is a fellow of the American Anthropology Association and of the Royal Anthropology Society of Great Britain and Ireland. He is a member of the American Ethnological Society, and Sigma Xi. Manning Nash is the author of several books including *The Golden Road to Modernity*, 1965, *Machine Age Maya, second edition*, 1967, and *Unfinished Agenda: The Dynamics of Modernization in the Developing Nation*, 1984.

Contributors

Fatimah Daud

Associate Professor
Department of Anthropology and Sociology
University of Malaya
Kuala Lumpur, Malaysia

Mohammed Fauzi Haji Yaacob

Associate Professor
Department of Anthropology and Sociology
University of Malaya
Kuala, Lumpur, Malaysia

K. T. Joseph

Professor of Land Use Studies
Department of Geography
University of Malaya
Kuala Lumpur, Malaysia

Khoo Kay Kim

Professor of Malaysian History
Department of History
University of Malaya
Kuala Lumpur, Malaysia

Mokhtar Tamin

Professor of Rural Economics
Faculty of Economics and Administration
University of Malaya
Kuala Lumpur, Malaysia

Nik A. Rashid Ismail

Deputy Vice Chancellor
(Development and Training)
National University of Malaysia
Bangi, Malaysia

G. Sivalingam

Associate Professor
Faculty of Economics and Administration
University of Malaya
Kuala Lumpur, Malaysia

Shamsul A. Baharuddin

Associate Professor
Department of Anthropology and Sociology
National University of Malaysia
Bangi, Malaysia

Index